Classic Failures in
Product Marketing

CLASSIC FAILURES IN PRODUCT MARKETING

Marketing Principles Violations and How to Avoid Them

DONALD W. HENDON

QUORUM BOOKS

New York
Westport, Connecticut
London

Library of Congress Cataloging-in-Publication Data

Hendon, Donald W.
    Classic failures in product marketing : marketing principles
violations and how to avoid them / Donald W. Hendon.
      p.   cm.
    Includes index.
    ISBN 0-89930-304-8 (lib. bdg. : alk. paper)
    1. Product management—United States. 2. Business failures—
United States. 3. Marketing—United States. 4. New products—
United States. I. Title.
HF5415.15.H46   1989
658.8—dc19   88-35469

British Library Cataloguing in Publication Data is available.

Library of Congress Catalog Card Number: 88-35469
ISBN: 0-89930-304-8

First published in 1989 by Quorum Books

Greenwood Press, Inc.
88 Post Road West, Westport, Connecticut 06881

Printed in the United States of America

∞™

The paper used in this book complies with the
Permanent Paper Standard issued by the National
Information Standards Organization (Z39.48--1984).

10 9 8 7 6 5 4 3 2

To Rebecca, my wife,
the joy of my life

I wish to acknowledge her great efforts in
researching and editing this book and
helping me prepare the final text
using our computerized word processor.

Contents

Figures   ix

PART I: INTRODUCTION

  1   What This Book Is About   3

PART II: THE MARKETING SETTING

  2   Customers   11
  3   Competitors   37
  4   The Environment of the Market   53
  5   Disasters and Safety — Rumors and Reality   65

PART III: MARKETING TOOLS

  6   Product or Service — Launching It and Naming It   101
  7   Pricing   141
  8   Channels of Distribution   155
  9   Advertising   161
10   Personal Selling   185

Subject Index   193
Author Index   201

Figures

1   MDS Map   115
2   The Negotiation Matrix   186
3   The Difference Between the Hard-Sell Approach and the
    Marketing Approach   188
4   The Basics of Body Language   190

PART I
INTRODUCTION

1
What This Book Is About

If you ever visit the International Supermarket and Museum in Naples, New York, you'll find on its shelves more than 60,000 consumer products that have failed in U.S. supermarkets. How many of these soft drinks do you remember — Okeechobe Orange Pokem, Kickapoo Joy Juice, Hagar the Horrible Cola, Panda Punch, Sudden Soda, Nutrimato, and Yabba Dabba Dew? None of them are made anymore. They failed. So did Tuna Twist, Gimme Cucumber hair conditioner, Batman Crazy Foam, Moonshine aftershave, Moon Shine Sippin' Citrus, Oasis deodorant, Buffalo Chip chocolate cookies, designer diapers, Baker Tom's baked cat food, I Hate Peas, I Hate Beets, I Hate Spinach, Wild Life beans in sauce with wild boar meat, and Wine and Dine Dinner. All these products are in the museum, along with about 15,000 products that succeeded.[1]

This book is a search for the reasons why products and services *failed,* not why they *succeeded.* According to Dun & Bradstreet, over 250,000 new businesses were started in the United States in 1985, and the same year, nearly 60,000 businesses failed. Half of the products were less than five years old. I'm a business professor, and, like most professors, I also do a lot of consulting. I know from my 20-plus years of teaching that students in business schools in the United States and abroad don't study failure very much, even though my consulting tells me that failure is much more common in business than success. Most new products fail — every marketer knows that, and yet business schools tend to sweep the stories of failures under the rug.

There haven't been many books written about business failures, either. Only a few come to mind, and since they haven't sold as well as books about business successes, many more books have been written about success stories. One best-selling author, Thomas Peters, who coauthored *In Search of Excellence,* said that failure is almost a taboo subject in business: "There's still a frontier optimism. So we don't talk about failure, we don't write about it, we don't even think about it." When it happens, we deny it. When we *have* to talk about it, we use euphemisms. As one public relations (P.R.) executive said about how failures are handled in press releases, "Any time you sugarcoat it, you're going to get indigestion."[2]

Here are a few euphemisms I found in U.S. press releases: When the Three Mile Island nuclear plant near Harrisburg, Pennsylvania, almost exploded, its P.R. people described the fire as "rapid oxidation" and the explosion as "energetic disassembly." The damaged reactor core emitted no more heat than "17 home toasters." In 1985, when Coca-Cola U.S.A.'s old Coke had to be brought back under a new name, Coca-Cola Classic, the company said that new Coke was a "fighting brand" within a "megabrand." It had attributes that became a "strategic plank" in Coke's total marketing strategy. The press release never said new Coke was a flop.[3]

Why are so many of us like ostriches? Why do we bury our heads in the sand to avoid coming face to face with bad news? One reason is that we'd rather hear about positive things, but many students of the subject of failure think it's more than that — failure is personal and emotional to people. When we fail, our anxiety levels skyrocket. At times, we even deny that we failed. We talk about errors and mistakes instead — anything but that dreaded word, "failure." And this emotional response to failure keeps us from learning from it. We can learn much from it, though, if only we allow ourselves to learn. This book is written so that you'll allow yourself to learn about this unpleasant subject. There are three reasons why you'll learn:

First of all, chances are, your failure is not mentioned in this book. I do discuss in some detail more than 500 failures, from such nations as the United States, Canada, Australia, the Philippines, Japan, Indonesia, Hong Kong, Finland, Vietnam, Canary Islands, France, West Germany, the United Kingdom, Ireland, South Korea, Madagascar, Kenya, New Zealand, Belgium, Sweden, India, Taiwan, Italy, Switzerland, the People's Republic of China, Singapore, Malaysia, Brunei, Thailand, South Africa, Norway, the Netherlands, Egypt, Persian Gulf States, U.S.S.R., Colombia, Mexico, Chile, Argentina, and Brazil. But there's a high probability that none of your failures and none of your company's failures are mentioned in this book, and that means you can be detached and objective when you read about all the failures. You won't get emotionally involved because each failure you'll read about happened to somebody else, not to you — so you'll learn from somebody else's hard luck.

Second, hearing about failures is fun. And when something's fun, we get involved in it more, and the more we're involved, the more we learn. How do I know that hearing about failures is fun? Because I've taught tens of thousands of business executives in my seminars and even more university students than that over the years. Whenever I talk about failures, mistakes, errors, whatever you want to call them, I can see my audience's interest level rise dramatically. There are more smiles on their faces. They lean forward and use more positive evaluation gestures. I can tell this not only from their body language, which you'll learn more about in Chapter 10, but also because they always ask me more questions and want to discuss the failures more than any other part of what I've said. I've found out, too, that they remembered the concepts I talked about in conjunction with the failures more than they remembered the concepts I talked about in conjunction with the success stories I gave them.

And third, reading about failures is a lot better than learning the hard way — through experience. Why? It's not as painful!

Let's see how much fun failure can be. Here are a few people and companies that obviously made the wrong decisions:

- On January 1, 1962, the group later known as the Beatles auditioned for Decca Records. Decca turned the Beatles down. During the next four months, four other British record companies also declined to give them a contract.
- When Steve Wozniak was working for Hewlett-Packard in California in 1975, he built the first personal computer in his garage. He offered it to H–P, but was turned down. Wozniak and his garage partner, Steve Jobs, eventually started Apple Computer.
- Hollywood's Victor Fleming, who directed the movie *Gone with the Wind* in the late 1930s, turned down an offer of 20 percent of its profits and insisted on a flat fee instead. He thought the movie was going to be "the biggest white elephant of all time." Gary Cooper turned down the role of Rhett Butler. He said, "I'm just glad it'll be Clark Gable who's falling flat on his face, and not Gary Cooper."[4]
- Tris Speaker, the great U.S. baseball player said in 1921, "Babe Ruth made a big mistake when he gave up pitching."
- Lord Kelvin, President of the British Royal Society, said in 1885, "Heavier than air flying machines are impossible."
- Robert Milliken, who won the Nobel Prize in Physics, said in 1923, "There is no likelihood man can ever tap the power of the atom."
- Grover Cleveland said in 1905, several years after he had left the office of president of the United States, "Sensible and responsible women do not want to vote."

- Hollywood's Darryl F. Zanuck, head of 20th Century Fox Studios, said in 1946, "Video won't be able to hold onto any market it captures after the first six months. People will soon get tired of staring at a plywood box every night."[5]

- Gulf Oil wanted to use its "No-Nox" name to brand its gasoline in Indonesia. After all, Americans knew it meant no knocks occurred in the engine when they used Gulf No-Nox gasoline. However, after Gulf started using the "No-Nox" name in Indonesia, it found, to its chagrin, that "No-Nox" sounded like the Bahasa word, "nonok," which is a slang term for female genitals.[6]

- For many years, Guinness Stout, the popular Irish malty ale, had a difficult time in Hong Kong. British men liked it, so when it first entered the Hong Kong market, it positioned itself as a macho he-man's drink. However, women began drinking it because they thought it gave them the extra iron they needed during pregnancy and menstrual periods. Men were ridiculed as being effeminate if they ordered Guinness, and it took the company many years to overcome this stigma. An executive of the firm that markets Guinness in Hong Kong attended one of my seminars there in 1987. He told me it had finally overcome the problem, but it certainly took a lot of hard work.

- Former Baltimore Orioles baseball manager Earl Weaver said, "Managers are always learning, and mostly from our mistakes. That's why I keep a list of my mistakes at home for reference. I used to carry the listarfound in my pants pocket, but I finally had to stop. It gave me a limp."[7]

- Civil War General John Sedgwick's last words were about the enemy. He said, "They couldn't hit an elephant at this dist—." An enemy bullet killed him before he could finish his sentence.

Failures aren't all bad, though. There is often a silver lining within every failure cloud; for example, Christopher Columbus found America instead of India. Penicillin, rubber, Belgian endive, photography, X rays, the telescope, and electric current were all discovered by error. It may be possible that aging occurs because of an accumulation of errors in deoxyribonucleic acid (DNA). To prolong life, a few scientists began to experiment with ways of improving our body's ability to repair errors in the DNA molecule.[8]

Yes, as the old saying goes, to err is human. Errors will always be with us. Some people even became famous for failing, for making mistakes, like Douglas "Wrong Way" Corrigan who was flying from New York City to Los Angeles in 1938 but landed in Ireland instead. Some products have become famous *because* they failed — like the Edsel. (An Edsel in mint condition commands very high prices on the collector's market.) The Leaning Tower of Pisa is a symbol of error, but it's also a money-making tourist attraction in Italy. So, since failure is all around us in our everyday lives, why not make the best of it and learn from it?

In the next nine chapters you'll learn about many important mistakes that you should try to avoid at all costs. This book is a little different from what you might expect a book about errors to be about because most of the examples that illustrate the kinds of mistakes happened in the 1980s — although a few "old classics," like the Edsel, rear their ugly heads. Also, most of the examples will probably be unfamiliar to you. I've got thousands of examples in my files, but in this book, I've tried to give you little-known and very recent examples from companies both big and small, in the United States and abroad, from industrial marketers and consumer marketers, from products and services, and from profit-making and not-for-profit organizations. I've made sure these different examples have one thing in common — they teach you something about failure and how to avoid it.

To make sure you avoid failure, there's an important section after each mistake and accompanying examples entitled "What to Learn, What Action to Take." These sections tell you what you should have learned from reading about the mistakes made by different companies and how to avoid making similar mistakes. Finally, following these sections, there's a "How to Learn Even More by Digging Deeper" section, listing additional books and articles for you to look up in your search for learning through the failures of others.

Mastering the lessons you learn in this book will make you a better marketer and your company more profitable — that's my wish for you. That should be your wish, too. So go ahead and start turning that wish into reality.

NOTES

1.   Michael M. Miller, "What a Museum! Panda Punch, I Hate Peas, Nutrimato, and More," *Wall Street Journal*, 15 December 1986, p. 30.

2.   Janice C. Simpson, "Business Schools — and Students — Want to Talk Only About Success," *Wall Street Journal*, 15 December 1986, p. 29.

3.   Joanne Lipman, "In Times of Trouble, Candor is Often the First Casualty," *Wall Street Journal*, 15 December 1986, p. 29.

4.   Michael M. Miller, "Sometimes the Biggest Mistake is Saying No to a Future Success," *Wall Street Journal*, 15 December 1986, p. 29.

5.   "Tracking Hi-Tech: Digital Paper and Plastic Batteries," *World Executive's Digest*, August 1988, p. 14.

6.   David A. Ricks, *Big Business Blunders*, (Homewood, Ill.: Dow Jones-Irwin, 1983), p. 42.

7.   Earl Weaver, *It's What You Learn After You Know It All That Counts*, (New York: Simon and Schuster, 1983), p. 300.

8.   M. Hirsh Goldberg, *The Blunder Book*, (New York: William Morrow and Co., 1984), pp. 13–14.

PART II
THE MARKETING SETTING

2
Customers

You learned when you first started studying marketing that you always start out by finding out what your customers want and need — only after that should you attempt to build your marketing mix. Businesses ignore the consumer at their peril.

There are many mistakes you can make when you deal with your customers. Four important ones that have cost firms billions of dollars are covered in this chapter: offending community groups and other pressure groups, offending minority groups, offending women by sexism, and misreading your customers' deeply held values. Learn from these mistakes — read what other firms have done, and do your best *not* to copy them.

OFFENDING COMMUNITY GROUPS AND OTHER PRESSURE GROUPS

Many marketers have offended certain groups without meaning to do so. Some groups are more important than others, of course, and it's almost impossible to avoid hurting the feelings of somebody when you're marketing to millions. Marketers can become paranoid trying to anticipate all eventualities. It's better to err on the side of caution most of the time, but it's impossible to anticipate all the pressure groups you may alienate. Make sure, though, that you don't alienate pressure groups that live up to their name — that will put downward pressure on your sales and profits. Some important and less important pressure groups and spokesmen who have been offended by marketing techniques are discussed in the following paragraphs.

For two years, I was a Visiting Professor of Marketing at Memorial University of Newfoundland in St. John's, Canada, where once a year the residents look forward to eating the local delicacy, flipper pies. They are made of the flippers of seals, and since Newfoundland's main industry is fishing, it is even patriotic to eat flipper pies. Once a year seal hunting season arrives, and the men of Newfoundland in the fishing industry go out to sea and kill seals with clubs. This has raised protest in some parts of the world, but not in eastern Canada.

Mattel Inc., the U.S. toy manufacturer and marketer, created controversy in Newfoundland in 1986. Its Barbie Sticker Album included a story, starring Barbie, called "Amid Snow and Ice." Part of the story reads like this: "Barbie is particularly concerned for the pretty seal pups. She has come to help protect them from the ruthless hunters that slaughter the young seals for their soft, white skins." Along with "her wildlife-loving friends," Barbie sprayed the seals with dye to make the skins worthless, and so "a thousand seals have been saved from a cruel death."

When a St. John's TV station found out about it, it ran the story. It also mentioned that every time one of Mattel's stuffed animals, Snuggles the Seal, was sold, $1 was contributed to the Humane Society in the United States. Soon stores throughout the province pulled the sticker album from its shelves and returned them to their suppliers. Newfoundland's minister of fisheries asked Mattel to withdraw the publication from the world market, saying, "There hasn't been a white-coat seal hunt for four or five years," that seal pups are no longer killed, and that the Barbie story "perpetuates the lie that harvesting seals is somehow worse than harvesting other animals." The Canadian book distributor told Mattel that in the future Barbie "should stick to Ken and cars and clothes," and not tackle ecological issues.

An Italian licensee published the album, and Mattel reviewed the contents of it before it was published. However, it didn't find a problem. Very few people outside of Canada know much about Newfoundland, which is Canada's poorest province and which has a very small population, so it's understandable that people at Mattel's headquarters in southern California didn't know how strongly Newfoundlanders felt about its annual seal hunt. Newfoundlanders find themselves the butt of many jokes told by fellow Canadians, because of its poverty and perceived backwardness, and they strongly resent any criticism from people who live "off the island."[1]

When Ralston Purina Company, maker of Meow Mix cat food, decided to hold a Meow Off contest at Lincoln Center in New York City in 1986, with the winner receiving $25,000 and a role in a new cat food commercial, it thought it had covered all eventualities. First, it donated $25,000 worth of Meow Mix to four organizations that shelter homeless cats. Second, it made sure that the 40-piece orchestra's stringed instruments were equipped with nylon or steel strings instead of catgut.

It anticipated *that* eventuality, but that wasn't enough to keep the Anti-Cruelty Society of Chicago from complaining that the cats were being treated cruelly. To produce meowing from finicky cats, it offered each cat some Meow Mix, then some tuna fish, then locked it in a closet, and then put it in a travel box. The executive director of the society said, "It's degrading to the animals." Whether it's degrading or not, it's dangerous to aggravate organizations that try to prevent cruelty to animals when you make animal food. It's almost like biting the hand that feeds you.[2]

Harcourt Brace Jovanovich Inc. is not only a large textbook publisher — it also owns Sea World, an aquatic park in San Diego, California, and other aquatic parks in Texas and Florida. In 1986, it purchased another aquatic park in Rancho Palos Verdes, California, named Marineland, 100 miles north of San Diego's Sea World, and announced plans to renovate it. However, two months after buying the famous tourist attraction, it closed Marineland, fired its 300 employees, and decided to develop the prime ocean-front real estate instead. It shipped all the trained animals to Sea World.

That aggravated people in the community. A citizen's group collected 25,000 signatures against the closing and threatened to boycott Harcourt textbooks. Harcourt realized chances of getting local clearance for a real-estate development were poor, so it decided to sell the land instead. It explained to the public that it *had* planned to continue operating Marineland, but then found that $25 million — which was more than the initial purchase price — in unexpected improvements were needed. In a press release, it assured the community that "the publisher of Carl Sandburg and T. S. Elliott does not desecrate what it touches." A Rancho Palos Verdes city councilman said, "Who can believe Harcourt when it can't even get T. S. Eliot's name right?"[3]

Harcourt hoped that the fuss would soon blow over, but it took quite a while for tempers in the community to cool down.

Australia celebrated its bicentennial in 1988. In 1987, the New South Wales Bicentennial Authority approached Sid Londish, a land developer, for permission to erect a giant steel birthday cake on vacant land owned by his company in Sydney. He agreed, and even offered to set aside A$220,000 for the project. People didn't like the idea, though, and so Comrealty Ltd., his company, staged a contest with a radio station to come up with an alternative. The winning entry was an oversize echidna (anteater) with 200 candles in place of its spines. That cost too much, and the next alternative, a neon map with the cake and anteater, was rejected.

By this time, Londish came under pubic attack for throwing his money away on frivolous eyesores instead of donating it to worthy causes. To quiet public opinion, he decided to pay for two decorative metal archways in a park and to donate any leftover funds to charity. Mr. Londish didn't anticipate his good intentions would backfire so much. It's best, when you donate to a public cause, to make sure that the great majority of the public *supports* the cause.[4]

When the New York Giants professional football team won the National Football Conference title and the right to play in the 1987 Super Bowl against the American Football Conference champion Denver Broncos, New York City's mayor declared that if the Giants won, he would not allow them to have a ticker tape parade in Manhattan, since the Giants had moved from New York City to a suburban New Jersey location several years earlier. American Express sensed a marketing opportunity, and got the mayor's promise to support a full ticker tape parade in Manhattan if American Express, and not New York City, paid the $700,000 estimated cost.

After word of American Express' offer got out, the owner of the Giants said if they won the game, they didn't want to celebrate with a ticker tape parade in Manhattan — they would celebrate at the stadium in New Jersey.

Then, the governor of Colorado publicly asked American Express at a press conference, "What are you going to do for *us*?" Several Denver radio stations asked their listeners to stop using their American Express credit cards, and some local restaurants started rejecting the cards. American Express officials flew from New York to Denver to meet with state and city officials. They offered to pay for a ticker tape parade if the Broncos won. Eventually, American Express contributed money to both states and to charities. It got them a lot of exposure for a few days, but what kind of exposure? One American Express official said, "The whole thing was a disaster." Another one said, "My guess is that if they decided to do this again, they would do it with great trepidation."[5]

FMC Corporation, a large industrial marketer in the United States, produces Commence, a herbicide. When it introduced the product, it ran a series of TV commercials that were intended to be a humorous look at what happens when two farmers make a friendly wager. One farmer bet several friends that Commence can get rid of three types of troublesome weeds. Of course, Commence *did* get rid of the weeds, and one loser had to paint his tractor pink. Another loser had to literally eat his hat. Still another loser had to get a Mohawk haircut. The purpose of these ads was to get attention, to set the new herbicide apart from the traditionally bland advertising in the field.

Although the ads *did* get attention, some of it was unfavorable. Some farmers found the ad's portrayal of farmers objectionable and abusive, and ten of them wrote and complained. Although ten was a small number, FMC was especially sensitive to the criticism because Commence was a joint project with another firm, Elanco, an agricultural division of Eli Lilly & Co. So in February 1988, it pulled the ads and replaced them with something less controversial.[6]

Australia's unions are very strong, and marketers need to take their reactions into account when they formulate their marketing strategy and tactics. The insurance industry didn't do that in the middle 1970s and learned the hard way how unions can put a crimp in their plans. The Labor government of then Prime Minister Whitlam announced plans for the government to become involved in the insurance business. The insurance trade association decided to mount a counterattack by convincing the public that this was a very bad idea.

At the time, the Australian postal service was chaotic, and the trade association used this in their counterattack. I was living there at the time as a visiting professor, and I counted ten nationwide postal strikes in a 12-month period. I didn't even bother to count the even more numerous local strikes in Sydney, where I lived. It seemed the Redfern Post Office, which handled most of the mail for businesses in downtown Sydney where I worked, was grossly mismanaged at the time and seemed to be continually on strike. I began mailing two additional copies of every letter several days apart to increase the probability that my letters got delivered.

So the trade association ran a series of ads in the Sydney *Morning Herald* and other newspapers with this message: "If you don't want to see Australia turned into one giant post office, do something about it. Tell your representative in Parliament that you are against the government's plan to go into the insurance business." Their logic went like this: Private insurance companies provide the bulk of financing to businesses in Australia. If the government gets into the insurance business, it will sell policies at such a low cost that the private insurance companies could not match them, and eventually the private insurance companies would have to go out of business. Only the government's insurance monopoly would be left, and it would decide which businesses get funding and which don't. This is the first step toward the socialization of Australia — or so the ads said.

The headline, about turning Australia into "one giant post office" got the telecommunications unions very angry. They told the trade association if it didn't pull the ads immediately and issue a public apology, they would not deliver any mail or telegrams to any insurance company and would cut off their telex and local and long distance telephone service. The powerful insurance industry immediately capitulated and did as the unions asked.

In the early 1980s, I remember reading that Ralph Nader, the consumer advocate and frequent flyer, was bumped from his flight in the United States because of overbooking. Of all the people in the world *not* to bump, it's Ralph Nader. He sued, and the airline got a lot of unfavorable publicity.

In Canada in 1985, David Reville, a left-leaning member of the Ontario Parliament, spoke in support of striking bank employees in front of two branches of the Canadian Imperial Bank of Commerce. He also opened a "nuisance" account into which strikers would repeatedly deposit and then withdraw a few cents. The bank retaliated by closing not only his "nuisance" account, but also his three other accounts. It also called in his $10,000 loan.

It was a mistake to anger this powerful person. He began to wonder, "If they do this to me, how does one suspect they treat people with less access to news conferences?" Mr. Reville talked about it in several news conferences. He talked about it in Parliament, which set up a committee to investigate the matter. Ontario's attorney general began investigating whether there were grounds for taking legal action. Mr. Reville also talked to Ontario's premier, David Peterson. Mr. Peterson called the chairman of the bank about the matter. The chairman then conceded his bank had "made an error in judgment and will take every reasonable step to rectify it."[7]

What to Learn, What Action to Take

There are five major things you can learn from these nine examples:

- It's very easy to overlook at least one pressure group in your marketing (and other) plans.
- Some pressure groups are more important and more vocal than others. Make sure you are sensitive at least to the needs of the more important and more vocal groups.
- Never alienate powerful spokesmen of pressure groups, including Ralph Nader, congressmen, senators, and members of parliament.
- Try to handle well all situations in which you gave inadvertent offense. You should apologize, even if you don't want to, so you don't antagonize the groups

any more. That's the way to make the best out of a bad situation.

- Monitor the effect your action has on sales. The stronger the negative impact, the more you'll have to do.

OFFENDING MINORITY GROUPS

Offending community groups and other pressure groups is bad enough, but it is almost suicidal when you offend a minority group in the United States because many of these groups are very well organized and can launch boycotts against your company's products. From the following examples, note that three important minority groups with lots of clout are gays, blacks, and Italian-Americans.

The January 26, 1988, issue of the *Wall Street Journal* quoted Michael Lesser, chairman of the Lowe Marschalk advertising agency, as disputing the effectiveness of marketing beer to homosexuals and lesbians. He said, "I'm surprised beer companies would think seriously of advertising in the gay media. Beer imagery is so delicate that getting associated with homosexuals could be detrimental." Lowe Marschalk handled all advertising for Stroh's Beer, a major factor in beer sales in the United States.

When members of the Chicago gay community heard about this, they decided to launch a public awareness campaign to draw attention to what they said is an anti-gay bias in the marketing and advertising industries. So, they organized CAMMP, the Coalition Against Media/Marketing Prejudice. A weekly Chicago gay newspaper, *Windy City Times,* ran a full-page story in its February 4 issue to publicize this cause and featured a photo showing CAMMP members emptying bottles of Stroh's beer. CAMMP contacted Stroh's headquarters to protest, telling its managers that they were soliciting support from regional and national organizations, activists, and businesses.

Stroh's managers were worried. Gays in the United States have higher disposable incomes than most market segments, and it is an important market for beer and many other products and services. So it apologized in a letter to the *Wall Street Journal* saying that the agency's comments were contrary to Stroh's nondiscrimination policy and weren't made on behalf of Stroh's, and said that the agency was warned that "any similar public comments offensive to any group could have a serious adverse effect" on their relationship with Stroh's.

It also ran an apology in the form of an ad in the February 11 issue of *Windy City Times,* reiterating what it said in the letter to the *Wall Street Journal* and objecting to a boycott of its products as a result of the agency's comments. The ad said in part, "Stroh's fully understands the affront the gay and lesbian community must feel as a result of our agency's comments. However, we hope you understand that Stroh's has done nothing wrong and that the improper actions of a third party should not be the basis for concerted action against Stroh's. Stroh's will continue to make its advertising placement decisions without regard to the sexual preferences of the media readers. We assure you that we will continue to adhere to our strict policy of nondiscrimination for any reason, including sex, age, religious belief, and sexual preference."

That apology in *Windy City Times* was just one demand made by CAMMP. Other demands included a similar ad in the *Wall Street Journal*, ads saluting the gay community during Gay and Lesbian Pride Week in June, and financial support of the Gay and Lesbian Press Association. A CAMMP spokesman said, "The quick resolution of this matter underlines the determination and economic strength of our community. Let this serve as a notice that the lesbian and gay community will not tolerate attacks upon us or those who support us."

Homosexuals are definitely big in spending power, and so many marketers are doing all they can not to offend this powerful group. However, it's hard to draw the line between supporting one group — which might offend a much larger group, in this case, heterosexuals and Bible Belt Christians — and not offending the minority group. It makes marketing much more difficult.[8]

The U.S. Army doesn't want to be controversial, either. It was planning to run a full-page ad in the February 1988 issue of *Student Lawyer* magazine but pulled the ad when it learned that the February issue had an article about gay law students. Apparently, the U.S. Army didn't want to offend the heterosexual community more than it didn't want to offend the gay community. Although some gays took offense, it was not made into a major issue by them, mainly because the U.S. Army does not want homosexuals and lesbians to join its ranks anyway.[9]

Irving Bottner, president of Revlon's Professional Products Division was quoted in the October 13, 1986, issue of *Newsweek* magazine as saying that black hair-care companies face extinction because they make inferior products. "In the next couple of years, the black-owned businesses will disappear. They'll all be sold to white companies." A Chicago-based black organization promoting social change, Operation PUSH (People United to Save Humanity), Inc., accused Revlon of racism and began a boycott by blacks of Revlon products in Chicago and tried to extend the boycott to all 50 states. Several black churches staged mock funerals to "bury Revlon" with a nationwide boycott. Although

Revlon issued an apology from Bottner, claiming his remarks were taken out of context, the boycott kept escalating. Several black publications, including *Ebony, Essence,* and *Jet,* refused to accept Revlon advertising.

Revlon hired a public relations agency to handle the fallout, promoted a black to vice president, promised more minority hiring, increased contributions to black charities, and agreed to sell its manufacturing plant in South Africa. It tried to place ads saluting Martin Luther King, Jr., in black newspapers on the King national holiday, but most of the publications rejected it.

Things got worse. The American Health and Beauty Aid Institute, a consortium of black beauty companies, increased its budget for its "buy black" campaign by $1 million. Operation PUSH accelerated its campaign urging blacks to buy products manufactured by black-owned companies, with the Revlon boycott as its centerpiece. It seemed to work. Revlon's ethnic hair-care division and its two lines of beauty products, Realistic and Roux, lost market share.[10]

Shortly after the Revlon episode, an official of professional baseball's Los Angeles Dodgers team, Al Campanis, was interviewed on national television and said that blacks had good ballplaying talent but poor managerial talent. He also said blacks were poor swimmers because they lacked natural buoyancy in the water. He was fired. About a year later, a CBS Television Network sportscaster, Jimmy "The Greek" Snyder, was fired because of similar remarks he made in a television interview about blacks. The Dodgers and CBS apparently didn't want a repetition of the Revlon boycott by blacks. These two employees made a mistake, but at least their employers learned the Revlon lesson and minimized the damage, as did Quaker Oats. In the late 1960s, it reacted to black criticism by changing its Aunt Jemima figure to look less like a plantation house cook. Clearly, it's bad business to offend large minority groups that are well organized and have used boycott tactics in the past.

U.S. blacks have also gotten angry at products they deem offensive marketed entirely in other countries, for example, Japan, a nation in which there are very few blacks. The blacks who do live there are definitely not part of the Japanese race. In 1986, Japan's prime minister, Yasuhiro Nakasone, suggested that U.S. blacks and other minorities there were dragging down the intellectual level of the United States. In July 1988, Michio Watanabe, a leading Japanese politician, said that U.S. blacks had no qualms about going bankrupt through excessive spending. Both men apologized after media reported black anger in the United States.

Then, in August 1988, U.S. media reported that "Little Black Sambo" and "Little Black Hanna," two black cartoon children with exaggerated racial features that U.S. blacks felt were offensive, were used on a line of children's toys and beachware in Japan. The manufacturers, which also marketed Smurf products there, defended the cartoon caricatures as appearing "cute" to the Japanese, but decided to withdraw them from the market after the chairman of the Black Caucus in the U.S. House of Representatives suggested a black boycott of all Japanese imports to the United States. In 1989, Japanese publishers stopped printing all "Little Black Sambo" books.

The Black Caucus was also upset by U.S. news media reports in August 1988 of Yamato Mannequin Company's black store mannequins with exaggerated facial features. The company recalled all black mannequins and discontinued their manufacture and marketing. The Black Caucus also suggested that the Japanese government start a public education program on racial issues. The new Japanese prime minister, Noboru Takeshita, sent a letter of apology to the Black Caucus, and the boycott didn't happen. The Japanese seem to be quite sensitive to foreigners' perceptions. The nation's second-largest tourist agency, Kinki Nippon Tourist Company, uses the name Kintetsu International overseas, because "Kinki" sounds like "kinky," an English term for bizarre sexual practices.[11]

Sambo's Restaurants are no more. The name "Sambo" became very offensive to blacks at the height of the civil rights movements of the 1960s. The chain's name came from its excellent pancakes. The 1890s children's story, "Little Black Sambo," was about a young black boy who loved pancakes. He fooled a ferocious tiger, who turned into butter. Sambo then used his "tiger butter" on his huge stack of pancakes. Sambo's didn't want to change its name, so it changed Sambo into a little Indian boy with light skin, the son of a maharaja. Its logo featured an Indian-looking Sambo in a turban playing with a tiger. That didn't work, and blacks were still offended. Eventually, the chain gave in and changed its name to No Place Like Sam's and then to Seasons, but it was too late. It eventually went bankrupt in 1981.

Godfather's Pizza almost made the same mistake. Founded in Omaha, Nebraska, where very few Italian-Americans live, it originally sought to capitalize on the popularity of the movie, *The Godfather*. In its TV commercials, a gangster "made you an offer you couldn't refuse" — a succulent Godfather's Pizza. It was surprised to learn that Italian-Americans found the ads offensive, but it changed the ads and never stressed the gangster stereotype again. It didn't change its name, and it continued to grow throughout the United States, including areas where many Italian-Americans live.

Sometimes, it's "damned if you do and damned if you don't." Coca-Cola found this out when it introduced a contest in March 1980, promoting its poorly selling Mr. PiBB soft drink. It was called "Find the PiBB Girl," and it offered $10,000 to a young woman possessing the facial features of five white actresses and singers. Blacks protested, and the company quickly withdrew all its promotional material. According to law, though, it still had to award the prizes.[12]

Colgate learned from this. In 1985, the U.S. consumer products firm bought 50 percent of the Hong Kong-based Hawley and Hazel Chemical Company in order to get a much bigger share of the toothpaste market in southeast Asia. Hawley and Hazel had marketed Darkie Toothpaste since the 1920s throughout the region and enjoyed large sales and market shares ranging from 20 to 70 percent in Hong Kong, Malaysia, Singapore, Brunei, Taiwan, Thailand, and many other nations in that part of the world. Although the toothpaste's Chinese characters are literally translated as "Black Man Tooth Paste," and although the logo features a top-hatted and gleaming-toothed smiling likeness of the late white singer Al Jolson in blackface, the Interfaith Center on Corporate Responsibility, a related movement of the National Council of Churches in the United States, took offense. In late 1985, it said the brand name is racist and that the use of Jolson in blackface is demeaning to blacks. It demanded that the name and logo be changed so that Colgate would "not be associated with promoting racial stereotypes in the Third World."

Colgate was caught on the horns of a dilemma. The use of a black person — and Asian buyers perceive the top-hatted Jolson as a black man, not a white man in blackface — for a toothpaste in Asia, where few black people are seen, is a marketing plus. According to market studies, one of the first (and pleasant) things Asians notice in black people is their beautiful smiles, as a result of the contrast between their dark skin and white teeth. Darkie is positioned as a "bright-smile" toothpaste in many markets there, and it's important to stress this in its packaging. It did by using a black man. Furthermore, changing the name of the toothpaste and logo would do away with more than 60 years of good will that the brand had built up. The Chinese-speaking buyers, who don't know English anyway, pay no attention to the English "Darkie" name and only look at the "Black Man Tooth Paste" name in Chinese characters, and Colgate had no intention of marketing Darkie outside of southeast Asia, where it knew it would offend black people.

Colgate explained all this to the Interfaith Center on Corporate Responsibility, but the group continued its pressure. It filed a shareholder resolution challenging the company's practice. Finally, in early 1987, Colgate-Palmolive agreed to change the name of the toothpaste and remove Al Jolson in blackface from the label, and the church group agreed to withdraw its shareholder resolution. Hawley and Hazel began extensive consumer testing to find a name and a logo that would both eliminate the offense to U.S. blacks but was still close enough to the original to be quickly recognized by Darkie's brand-loyal customers in its Asian markets. In January 1989, Colgate announced it would rename Darkie and redesign its logo to show a smiling "racially ambiguous" man in a silk top hat, tuxedo, and bow tie. (I showed the new man to 73 people in Chattanooga, Tennessee, and 84 percent of them perceived him as black.) To reduce confusion and avoid lost sales, the new name, Darlie, would be changed in stages over twelve months, and the new logo would appear in 1990. Colgate would pay for all redesign and repackaging costs and reimburse Hawley and Hazel for any loss in profits caused by the change. The Chinese characters, "Black Man Tooth Paste," would remain unchanged.

It's interesting that a black group didn't challenge Colgate-Palmolive, although a member of the Congressional Black Caucus criticized Darkie and its logo in 1988. If a black group had challenged Colgate, this issue would have received much more publicity, and the company might have moved faster.

Time will tell if the new name and logo will work or not. But Colgate took a middle ground. It didn't make a drastic name and label change. A drastic change would have been a major mistake. It would have meant the loss of 60-plus years of marketing goodwill in southeast Asia from that market's viewpoint. And after all, the old label reinforced the positive perception that people in the Far East have of black people and their friendly smiles. But of course Colgate was thinking of its bigger market in the United States when it made its decision.[13]

What to Learn, What Action to Take

Minority groups are very sensitive because they are in the minority. If you aren't a member of a minority group — and all of us are, to some extent — try to empathize with them. If you aren't that sensitive to others' needs and feelings, ask members of minorities for help. There are probably members in your company. One source to tap is the vice president of "special markets." This title is almost always a euphemism for "minority markets," and most larger firms have this position in their organization charts. If you're getting ready to run an ad, pretest it. Make sure a sufficient percentage of respondents are members of heavily organized minority groups.

And remember this — many nations are melting pots these days. Toronto, Ontario, Canada, has a very large ethnic population. Australia's immigration rules have been liberalized over the years, and there are many Greeks, Turks, and Asians living there now. India has over 300 languages. Hong Kong residents are migrating abroad in great numbers before the People's Republic of China takes over in 1997. Large numbers of Vietnamese refugees live in many nations. Many cities in the United States have elected mayors who are members of minority groups.

In the United States, there are many minority groups, including blacks, Hispanics or Latinos, and Asian-Americans. Blacks are the most organized and vocal, but such organizations as the League of United Latin American Citizens, the American G.I. Forum, and the Mexican-American Legal Defense Fund indicate that Hispanics are moving in that direction, too. In fact in 1988, the Chicano Caucus of the Democratic Party of California called for a boycott of Citibank until the bank agreed to an "equitable adjustment" of the $2.6 billion in loans it is owed by Mexico. The caucus accused the bank and other U.S. corporations of contributing to Mexico's economic woes by loaning it billions of dollars after the great oil price drop. Citibank was targeted because it is Mexico's largest creditor. At that time, Mexico owed all its creditors more than $103 billion, including nearly $45 billion in interest.[14]

The fastest growing minority in the United States is Asian-Americans, and they are especially noticeable in Hawaii (where they form a majority) and in large cities on the West and East Coasts. Immigrants from the Indian subcontinent are a powerful presence in the motel business. So there are more and more minority groups to worry about offending than ever before. The need for caution is great.

SEXISM

This is a special case of offending minority groups. Technically, women are *not* a minority, since they make up 51 percent of the human race, but sexism is a very special issue. Marketers have to be careful of making sexist remarks. Women can be offended by them, especially in nations where the feminist movement is well established, such as the United States. Pressure from women's groups and a near doubling of women in the work force from the 1970s to the 1980s have forced U.S.

advertisers to sell their products and services using women modeling confidence, success, and security, as well as sexuality. It's important not to offend women anywhere, of course, but an ad or remark that is considered sexist in the United States and Canada may be considered complimentary in Mexico, Brazil, and the Philippines, where the feminist movement is still in its infancy.

For example, Charles Anderson of Fallon McElligott, the second largest advertising agency in Minnesota, with $130 million in annual billings, made a presentation at a seminar in October 1987 to show off its creative flair. It showed three female stars of the TV series, *Dynasty*, with the headline "Bitch, Bitch, Bitch" in one slide. The director of the Mankato Women's Center, Neala Schleuning, wrote a letter complaining about the negative stereotypes of women in its presentation and accused the agency of having a "male gonad style of doing business." She wrote, "While I was generally impressed with the creative level and quality of the work of your organization, I was both annoyed and offended by the persistence of negative stereotypes of women in your audiovisual presentation. It's a shame that you have to resort to such shop-worn ideas to convince us of your creativity."

Mr. Anderson wrote back, thanking her for her "deeply thoughtful and perceptive letter." He went on to say that Mrs. Schleuning should visit an African tribe to spread the feminist gospel and referred her to the enclosed photo of a naked African boy kissing the backside of a cow. "I pass the picture along to you believing that you will be able to deal with these people in the same firm, yet even-handed, manner in which you dealt with us."

Mrs. Schleuning discussed the reply with a statewide group of women's organizations, which wrote to the agency asking whether Anderson's letter represented its true feelings. Evidently it did, because Patrick Fallon wrote her back, volunteering to pay half of her travel to Africa, "or full expenses, one way." His partner, McElligott then sent her a pith helmet and mosquito net, calling her "our brave missionary" to the tribe.

She showed these responses to the organizations, which began sending copies of all the correspondence to Fallon McElligott's clients, urging them to question continuing their relationship with the agency. Judi Servoss, vice president for advertising at US West, one of the agency's largest accounts, recommended that Fallon McElligott be dropped, and her superiors concurred unanimously. She said, "We were extremely uncomfortable with the incident. We're a company that strongly espouses pluralism and equal opportunity, and the reaction by the agency to its critic was one that flies in the face of all that. We just didn't feel it was appropriate behavior for somebody that we work with."

At this point, the agency began worrying that it might lose such other clients as Porsche USA, Lee Jeans, First Tennessee Corporation, Continental Illinois Bank & Trust Co., the Wall Street Journal, and Federal Express. So it contacted all its clients, apologizing for its response and advising them to expect inquiries from the media when word of US West's decision was made public. Fallon personally apologized to Mrs. Schleuning, and he and McElligott met with the coordinator of the Minnesota Women's Consortium to apologize. Fallon said, "There really can be no excuse of explanation for our behavior, except that we allowed our reaction to your criticism to sweep us beyond the bounds of judgment, taste, and common decency. It shouldn't have happened, and it won't happen again. . . . We just overreacted and used bad judgment. We made a mistake, and it became public. Hopefully we're good enough that one mistake is something our clients don't have to understand but will forgive." That seemed to have worked. The agency just lost the one account, but that account made up a large percentage of its billings. In 1988, Fallon resigned from the agency.

What did Mrs. Schleuning think about all this? She said she never intended to "bring the agency to its knees. I don't wish anyone ill. But, we all have to live with the consequences of our own actions."[15]

Joseph Bento's Michelin tire retail store in Toronto, Ontario, Canada, sent out 20,000 flyers in late 1979 showing "Bib," the Michelin tire man popping up through one stack of Michelin radial tires and a nude woman popping up through a second stack. The ad attracted a lot of attention, and Mr. Bento sold all his inventory. However, Michelin revoked his license and refused to sell him more tires because "he was jeopardizing the image of our product." A company spokesman was embarrassed by the wrong kind of attention and told the media it had not authorized Bento to use "Bib" and the nude woman together in the ad.[16]

Several feminist groups protested when a northern California mall, Vallco Fashion Park, ran an ad in 1986 in the San Jose *Mercury-News* showing a model in handcuffs under the headline, "Crimes of Fashion." Sales at the mall were reported down slightly for the next few weeks.[17]

In 1985, Famolare shoes ran an ad showing the legs of a female runner in a starting position next to a man's hand holding a gun. They were shown in regional magazines in the northeastern United States. Shortly thereafter, several women's groups began criticizing the ads for what they perceived to be as sexual inequality. The company quickly replaced the ads.[18]

Here is a more blatant example of sexual inequality. In November 1985 in Argentina, Piña Colada American Club, a premixed alcoholic cocktail marketed by Dellepiane, a local distillery, created a lot of controversy with its ads in a nation where the feminist movement is not very strong. Because of this, the ad did *not* backfire. It's discussed in this book, though, to show you that you've got to know the culture of the nation in which you're running your ads. This kind of ad probably wouldn't work in the United States, but it *did* work in Argentina.

The ad campaign was based on a pun — the word "piña" in Argentine Spanish usually means "punch." Several nine-second spots show different women, each with a shiny black eye (obviously painted on) asking her man to "Give me another piña." The women lie in bed, emerge from a swimming pool, and are at a party, and their tone of voice ranges from sultry to submissive. Feminist groups, especially organizations that assist abused women, called for a boycott of the product and threatened to take legal action against the ad agency, Schussheim-Braga Menendez, for "incitement to violence." One organization said the ad "reinforces the common notion that women find pleasure in blows."

The ad agency decided to mollify critics by showing a man with a black eye painted on, also asking for another punch. But the company kept the ad running because sales quadrupled in one month. The agency explained, "The ad's clearly a joke. The black eye was obviously painted on, and by asking for a piña, the model undoubtedly means she wants more sex. Besides, you have to come up with a really bold commercial to sell a product on a small budget." (Its budget was only $10,000.) Furthermore, research shows that Argentine women reject ads showing females in decision-making positions and prefer traditional sex object and housewife roles. As a result, marketers reject emancipated female characters in ads in that nation. For example, when an ad agency proposed a beer commercial in which the female character was moving all her things into an apartment where she would be living alone, the client rejected it by saying, "If she is moving out of home to live all by herself, she must be a whore."[19]

There's a difference in viewpoints as to whether Nude Beer and Nude Nuts made a mistake or not. Both products, made by Golden Beverage Company of Irvine, California, feature photos of women in their bathing suits on their packages. You can scratch the tops off their bathing suits to reveal their breasts. In Denver, Colorado, the products were average sellers. Then, local police removed them from stores because they were judged to be obscene. A short time later, a state judge ordered that they couldn't be banned. When they were put back on the shelves, sales soared. The New York chapter of the National Organization for Women ingored Nude Beer until 1988 when Nude Nuts were introduced. They then decided to protest. At the time I wrote this book, the result of the protest was unclear. Will it be like Denver and Argentina, or will it be like the Fallon McElligott ad agency?[20]

Ads that U.S. feminist groups would have perceived as sexist also work fairly well in Australia, where the feminist movement is still in its infancy. In 1977, the Victoria Dairy Industry Association (VDIA) launched a highly successful campaign promoting flavored milk under the "Big M" label. Its radio ads used many double entendres, and its TV, print, and outdoor ads were very heavy on surf and sun, full of beautiful young women in extremely skimpy bikinis. Sales of flavored milk increased dramatically in Melbourne and other Victoria cities after the campaign began.

The VDIA campaign was copied almost verbatim in Nova Scotia, Canada, in 1982, but it was a dismal failure. Many women complained, and a new campaign was substituted.

Several years before Texas Air Corporation bought Continental Airlines, Continental called itself the "Proud Bird with the Golden Tail" in its U.S. ads. Soon after its initial campaign, it decided to change the copy but keep the theme. Taking a tip from Singapore Airlines, whose "Singapore Girl" ads have become famous the world over, it showed several of its female flight attendants with the headline, "We really move our tails for you." This irritated the flight attendants union and several feminist groups, and Continental was forced to drop the ads. Continental didn't appear to learn from this mistake. In early 1986, it ran a radio ad that many listeners perceived as depicting a telephone caller trying to make a date with a prostitute. A Continental spokesman said the person in the ad was really calling a Continental reservation agent and asking for a cheap no-frills fare. After numerous complaints, radio stations in New York City, Denver, Los Angeles, and Chicago refused to run the ads.[21]

In 1988, Peterson Outdoor Advertising Company put up three billboards in Chattanooga, Tennessee, featuring Oggi hair care products. The boards showed a nude female with long blonde hair covering her private parts. After receiving many complaints from women, Peterson removed the boards. This cost the outdoor advertising plant $5,000 in billings.[22]

What to Learn, What Action to Take

What can you conclude from these examples? First of all, know your market. In some countries, such as Argentina and Australia, women are still looked upon as sex objects and housewives, and sexist remarks will not offend — they might even increase sales. In others, beware — even showing a female athlete ready to run, just waiting for the starting gun, can create criticism and hurt sales. Second, remember that sexist remarks are most visible in advertising, but marketing executives must be astute enough not to write sexist letters to women who can exert pressure on them if offended. Finally, when in doubt if your communication is going to be perceived as sexist or not, either research the issue or err on the side of caution and don't use that communication at all.

MISREADING CUSTOMERS' DEEPLY HELD VALUES

Although this book is being read by marketing executives from many different nations, it's being published first in the United States, and the majority of its *initial* readers, at least, are Americans. So, most of the examples are from the United States. Executives from other nations often do business with Americans, and are interested in how U.S. marketing executives behave and how U.S. consumers react to marketing techniques. Therefore, I'm going to concentrate on U.S. values in this mistake, not on values from other nations.

What are values? They are the states of being that people want to achieve. They describe the overall goals of society and of subgroups within that society. At the deepest and most enduring level are the cultural values held by most people in a society, such as ideas about security and freedom. The next level are values that relate to consumption activities, such as convenience and service. At the most superficial level are values that pertain to a certain product or product category — they're the benefits people feel a product should possess.[23]

At the risk of oversimplification, there are seven main U.S. cultural values — the "Can-do" spirit, hard work for its own sake, love of sports, love of children, fundamentalism in religion, money as a visible reward, big dislike of wasting time, high level of patriotism, and a thin web of social relationships.[24] Violate these values at your own risk. The following are examples of firms that misread consumers' deeply held cultural values.

In 1986, all-talk radio station WHBQ in Memphis, Tennessee, promoted its ten different topics under the overall format, "Talk . . ."

There was "Talk Jobs," "Talk Dirt," "Talk Fun," "Talk Money," "Talk Sex," and five more. It ran "Talk Sex" ads on the sides and backs of city buses and received many complaints. The station promptly removed the "Talk Sex" posters.[25]

It's been traditional to eat hot dogs and unshelled peanuts at baseball parks in the United States — even if you never eat them at home or in restaurants. The peanuts have traditionally come in shells, and spectators discard the shells on the stadium's floor. During the 1986 major league baseball season at New York's Shea Stadium, where the Mets play their home games, the concessionaire, Harry M. Stevens, Inc., began selling preshelled peanuts in cellophane packages. Sales fell 15 percent and complaints escalated.[26]

In 1987, in the spirit of *glasnost,* American Bullion & Coin began selling a five-ounce Soviet-made silver medallion showing two clasped hands backed by the U.S. and Soviet flags and the words "For peace and cooperation" in both Russian and English on one side. The other side has a mother polar bear with her cub. It cost $195. It created a lot of controversy, and sales were quite low. Here are some of the comments.

An American Legion official said, "I guarantee you that at whatever price, I wouldn't buy it for intrinsic or investment value at all. If given one free, I'd melt it down before I sold it. Veterans will be offended that the flags of the U.S. and Russia will be together in perpetuity." A precious-metals analyst at a stock broker said that the design "doesn't appeal to most Americans' sense of patriotism." The director of the U.S. Mint said, "It's easy to see why Americans would feel a little queasy." Its press secretary said, "Most precious-metals collectors are conservatives."[27]

The Better Business Bureau is a well-known U.S. institution. The Council of Better Business Bureaus, organized in 1913, has espoused consumer protection and business ethics. It's one thing to be victimized by con artists, but it's another to be victimized by the BBB itself. Many businesses in California felt the BBB victimized them when a promoter got the idea of publishing local directories that resemble the telephone Yellow Pages listing nothing but BBB members. It also contained consumer tips on such activities as buying cars and choosing schools. Distributed free, the promoter made money from selling ads. The local BBBs liked it because it raised money and increased membership. By 1988, some 30 local BBBs had published directories.

But the idea was controversial. In 1982, the national Council sent a memo to all its local chapters urging them to delay signing contracts with promoters. It feared "outright misrepresentation by the directories' ad sales reps, because local bureaus couldn't exercise adequate control over selling practices."

The warning was well founded. Better Book, Inc. contracted with 12 BBB chapters, mostly in California, to publish directories. It promised to print and distribute the directories to every home and business in each of the 12 geographic areas and keep all ad revenue in return. It also promised to sell BBB memberships. After deducting a sales commission, membership fees would go to the local BBBs. But directories came out months late. They distributed far fewer directories than they promised. They told local businesses they had to join the local BBB in order to advertise, which wasn't true. They told many an advertiser that they would be the only business of its type to appear in the directory, which also wasn't true. Instead of a promotional campaign that would "blanket" local media, the company usually ran just one small ad once in a local newspaper. Several BBBs sued Better Book, alleging that the company took money due to the BBBs, even going so far as to forge endorsement signatures on checks made out to the BBBs. Better Book filed for bankruptcy in 1986.

Needless to say, businesses were extremely unhappy about the situation. One person said, "I always thought the BBB was an elite group. Now I feel completely ripped off." Another said, "It's one thing to get cheated. But it's another thing to get cheated by a consumer-protection agency." Weakened by the defection of 2,000 members unhappy about the directories, the Los Angeles BBB closed down.[28]

In 1985, California parents complained to the telephone company when their children ran up huge phone bills by calling such information services as "Dial Santa" without asking or telling them first. The phone company's ads didn't contain price information and encouraged children to use their services. The state made the phone company display price information on all ads, place a voice-over price message on televised ads aimed at children, and provide a one-time credit on any bill when a customer proved he or she wasn't aware of a charge or that the children made the calls without the parents' consent. This incident created a lot of ill will for Pacific Telesis, the phone company.[29]

In 1985, Coca Cola unveiled a medium-priced line of men's and women's casual clothing bearing the Coca-Cola logo. Murjani International of New York manufactured the items under license from Coca-Cola, and they were advertised as "All-American," though they were made in Asia. This was especially upsetting to U.S. textile companies and workers, since thousands of textile employees have been laid off because of slow sales caused by competition from lower-priced imported garments and textiles. In fact, several textile manufacturers removed all Coke machines from their plants. One textile worker wrote, "I once had a dog who bit my hand when I fed him, and now it seems as if your company is doing the same thing to my company. I got rid of the dog."

After a wave of bad publicity and a meeting with 30 representatives of textile companies and unions, Coke announced that all Coca-Cola clothes sold in the United States would henceforth be made in the United States. Only Coca-Cola clothes sold outside the United States would be made in Asia. An executive of a stock brokerage firm said, "Coke is an American symbol. The company opened itself to a lot of embarrassment by putting its name on foreign-made clothes. It was plain dumb."[30]

A Vancouver, Washington fast-food chain, Burgerville USA, ran an ad in 1988 showing President Ronald Reagan with his eyes closed, wearing head phones. The headline said, "You can usually tell when someone skips breakfast." It cancelled the ad after many people complained, saying the ads were in bad taste.[31]

Remember that Coke is a U.S. symbol when you read this next example. In 1985, Coca-Cola replaced its old Coke with a new Coke, which had a new sweeter formula. This was a big news story, and several books have already been written about it, including Thomas Oliver's *The Real Coke, the Real Story,* and Roger Enrico and Jesse Kornbluth's *The Other Guy Blinked: How Pepsi Won the Cola Wars.* (Enrico is President and CEO of the Pepsi Cola Company.) All of you already know the story. What more can be said about it? And why did I put this famous story in the misreading consumers' deeply held values mistake category? Well, because of my great and long-time interest in business mistakes, I've read almost everything that's been written in major trade journals, books, and newspapers about the 1985 incident in which Coca-Cola dropped old Coke, introduced new Coke as its replacement, and then, "by popular demand," brought back old Coke as "Coca-Cola Classic." I think I've got something a little different to say here that you may not have read or heard about before.

In my book, *Battling for Profits,* I apply military principles of war to marketing, so I'm going to use some marketing warfare terminology to talk about Coke versus Pepsi in the ongoing Cola Wars. Hindsight tells us that the momentum — one of the U.S. Army's nine principles of war — shifted to Pepsi after the "Pepsi Challenge" (1974) and the Michael Jackson/New Generation ads (1984). Pepsi's frontal attacks succeeded, and by 1984, Coke had lost its 1950s two-to-one lead over Pepsi. Pepsi was number one in U.S. supermarkets and trailed Coke only by a slim 5 percent nationwide because of Coke's big institutional sales lead.

Then, Coke's powerful conservative leader Bob Woodruff died, and the new top management at Coke — mostly foreign born — felt free to rock the boat to regain the momentum it had lost to Pepsi. What did the managers do? They ignored their ad agency's (McCann-Erickson) advice about introducing a Pepsi clone as a flanker brand, giving them two Coke brands instead of one. Coke decided on only one, dropping old Coke and replacing it with what they thought was a thoroughly tested, better tasting new Coke. Actually, during its 100 years, Coke had often changed its "7X" formula — but it never told the public. *This* time, it *told* the public. In late April 1985, it said there's not going to be any more old Coke, only a Pepsi-tasting new Coke.

And that's where the *real* story begins. By the end of May, Coke was getting an average of 8,000 negative phone calls per day. In June, the management decided to bring back old Coke, while keeping new Coke, and the day after they made the announcement, they got 18,000 friendly phone calls.

Did they make a mistake? Yes — three, in fact. First, they didn't ask their focus groups, "What would you think if new Coke were to replace old Coke?" and so they didn't realize the passionate attachment Americans had to old Coke. Coke was revered almost as much as the flag. It's part of the patriotic feeling of being an American, it seems. And, of course, Coke's top executives were all foreign born.

They also failed to heed General George Patton's advice, "The way to win a war is not to die for your country but to make the other poor bastard die for *his* country." In other words, the battle should be for the profits of your *competitor's* product, not your own. New Coke — the Pepsi clone — was aimed at switching Pepsi drinkers to Coke. However, when old Coke was dropped, people judged new Coke against the memory of old Coke, not against Pepsi. Pepsi could then sit back and enjoy the battle because it wasn't involved and would eventually reap the spoils.

Third, Coke's top managers let their *emotions* rule when they threw out McCann-Erickson's advice to have "two Coke brands." They thought that Pepsi would end up number one if they let the two Cokes cannibalize each other — even though they did no market research on product line extension and cannibalization. In the end, they ended up with two Coke brands anyway — not to mention the third and fourth, Diet Coke and Cherry Coke.

Who won that skirmish? Pepsi did outsell Coke in supermarkets in 1985 and 1986, but Coke won the 1987 skirmish for supremacy as Classic (old) Coke outsold all other colas.[32]

In 1987, it was revealed that Japan's Toshiba Machine Company sold militarily sensitive technology to the Soviet Union that enabled that nation to make quieter running submarines that were harder to detect. The incidents occurred between December 1982 and May 1984. U.S. officials accused Toshiba and another company, Norway's Kongsberg Vaapenfabrikk, of compromising the security of the United States and its allies by violating rules of the Western nations' Coordinating Committee for Export Control.

Americans were visibly upset. Some congressmen physically destroyed Toshiba electronic products (made by Toshiba Machine's parent company) with bats and axes. The destruction took place on the steps of the U.S. Capitol building in Washington, D.C. Congress banned the sale of Toshiba products in the United States for several months. Sales declined as consumers began an informal boycott. In 1988, a Japanese court fined the company approximately $16,000 and imposed prison sentences on two of its employees. Both sentences were suspended.

Even though Toshiba and the two executives received only wrist slaps, the parent company's sales in the United States were greatly damaged for awhile. Both the president and the chairman of Toshiba Corporation, the parent company, resigned. In a full-page ad in the July 20, 1987, issue of the *Wall Street Journal* and other major U.S. newspapers, the company apologized and told its readers that the resignations were the highest form of apology in the Japanese business world.[33]

What to Learn, What Action to Take

The examples you just read about — "Talk Sex" radio, shelled peanuts at the ballpark, the U.S.-Soviet medallion, the Better Business Bureau scam, the expensive Santa Claus phone calls, and Coca-Cola's "All-American" clothing — indicate that even U.S. executives can misread their fellow countrymen's deeply held values. (The Coca-Cola executives mainly responsible for the old Coke–New Coke decision were Brazilian, Mexican, Argentinian, and Egyptian, however, and the Toshiba incident did not occur in the United States, but its revelation affected U.S. public opinion.)

If you're not a U.S. citizen and you do business in the United States, you're going to have an even more difficult time understanding and adapting to U.S. value systems, just as any marketing executive doing business in a foreign country has a difficult time reading the nation's deeply held values.

Even people who were born and reared in the United States in a family that adhered to mainstream U.S. values sometimes "can't see the forest for the trees." They are too closely involved to be able to step back and look at values from an objective standpoint. For that reason, it's good to occasionally re-examine our roots. The following excellent books and articles on the U.S. cultural value system should help you gain a deeper understanding of what Americans are really like.

Pusateri, C. Joseph. *A History of American Business.* Arlington Heights, Ill.: Harlan Davidson, 1984.
Trost, Cathy. "All Work and No Play? New Study Shows How Americans View Jobs." *Wall Street Journal,* 30 December 1986, p. 17.
Cavanaugh, Gerald F. *American Business Values in Transition.* Englewood Cliffs, N.J.: Prentice-Hall, 1976.
Magnet, Myron. "The Money Society," *Fortune,* 6 July 1987, pp. 29, 30.
Fisher, Glen. *International Negotiation: A Cross-Cultural Perspective.* Chicago: Intercultural Press, 1980.
"Special Report: The Year of the Yuppie." *Newsweek,* 31 December 1984, p. 17.

HOW TO LEARN EVEN MORE BY DIGGING DEEPER

Henry, Walter A. "Cultural Values Do Correlate with Consumer Behavior." *Journal of Marketing Research,* (May 1976): 121–27.
Mitchell, Arnold. *The Nine American Lifestyles.* New York: Macmillan, 1983.
Richins, Marsha L. "Negative Word-of-Mouth by Dissatisfied Consumers: A Pilot Study." *Journal of Marketing,* (Winter 1982): 68–78.
Shay, Paul. "The New Consumer Values." *Advertising Quarterly,* (Summer 1978): 15–18.
"Special Report: Marketing to Women." *Advertising Age,* 2 April 1984, pp. 9–36.
Venkatesh, Alladi. "Changing Roles of Women — A Life-Style Analysis." *Journal of Consumer Behavior,* (September 1980): 189–97.
Vinson, Donald E., Jerome E. Scott and Lawrence M. Lamont. "The Role of Personal Values in Marketing and Consumer Behavior." *Journal of Marketing,* (April 1977): 44–50.

NOTES

1. Alan Freeman, "Next, Barbie Travels to Chernobyl to Protest Against Nuclear Energy," *Wall Street Journal,* 6 October 1986, p. 31.
2. Robert Johnson, "And Now Here's the Winning Cat, Screaming to be Let

Out of the Box," *Wall Street Journal,* 25 September 1986, p. 33.

3.   Roy J. Harris, Jr., "It's a Cold, Cruel World: Corky and Orky are Shipped Up River," *Wall Street Journal,* 9 March 1987, p. 21.

4.   S. Karene Witcher, "This Could Mean Comeback Time for Those 200 Elvis Impersonators," *Wall Street Journal,* 6 January 1988, p. 17.

5.   Steve Swartz, "In the Super Bowl, is American Express a Winner or Loser?" *Wall Street Journal,* 23 January 1987, pp. 1, 11.

6.   Cyndee Miller, "Humor in Herbicide Ad Campaign is Not a Big Joke to Some Farmers," *Marketing News,* 29 February 1988, p. 6.

7.   "Shop Talk: Reville's Revenge," *Wall Street Journal,* 5 December 1985, p. 31.

8.   Joe Agnew, "Stroh Brewery Apologizes for Anti-Gay Remark," *Marketing News,* 29 February 1988, p. 3.

9.   Ibid.

10.   "Unintentional Insult Inspires Boycott," *Marketing News,* 5 December 1986, p. 1; Penelope Wang and Maggie Malone, "Can Revlon Repair Its Image?" *Newsweek,* 23 February 1987, p. 53.

11.   "Japan Vows Sensitivity to U.S. Racial Images," *International Herald Tribune,* Hong Kong, 5 August 1988, p. 5; James Risen, "U.S. Blacks to Strike Back at Japan," *International Herald Tribune,* Hong Kong, 10 August 1988, pp. 1, 2; David E. Sanger, "Takeshita Apologizes for Slur on U.S. Blacks," *International Herald Tribune,* Hong Kong, 17 August 1988, pp. 1, 2; "Japanese Publishers End 'Sambo,'" *Times-Picayune,* New Orleans, 27 January 1989, p. A-6; Yumiko Ono, "Truth in Packaging Is One Thing, But This Could Give It a Bad Name," *Wall Street Journal,* 25 January 1989, p. B-1.

12.   "For the Record," *Advertising Age,* 28 April 1980, p. 87.

13.   "Colgate Criticized; Name of Toothpaste Termed Racist," *Arkansas Gazette,* Little Rock, 17 February 1986, p. 8-B; "Business News Digest: Colgate to Drop 'Darkie' Product Label," *Arkansas Gazette,* Little Rock, 25 February 1987, p. 1-C; Douglas C. McGill, "Colgate Will Change Toothpaste's Name," *Times,* New York, 27 January 1989, pp. 25, 29; "New Look for Colgate," *Times-Picayune,* New Orleans, 27 January 1989, p. C-1.

14.   "Chicano Group Calls for Bank Boycott," *The Nation,* (Bangkok, Thailand), 16 July 1988, p. 18; "Citibank Attacked on Mexico's Debt," *Bangkok Post,* 16 July 1988, p. 15.

15.   Richard Gibson, "Fallon McElligott Loses a Major Client Over 'Stupid' Reply to Sexist Ad Charge," *Wall Street Journal,* 14 January 1988, p. 10; "Woman's Complaint Causes Ad Agency to Lose Account," *Marketing News,* 1 February 1988, p. 8.

16.   "Tiresome, Ain't It?" *Advertising Age,* 18 February 1980, p. 55.

17.   Reported on *CNN News,* March 8, 1986.

18.   Memphis *Commercial Appeal,* May 19, 1985, p. C-5.

19.   Christina Bonasegna, "Black Eye Spot Sparks Big Uproar in Argentina," *Advertising Age,* 9 December 1985, p. 40.

20.   Andrea Rothman, "So This is Why Some People Carry Beer Around in a Plain Brown Bag," *Wall Street Journal,* 8 August 1988, p. 19.

21.   "Airline to Keep Controversial Ad," *Arkansas Gazette,* Little Rock, 11 January 1986, p. 6-C.

22.   "Provocative Billboards Rejected," *Business Weekly*, Chattanooga, 15 August 1988, p. 3.

23.   David J. Reibstein, *Marketing*, (Englewood Cliffs, N.J.: Prentice-Hall, 1985), p. 179; Henry Assael, *Consumer Behavior and Marketing Action*, (Boston: Kent Publishing, 1984), p. 288.

24.   Donald W. Hendon and Rebecca A. Hendon, *How to Negotiate Worldwide*, (London: Gower Publishing and New York: John Wiley & Sons, 1989).

25.   "Talk Sex Ads Offensive: WHBQ Manager Promises New Signs are in the Offing," *Commercial Appeal*, 5 October 1986, p. C-8.

26.   Scott Wenger, "And if This Catches on, They Plan to Ban Cheering the Home Team," *Wall Street Journal*, 15 September 1986, p. 25.

27.   William Power, "Don't Read This if You Still Have High Hopes for the Next Summit," *Wall Street Journal*, 23 November 1987, p. 31.

28.   John R. Emshwiller, "If You Can't Trust the BBB, to Whom Do You Turn Then?" *Wall Street Journal*, 5 January 1988, pp. 1, 8.

29.   "California Sets Restrictions on Phone Call Service Ads," *Wall Street Journal*, 7 November 1985.

30.   Barbara Rudolph and Leslie Cauley, "Tempests in a Pop Bottle," *Time*, 26 August 1985, p. 37; "Coca-Cola Pledges Effort on Making Apparel in U.S.," *Wall Street Journal*, 12 August 1985, p. 8; "Textile Plants Flip Their Tops at Coke Clothing," *Commercial Appeal*, Memphis, 10 August 1985, p. B-4.

31.   "Food Ads Drop Sleepy Reagan," *International Herald Tribune*, Hong Kong, 15 August 1988, p. 6.

32.   Donald W. Hendon, "Strategies in the Cola War," *World Executive's Digest*, April 1987, p. 6.

33.   "U.S. Senators Urge Ban on All Toshiba Products," *China News*, Taipei, Taiwan, 18 June 1987, p. 3; Clyde Haberman, "Toshiba is Found Guilty of Selling Technology to Soviets, Receives Small Fine," *Chattanooga Times*, 23 March 1988, p. C-2.

3
Competitors

Two errors stand out here — passively letting your competitor set the rules and then playing by those rules instead of seizing the initiative yourself, and letting your guard down so your competitor can more easily steal your trade secrets.

PLAYING BY YOUR COMPETITOR'S RULES
INSTEAD OF BY YOUR OWN

Sun Tzu Wu, a very famous Chinese general, said 2,500 years ago, "A wise general makes sure his troops feed on the enemy, for one cartload of the enemy's supplies is equal to 20 of our own." And, as you just read, U.S. General George S. Patton said, "The way to win a battle is not to die for *your* country. The way to win a battle is to make the other poor bastard die for *his* country." This means the marketing battlefield should be over your competitor's profits, not over your profits.[1] Don't play your competitor's game. Make him or her play your game, by your rules, instead. Pick the battlefield yourself.

The following examples illustrate what can happen when you let your competitor pick the battlefield and you end up playing by his or her rules. The United States was the undisputed market leader in many fields for many years after World War II. Perhaps it grew fat and sassy because it was used to success. Little by little, market by market, Japan conquered the United States. Many observers think Japan, not the United States, is the leading marketer in the world today. For example, the governments of Singapore and Malaysia adopted a "Look East" commercial policy in the middle 1980s and decided to try to emulate Japan instead of the United States. Japan, a classic David to the U.S. Goliath, made the United States play a new game with a new set of rules — Japan's. How did it happen?

How did the United States make this mistake, perhaps the biggest and costliest strategic mistake talked about in this book?

Japan's success has been built upon economic assumptions that are quite different from U.S. economic assumptions. No government is good at picking economic winners and losers — only the market is. Some governments — Japan's, for example — are good at making sure that their industries ride with the winners. So when the Japanese government knew for sure that such industries as telecommunications, biotechnology, computers, aircraft, and advanced ceramics were long-term winners, it helped the country's businesses all it could to succeed in these industries.

It helped Japanese corporations sell products in foreign markets at prices below the home-market prices — sometimes, below cost. The U.S. government won't subsidize U.S. firms that want to dump abroad to gain a foothold, however. It thinks this is not playing fair. This is the first way that the two nations are different in their economic assumptions. As you'll see, the United States made the wrong assumption, and Japan made the right assumption.

Now, dumping usually means a windfall for consumers in the foreign markets. In 1988, a former member of the U.S. Council of Economic Advisers recognized this when he said at a Washington seminar for touring Japanese executives, "If Japan is willing to sell semiconductors below cost in the U.S. market, Americans should be grateful and turn their attention to making something else."

The Japanese simply couldn't understand what he was talking about. Such dumping allowed a Japanese industry to get and keep a lock hold on an important U.S. market — television. And the conquest of the TV set market, partly by dumping, paved the way for Japan's monopoly on videocassette recorders. U.S. firms who now want to build and market improved VCRs or peripherals can't do it because of the Japanese monopoly — the Japanese companies won't provide the needed parts or licenses.

Japanese firms also drove U.S. manufacturers out of the market for key semiconductor products by dumping. This has made U.S. manufacturers dependent on their biggest competitors — Japanese suppliers, who will find it easy to keep new U.S. entrepreneurs out of the market. Japan is now the dominant supplier of many critical items, and so it's hard for foreign customers to switch to other suppliers.

Dumping products overseas also serves another purpose — it protects existing market shares of Japanese companies while an industry is in flux and adjusts to change. For example, during the period from 1986 to 1988, the yen appreciated rapidly in value, but Japanese automobile marketers, didn't raise prices. They took lower profits home from the United States but enjoyed higher profits at home as their partner, the Japanese government, stimulated the domestic economy, not only for automobiles but for all products. And they knew that higher profits were around the corner because they began to cut costs dramatically. One Japanese industrialist said, "We have cut our costs by 30 percent over the past two years, and we are aiming for another 20 percent. We will be able to compete with the yen at 90 to the dollar."

Japan's consumers pay a heavy price for having its government subsidize overseas dumping because government subsidies weren't enough to keep Japan's firms profitable when they were struggling to get footholds in such large overseas markets as the United States. They needed subsidies from Japanese consumers, so the cost of living in Japan is one of the highest in the world. Most of you have heard of beef selling for over $50 a pound, million dollar prices for tiny homes in Tokyo, $12 cinema tickets, and so forth. What you've heard is true. Japanese consumers will put up with these things, but U.S. consumers won't. That's because of the second difference in economic assumptions between the two nations — the consumer is king in the United States, and the producer is king in Japan. In the United States, middlemen can't be controlled or pressured in many ways by manufacturers, and so Hyundai, a South Korean car, was able to persuade Chrysler, Ford, and General Motors dealers to carry its models in the United States. Although the yen was rising steadily during the time period that Hyundai was invading the U.S. market, it couldn't sell its cars in Japan. Why? Because dealers who decided to carry Hyundai would lose their Toyota or Nissan franchises. The result? Less competition in the local market and a worse deal for Japanese consumers. But that's acceptable in Japan because the producer, not the consumer, is king.

Closely related to the second difference in economic assumptions between the two nations is this — because the customer is king in the United States, antitrust laws there won't let competitors get together and collude on business matters. Japan thinks this is great, because, remember, the producer is king! The presence of antitrust laws in the United States and the lack of them in Japan is the third difference between the two nations in economic assumptions. Antitrust laws were good for the U.S. domestic market for many years, until the invasion gave Japanese firms such big advantages over U.S. firms. What would the federal government do if the chief executive officers of General Motors, Ford, Chrysler, International Business Machines, Apple, Citibank, Bank of America, and Chase Manhattan Bank got together once a month to discuss business matters? They'd probably put a stop to it because they'd look upon it as collusion. But what's collusion to the people of the United States is simply the basis of Japan's industrial structure. For example, the Sumitomo group's "White Water Club," which includes the heads of Sumitomo Bank, Nippon Electric Company, and Mazda, among others, meets monthly to discuss business matters.

Another difference in economic assumptions concerns foreign investment. The United States welcomes it because it thinks it strengthens its economy. The Japanese completely disagree — they don't want to be dependent on another nation. They prefer to be self-sufficient, to control their own destiny. For example, Japan needed capital to rebuild its economy after World War II, but it strictly limited the inflow of foreign investment. It still does.

Its huge export surpluses have given Japan enormous cash inflows of many different foreign currencies. Its major companies and its government know that Japan's manufacturing costs are much higher than costs in nations in southeast Asia and in Africa. They can't hope to match those costs anymore — Japan is too rich. So, to protect themselves against future lower-cost competitors who hope to repeat the so-called Japanese miracle, they are investing their money in their foreign markets by building manufacturing facilities. Instead of being the outsider, they have *now* become part of the establishment, much like British and then U.S. firms did throughout the world years ago. Remember, the United States welcomes foreign investment, and the weak U.S. dollar of the late 1980s made the United States a debtor nation for the first time in this century. Citizens of third world nations find it normal to wake up, go to work in foreign-made motor vehicles, pick up a paycheck from a foreign-owned multinational employer, enjoy foreign fare on television and in the movies, and buy foreign products at the store. Americans were beginning to get used to it for the first time in the late 1980s, and they'll eventually think it's normal, just as third world nations do.

Economic assumptions about how business is done differ. The Japanese work harder than Americans do. Some experts said that after they were defeated in World War II, the Japanese turned their allegiance from the military to businesses. They work hard and get job security. Male executives — and most executives *are* male — are expected to arrive early and stay late. They are expected to go drinking after work with their colleagues. They stay out late almost every night, and only see their spouses on weekends. They perform calisthenics together in the morning, while singing the company song. They go on holidays together at the company resort. Their funerals are arranged by their employer.

They are loyal to their company, and they don't often change jobs. They work hard in return for what they get.

People in the United States don't work nearly as hard. They job hop. They leave promptly at 5 P.M. and like to take long weekends. The U.S. general manager of a company producing artificial kidneys in Japan pointed out the differences between the two countries in the way they view the work ethic by saying his customers were physicians. His company's sales representatives were expected to do anything the physicians wanted them to do. For example, if a doctor wanted his car washed, the sales rep would do it. One rep even slept in front of one doctor's hotel room at night to guard it from intruders at the doctor's request. A U.S. sales rep would simply laugh at these requests, regard them as unreasonable, and refuse to do them.

Another difference in economic assumptions concerns patent policy. The Japanese patent system is designed to encourage copying, while the U.S. system sets up a legal monopoly to give the inventor a chance to get some market advantage for several years. Japan encourages copying because its culture avoids conflict and promotes cooperation — and that leads to cross licensing. This means granting your competitor a license to use your patents in return for royalty payments.

How does this happen? First, while the U.S. Patent Office honors the first inventor, the Japanese patent office honors the first one to apply. Unlike the United States, which makes inventors disclose all "prior art" to prove they have something distinctly different and new, in Japan, you can patent a relatively minor change, such as a bicycle with red pedals instead of black pedals. While the U.S. Patent Office keeps information in patent applications secret, Japan makes it available to competitors. Finally, while the average patent processing time in the United States is two years, it usually takes longer than six years in Japan. During this time, the Japanese applicant is vulnerable to several competing applications with minor variations. In fact, many large Japanese firms use a "patent flooding" strategy, filing for many patents on inventions of smaller companies, eventually enjoying the benefits of the markets first created and developed by the smaller companies. The latter's only alternative is the crosslicense — but that means competing against larger firms with identical products.

The small U.S. firm, Fusion Systems Corporation, which makes lamps and related equipment for lithography, drying labels, and fusing semiconductor wafers and coatings to optical fibers, faced this problem in Japan in the late 1980s. After it captured 80 percent of the market for ultraviolet lamps there, the giant Mitsubishi Electric Corporation began "patent flooding" to take away market share from them. At the time I was writing this book, it was uncertain how to respond. What would you do if you were faced with this situation?[2]

The United States beat Japan in World War II, and then Japan turned around and beat the United States in marketing warfare not too many years later. Although the United States was an extremely superior industrial power, Japan ignored U.S. rules and began playing by its own rules in the U.S. market. It made certain the battle was for profits in the U.S. market, not in the Japanese market, which it effectively closed to foreign entry. And it won. It is so powerful now that it's not very worried about what the fall of the dollar and the rise of the yen during 1986–1988 would do to its export-led economy. Many Japanese forecasters predicted in mid-1988 that after a slight dip, Japan's trade surplus will begin to rise again in 1989 because exports will rise dramatically again. Why? Remember, while the government stimulated the domestic market, manufacturers cut costs; foreign customers can't switch to other suppliers while Japan is the dominant supplier of many critical items. Japan is now very, very rich and is investing in manufacturing plants abroad, and all foreign nations, including the United States, need their money.[3]

After that mistake, the rest of these examples will seem quite tame, but they were spectacular when they were in the news. Many readers will remember playing with American Flyer trains and Erector sets. They were made by the U.S. firm, A. C. Gilbert Toy Company, which had a reputation for high quality, expensive toys. The market changed greatly in the 1960s, though, and at first Gilbert didn't change with the times. It kept to the status quo when retailers were mainly interested in low-priced, heavily advertised (on expensive TV) toys with attractive packaging that would move off self-service shelves. When it began to lose sales, it decided to play "me-too" and adopted its competitors' strategies and tactics. It sacrificed its major strength — its high-quality image — and overexpanded its line by bringing out an array of cheap new products. I'm using the word "cheap" in two ways — cheap in terms of price *and* cheap in terms of quality. The products were poorly made, and consumers recognzied it. That hurt the sales of its well-established, well-made products. It also began to spend heavily on TV advertising — 30 percent of sales was allocated to ads in that medium — and it emulated its competitors by paying more attention to the big discounters than to the established retail toy stores with which it was used to dealing. It tried to win the favor of the big discounters by guaranteeing the sale of its products. In 1967 it went bankrupt.[4]

Competitors can make you play their game in many ways. In 1987, Tanduay Rhum (Rum), the largest selling rum in the Philippines, was forced to deal with the problem of contaminated rum that killed several people. It turned out that a competitor put out the contaminated product in Tanduay bottles and labels. Tanduay was forced to abandon its marketing plan during the crisis and devote all its efforts to regaining the public's trust.

On occasion competitors also spread rumors. I have spent mid-May through mid-August in the Asia-Pacific region every year since 1972, and I hear the same rumor there every year. One year, a competitor spreads it about Coca-Cola. The next year, a competitor spreads it about Pepsi Cola. It's always the same rumor — that an employee of the soft drink bottler fell into the vat of syrup and his decomposed body wasn't found for several weeks. In the meantime, guess what you've been drinking? Something too horrible to contemplate. Sales always go down dramatically when the rumor spreads, and the affected company must abandon its marketing plan to fight the rumor. Much more is said later about how to combat rumors, including this one (see Chapter 5).

What to Learn, What Action to Take

These examples should make you think twice before you let your competitor call the shots. But there are no absolutes in marketing. There's always an "on the other hand," and this marketing mistake is no exception. So let me say it.

On the other hand, letting your competitor set the pace *can* make good sense at times, especially in such industries as chemicals and steel, because they are capital intensive and there's very little producers can do to differentiate their products, service, or image. Price wars are likely whenever one firm is greedy enough to disrupt the status quo. In these kinds of industries, market shares are rather stable, which indicates that most firms decide against attacking each other to gain extra market-share points. Instead, most firms try to do nothing that will rock the boat, and this usually means copying the leader in the industry. The key objective is not to create competitive reaction. When many firms do this, it's called "conscious parallel action." Some successful market followers in the United States include Burroughs (computers), Crown Cork & Seal (metal containers), and Union Camp (paper). One study reported that many companies with less than half the market share of the industry's leader had a five-year average return on investment (R. O. I.) that was larger than the median in the industry.[5]

A "Me-Too" Strategy can also pay off under these circumstances:

- In capital-intensive homogeneous product industries such as chemicals.
- When there's little opportunity to differentiate your product and its image.
- When all competitors' service quality is comparable.
- When customers are very price sensitive.
- When market shares are stable.
- When manufacturing costs are low.
- When product and service quality is relatively high.
- When you enter every new market you can.
- In markets where product piracy is common — foreign knockoff copies of globally popular products quite often succeed in many nations. In 1985, the top 16 nations in terms of manufacturing counterfeit goods were, in order: Taiwan, Hong Kong, the United States, Italy, Japan, the Philippines, Indonesia, South Korea, Thailand, Malaysia, Singapore, India, the Persian Gulf States, Mexico, Brazil, and Canada.
- Many low-market share firms follow a "me-too" strategy, and they are most profitable when
    - their high quality products and services also have medium to low prices.
    - their product or service line is narrow.
    - they have low total costs.
    - they focus on smaller market segments.
    - they're in low-growth markets.
    - they don't often change their products and services.
    - their products are mostly standardized with few extra services.
    - they're in industries with high value added.
    - most of them make industrial components or supplies.[6]

Therefore, it seems that this technique can be successful at times. But it wasn't successful for the United States and for the companies in the other three examples I gave you. It takes a special set of circumstances for this technique to be successful. I'm uncomfortable with it, and I don't really recommend it except under the circumstances just listed.

SECURITY — NOT PROTECTING YOUR TRADE SECRETS

Espionage is a dirty word everywhere. You've got to assume that your competitors are not only interested in learning your trade secrets — you've got to assume they're going to try to find them out. Sometimes, your employees sell your trade secrets — or use their knowledge of your operations when they move to a competing firm. Here's what can happen when you don't protect your trade secrets — and when you get caught trying to steal your competitor's trade secrets.

In 1986, Preco Turbine Services of Houston pleaded guilty in federal court to eight counts of theft of trade secrets from General Electric on how to make turbines. Three Preco executives used to work for GE, and it seemed they were using the knowledge they acquired there to help their new employer. The two companies settled a $36 million civil suit. Preco agreed not to hire anyone currently employed by GE and to destroy or return stolen documents.

In 1982, Philadelphia's Continental Data System introduced a software package for personal injury lawyers. Exxon Office Systems sent two employees, posing as law firm consultants, to Continental, which gave them a demonstration and a technical sales manual. That information enabled Exxon to come out with a competing product within two months. Continental sued Exxon, and in 1986, a federal judge ordered Exxon to pay $392,000 in punitive and compensatory damages to Continental.[8]

IBM suspected that Hitachi, a large Japanese company, stole some of its trade secrets and was trying to get more. It decided it wasn't going to let Hitachi get away with it, so in October 1981, IBM executives met with FBI agents to discuss evidence that Hitachi had illegally acquired documents that were IBM's property. They set up the groundwork for an elaborate sting operation.

The next month, in Las Vegas, Nevada, an engineer from Hitachi met with a special FBI agent posing as head of a dummy technology brokerage firm. The engineer asked the FBI plant for early information on IBM products. In March 1982, Hitachi officials from Tokyo came to Santa Clara, California, and handed a list of their requirements to an FBI agent, settling on a $525,000 "consulting" fee. In June 1982, San Francisco police booked three Hitachi executives after setting up a dummy exchange of IBM documents for the promised payment.

Two of them pleaded guilty, and a third pleaded no contest to conspiracy charges. Hitachi pleaded guilty and was fined $10,000 to federal charges of conspiring to transport the purportedly stolen IBM secrets across state lines. IBM also sued Hitachi, and they agreed on an out-of-court settlement of $300 million. Sales of Hitachi products in the United States fell when the FBI case against it was named public.[9]

Those three cases involved illegal activities. Most trade secrets and marketing plans aren't obtained through illegal means. That makes the job of protecting yourself difficult. For example, here's how Coca-Cola's competitors learned more about its formula. In April 1985, Coca-Cola announced that it was dropping old Coke and bringing out new Coke. Old Coke used more than 30 percent of the world's annual crop of vanilla beans. Madagascar produces 80 percent of the world's vanilla beans.

Demand there evaporated overnight. The conclusion was obvious — old Coke used vanilla beans and new Coke didn't.[10]

Here's another example of not guarding your trade secrets, this time from the Philippines. In the early 1980s, Asia Breweries, a large corporation that was part of the Lucio Tan group, allegedly owned by then President Marcos or by Marcos cronies, decided to mount a strong challenge to the leading beer manufacturer, San Miguel. Asia Breweries' Beer Hausen, was a premium beer with a golden foil wrapper over the cap. However, San Miguel's packaging division was the only source of supply for beer bottles, caps, and gold foil. Asia Brewery naturally had to reveal their plans to their competitor in order to get the containers and packaging they needed. San Miguel sold them what they needed; however, about two months before Beer Hausen was launched, San Miguel brought out a new premium beer, Gold Eagle, which had a golden foil wrapper over the cap. When Beer Hausen came out, Filipinos perceived it as just another "me-too" entry. Of course, as I said before, "me-too" can pay off — but in this case, it didn't. Beer Hausen never achieved the sales that its creators had hoped for, and a few years later, the Marcos regime collapsed.

What to Learn, What Action to Take

Marketing intelligence gathering is becoming more and more sophisticated. Unfortunately, the increasing sophistication has been accompanied by more unethical behavior. Microlab/FXR, a manufacturer of listening devices, estimated that U.S. firms spent over $50 million on electronic surveillance in the middle 1980s and that the figure was growing by 30 percent a year. Here are four popular bugging devices that can be legally purchased for less than $100 in Europe but which are illegal in the United States:

- The *spike* is pointed at one end. It's 3 inches long and 1/4 inch in diameter. It's usually inserted into furniture fabric or into carpeting.
- The *slab* is a transmitter that's often glued into the inside of book bindings. It's flat and about 1/8 inch long.
- The *picture hook* is the most common bug. It looks like a picture hanger. The metal wire is its antenna.
- The *rod* is inserted inside a ball-point pen or planted on an executive's desk. I've seen this one advertised in a daily newspaper in Taipei, Taiwan for less than $15.

All of these devices come with receivers, some of which can be miles away. Some bugs are voice activated.[11]

Stories of phony executive search firms interviewing disgruntled executives on the pretext of offering them better jobs, solely to find out their companies' marketing plans, also abound. There are many unethical or illegal ways of finding out competitive information.

Don't let this happen to you. Hire a security consulting firm and have it examine your premises. A good place to look for one is in the *Security Letter's Source Book,* a directory of services, suppliers, and manufacturers in the U.S. security industry. The consultant you hire will make several suggestions, including buying a paper shredder and even shredding carbon ribbons. But don't stop there. Much of your data is in computer files. If you're like most companies, with a cheap battery-powered TV set, a TV antenna, and about $200 to $400 worth of basic electronic gear, a person could get a duplicate of whatever's on a terminal screen from a few blocks away.

How can you guard your computer files? The National Security Agency in the United States set up a program, known by the code name Tempest, to establish standards for safeguarding terminals against high-tech surveillance. Federal law now permits sales of Tempest-approved equipment in the private sector. As of the mid-1980s, 139 companies were manufacturing 256 computer products that met the standards. However, this was only a small fraction of the entire computer industry. Shielding your terminals with Tempest-approved products is very expensive because it means practically remaking the equipment. It will cost you as much as three to six times the original price of the terminal.[12]

Don't feel safe if you've bug proofed your offices or shielded your computer terminals with Tempest-approved devices, though. There are many creative *legal* ways of getting competitive intelligence in the United States:

- Many companies subscribe to industry newsletters simply to get competitive information.
- Many companies get information about competitors in foreign nations by asking the commercial attaché at the embassy of the competitor's country. They usually answer questions on a per-inquiry fee basis.
- Companies find information in loan applications. Banks have to file a form that goes by different names in different states that gives data about the borrower. They're filed with the secretary of state's office in the state capital, and they can be examined.
- Trade shows are notorious for talkative salespeople. Many competitors pose as customers to get information. The trade show directory also gives lots of information.

- The Thomas Register is one of the best buyer's guides around. Almost every trade journal has a special annual issue that serves as a buyer's guide. These kinds of guides are indispensable tools in intelligence gathering.

- Many firms subscribe to newspaper clipping services just to look at the help-wanted ads of competitors.

- Companies have to file environmental impact statements when they are planning to build plants or change production processes that might affect the environment. These statements, on file with local, state, and federal agencies, can be examined by competitors, and they often are.

- Competitors can estimate how many products you sell by finding out what company makes the boxes you ship your products in. Then, they ask the box manufacturer how many boxes you buy.

- Companies have asked electric utilities about power consumption and usage to estimate production figures.

- Local chambers of commerce and various offices at city halls and county court houses give out data as well.

- Some companies buy one share of stock of their competitors just to get on their mailing list and to attend their stockholders meetings.

- In larger cities especially, several students who attend evening Masters in Business Administration classes are there because they know their competitors' employees are attending the class too. Many students write term papers based on current projects at their companies and present them orally in class.

- Often, competitors will simply observe your plant. They'll count how many employees enter and leave or estimate it by the number of cars in your parking lot. They'll observe the rust on rail sidings next to your plant to estimate how frequently boxcars pull up. They'll even pay the United States Geological Service a nominal fee, give them the correct longitude and latitude coordinates, and get an aerial or satellite photo of your plant. The service will even sell photos taken over time that reveal changes in your physical facilities.

How can you keep your employees from stealing your trade secrets and using them against you when and if they start working for one of your competitors? You may have to go to court as General Electric did against Preco. Will you win? Maybe. On one hand, the courts have generally recognized the unfairness of a prior employee using your proprietary information to compete with you, especially in industries where "intellectual property" is your most valuable asset. On the other hand, courts don't want to restrict a former employee's right to earn a living.

Most courts have ruled that if you make your employee sign a nondisclosure agreement ahead of time, then you *can* enforce it later. The May 1986 issue of *Personnel Administrator* had an article in it by Gary S. Marx and Stewart S. Manela entitled "Protecting Confidential Information in High-Tech Companies." It gave step-by-step methods to demonstrate conclusively in a U.S. court of law that an employee was fully apprised of a company's restrictions on postemployment disclosure of confidential information. It also gave three sample clauses you could use in your employment contract: a sample trade secret clause, a sample noncompetition clause, and a sample assignment clause. Have your attorney look at this article and the clauses and advise you what course of action to follow.[14]

HOW TO LEARN EVEN MORE BY DIGGING DEEPER

Alreck, Pamela L. and Robert B. Settle. *The Survey Research Handbook.* Homewood, Ill.: Richard D. Irwin, 1985.

Cohen, William A. *Winning on the Marketing Front.* New York: John Wiley & Sons, 1986.

Day, George S. *Strategic Marketing Planning.* St. Paul, Minn.: West Publishing, 1984.

Greenberg, Barnett A., Jac Goldstucker and Danny N. Bellenger. "What Techniques are Used by Marketing Researchers in Business." *Journal of Marketing,* (April 1977): 62–68.

Hershey, Robert. "Commercial Intelligence on a Shoestring." *Harvard Business Review,* (September–October 1980): 22–30.

Oxenfeldt, Alfred R. and William L. Moore. "Consumer or Competitor: Which Guideline for Marketing?" *Management Review,* (August 1978): 43–48.

Payne, Stanley L. *The Art of Asking Questions.* Princeton, N.J.: Princeton University Press, 1951.

Porter, Michael E. "How Competitive Forces Shape Strategy." *Harvard Business Review,* (March–April 1979): 137–45.

___. *Competitive Advantage.* New York: Free Press, 1985.

___. *Competitive Strategy.* New York: Free Press, 1980.

___. "A Good Competitor is Not Always a Dead Competitor." *Wall Street Journal,* (1 April 1985): 1.

Porter, Michael E. and Victor E. Millar. "How Information Gives You Competitive Advantage." *Harvard Business Review,* (July–August 1985), 149–60.

Rothschild, William. *How to Gain (and Maintain) the Competitive Advantage.* New York: McGraw-Hill, 1984.

Wall, Jerry L. "What the Competition is Doing: Your Need to Know." *Harvard Business Review,* (November–December 1974): 22–24ff.

NOTES

1.   Donald W. Hendon, *Battling for Profits: How to Win Big on the Marketing Battlefield,* 2d ed. (Jonesboro, AR: Business Consultants International and Singapore: Executive Data Centre, 1987), p. 151.

2.   George Melloan, "Business World: An American Views Japan's Copycat Culture," *Asian Wall Street Journal,* 15–16 July 1988, p. 6.

3.   Clyde V. Prestowitz, Jr., *Trading Places: How We Allowed Japan to Take the Lead,* and Clyde V. Prestowitz, Jr., "Traditional Trade Talks Won't Change Japan," *International Herald Tribune,* Hong Kong, 15 June 1988, p. 4.

4.   Robert F. Hartley, *Marketing Mistakes,* (New York: John Wiley & Sons, 1986), pp. 77–87; "Toymaker A. C. Gilbert Co., Poor Loser?" *Sales Management,* 1 May 1966, pp. 25–28.

5.   Philip Kotler, *Marketing Management: Analysis, Planning, and Control,* 5th ed. (Englewood Cliffs, N.J.: Prentice-Hall, 1984), p. 410; Richard G. Hammermesh, M. Jack Anderson, Jr., and J. Elizabeth Harris, "Strategies for Low Market Share Businesses," *Harvard Business Review,* May–June 1978, pp. 95–102.

6.   Philip Kotler, *Marketing Management,* 6th ed. (Englewood Cliffs, N.J.: Prentice-Hall, 1988), pp. 328, 341; Carolyn Y. Woo and Arnold C. Cooper, "The Surprising Case for Low Market Share," *Harvard Business Review,* November–December 1982, pp. 106–13; Carolyn Y. Woo and Arnold C. Cooper, "Market Share Leadership — Not Always So Good," *Harvard Business Review,* January–February 1984, pp. 2–4; Thomas C. O'Donnell, Elizabeth Weiner, Hazel Bradford, Amy Borrus, and Dorinda Elliott, "The Counterfeit Trade," *Business Week,* 16 December 1985, pp. 64–68, 72.

7.   "Business News Digest: Houston Firm Fined for Secrets Theft," *Arkansas Gazette,* Little Rock, 5 March 1986, p. 1-C.

8.   "Exxon Ordered to Pay Damages of $392,000 in Trade Secrets Case," *Wall Street Journal,* 31 January 1986, p. 4.

9.   Thom Nicholson, Jennet Conant and Frank Gibney, Jr., "A $300 Million Apology to IBM," *Newsweek,* 21 November 1983, p. 84.

10.   Steve Mufson, "Don't Thank Us, Pepsi; We Just Talked with a Few Bean Buyers," *Wall Street Journal,* 17 July 1985, p. 29.

11.   Michael Geczi, "Bug Sweepers Gaining Popularity as High-Tech Eavesdropping Grows," *Arkansas Gazette,* Little Rock, 8 January 1986, pp. 1-C, 2-C.

12.   John J. Fialka, "Study Sheds Light on Vulnerability of Computers to Electronic Spying," *Wall Street Journal,* 18 October 1985, p. 29.

13.   Synthesized from William L. Sammon, Mark A. Kurland and Robert Spitalnic, *Business Competitor Intelligence,* (New York: John Wiley & Sons, 1984); Jeffrey L. Kovach, "Competitive Intelligence," *Industry Week,* 12 November 1984, pp. 50–53; Richard Wolkomir, "Scouting the Competition," *American Way,* 8 January 1985, pp. 78–81; Leonard M. Fuld, *Competitor Intelligence: How to Get It, How to Use It,* (New York: John Wiley & Sons, 1985); Colin Rivers, "Technology: Killing Bugs in the Office," *Australian Business,* 20 June 1984, pp. 112–13; Mark Potts, "Were Cookie Secrets Stolen?" *Advertiser,* Honolulu, 22 June 1984, p. B-5; Robert L. Brown, "The Ugliest Competition: Marketing Espionage," *Sales Management,* 4 December 1964, pp. 23–26; "Business Sharpens Its Spying Techniques," *Business Week,* 4 August 1975, pp. 60–63; "Bugs are Everywhere, Says Firm That Sells De-Bugger," *Caller,* Corpus Christi, Tex., 6 January 1982, p. 2-A; Jay Stuller, "Gray Flannel Pirates," *Texas Flyer,* November 1980, pp. 52–55; Jeffrey N. Birnbaum, "Firms Try Shredders, Special Locks to Protect Valuable Mailing Lists," *Wall Street Journal,* 17 April 1981, p. 27; George J. Church, Jay Peterzell and Raji Samghabadi, "The Art of High-Tech Snooping," *Time,* 20 April 1987, pp. 22–24; Irene Pave, "How to Keep Spies Out in the Cold," *Business Week,* 25 April

1988, p. 144; Dody Tsiantar, John Schwartz, Bob Cohn and Lynda Wright, "George Smiley Joins the Firm," *Newsweek,* 2 May 1988, pp. 46–47; Doug Stewart, "Spy Tech," *Discover,* March 1988, pp. 58–65.

14.   Gary S. Marx and Stewart S. Manela, "Protecting Confidential Information in High-Tech Companies," *Personnel Administrator,* May 1986, pp. 35–36ff.

4

The Environment of the Market

When you read your very first principles of marketing text, you learned that there are five environments that were beyond your control, at least in the short run. They are the competitive environment, technological environment, economic environment, legal environment, and cultural and social environment. Some texts include the company's resources and objectives as an uncontrollable environment because often marketing executives are unable to influence top management to allow them use of a larger budget. This subject was so important that an entire chapter was devoted to this subject. Remember? And yet, many marketing managers have forgotten the obvious — you have to pay attention to what's beyond your control, or you'll fail badly.

IGNORING THE COMPETITIVE ENVIRONMENT

This first mistake shows what can happen when you don't pay close attention to the competitive environment. American Motors Company is no more. Its assets were bought by Chrysler Corporation in the late 1980s, mainly to get the rights to manufacture the Jeep. American Motors made three major mistakes that you need to know about. First, in the 1950s, when it was known as Nash Motor Car Company, it tried to buck the environment by educating the U.S. public about large cars' relative lack of economy by calling them "gas-guzzling dinosaurs." It was positioning itself (before the word was widely used) as the smart alternative to the dinosaurs, since its Rambler was low priced and delivered good gasoline mileage. It served that market niche well, but its mistake was that it couldn't make that niche larger.

Later, it tried financial measures to improve itself — it merged with Kaiser-Willys Motors and eventually called itself American Motors. It was bought by France's Renault, which kept the American Motors name, and which added Renault cars to its product line. Here's where it made its second mistake. Its image as a low-priced alternative was muddied. It offered too many cars that were quite different from each other, confusing the public. Its cars were as expensive as many of its competitors, whose mileage figures were more impressive.

The last sentence highlights American Motors' third and, I think, biggest mistake — it ignored its competitors. It didn't keep track of the things they were doing to undermine American Motors' old niche. Before they knew it, the niche was gone. One ad they ran, for their Jeep Wagoneer, which they called "America's luxury four-wheel drive sportwagon," showed they had abandoned their old economy image. But, worse, the ad's headline said, "We couldn't find a competitor." Of course, the ad agency was doing its job — puffing the product, indulging in a little hyperbole. But the headline, "We couldn't find a competitor" is symbolic and symptomatic of their shortsightedness.

If you are foolish enough to think you don't have a competitor, you're probably in the electricity business. Several years ago, I was one of several speakers at a one-day symposium sponsored by the electricity industry in the state of Queensland, Australia. I was the only marketing speaker. At the cocktail party the night before, I heard many people talking, "Who's this Hendon guy? What did they invite *him* for? He's going to talk about marketing. We don't need marketing. We don't have any competitors. We're the electric company."

The next day, I told them that they had many more competitors than the gas company and had them brainstorm some ideas as to who these other competitors could be. They did a poor job, for they ended up with the gas company and nobody else. Then, I told them that "doing without" is a competitor. In Australia, people like to go out of the house on weekends to sporting events, to picnics, and so forth. Whenever they left the house, they shut off many electricity-generating devices. So, one of their competitors was leisure-time activities outside the home. That got them thinking. The second brainstorming session was much better. In fact, one of the members of the audience said that since Australians like to make love with the lights out, they were also in competition with making love.

In my seminar, "How You Can Negotiate and Win," one of the 186 tactics that the business executive participants master is "Making the Other Side Aware of Their Competition." It's one of the most powerful of all negotiating techniques — even if the competition is phony. (Beware of price wars started not by your competitors, but by your buyers, who tell you your competitors have lowered their prices when in fact they haven't. See "Greed in Setting Prices" in Chapter 7.)

Even industry leaders have been known at times to ignore competition. Sometimes it's easy to ignore competition when you're already "king of the hill." In the United States, Xerox Corporation was almost a monopoly in the photocopying business for many years. It continued to sell directly to users, to lease its machines, and to service its machines itself. It ignored the Japanese invasion strategy exemplified by such firms as Savin. Savin and others knew it would be too hard to match Xerox's marketing strategy and tactics, for they couldn't afford starting their own sales and maintenance force from scratch. Instead, they got office supply retail stores to carry their photocopying machines. These retailers had their own sales and maintenance reps, and they were looking for a way to increase their presence in the very lucrative photocopying business on their own terms, not on Xerox's terms. Savin's proposal made a lot of sense, and so this company and other Japanese firms took a very large share of the market away from Xerox. Eventually, Xerox opened its own retail stores, started calling its reps TeamXerox, and decided to sell as well as lease photocopiers, but their competitive response came much too late to regain much of the market share it lost. Xerox ignored its new domestic competitors from overseas far too long.

IGNORING THE TECHNOLOGICAL ENVIRONMENT

There are many examples of firms that ignored the technological environment. One of the first examples in modern U.S. marketing history is Henry Ford, who founded the Ford Motor Company. His Model T motor car was the best-selling auto in the United States, so there is a lot of similarity between this example and the Xerox example. Even though the Model T was number one, Henry didn't change it for many years, while Chevrolet was making changes often, using new technologies. Ford made a now infamous remark, "We'll give the customer any color he wants, as long as it's black." It was an arrogant statement by an arrogant man who had been on top so long he thought nothing could dislodge him from the number one position. Chevrolet took over as number one in sales in the United States, and Ford didn't catch up with Chevrolet until the late 1980s. Ford tried. It introduced its Model A after Chevrolet had eroded its market share, but Henry Ford's heart wasn't in it, people say. He had a soft spot in his heart for the Model T, even after its heyday had passed.

Ignoring technology also proved costly for Gillette Company. Although it had the new stainless steel razor blade technology itself, it was reluctant to cannibalize its crown jewel, the Super Blue Blade. This happened in the early 1960s in the United States, and Gillette lost market share to competitors who embraced and used the new technology. This market share was never regained, even after it finally introduced its version of the stainless steel razor blade.

Perhaps Gillette's managers made a calculated effort to let competitors, such as Wilkinson, face the risks inherent in bringing out a new product. Perhaps they felt its marketing muscle would enable it to take away share from these upstarts if the new blade turned out to be successful. Any firm that is reluctant to embrace innovation is asking for trouble, whether it is an industry leader like Gillette or a follower like Personna. Marketers need to be aggressive to be successful, and Gillette didn't show this in the early 1960s. It learned form this mistake, though, and has been in the forefront of technological improvements in its industry ever since.

Filipinos attend more movies per capita than almost any other nation. By the late 1980s, however, attendance at cinemas in the Philippines was down significantly. The cause was the proliferation of retail shops renting movies at very low prices — less than the equivalent of 50 U.S. cents. Most movies were pirated — copied at little or no cost — so the stores could afford to rent for these low prices and still make large profits. They also rented VCRs to people who didn't have any. I advised several cinemas as a consultant and suggested they do what some cinemas in the United States have done — preempt the competition and rent cassettes, too. After all, those who attend cinemas are "heavy users" — dedicated movie fans. These heavy users might as well rent cassettes from the cinemas, where they go often, instead of making separate trips to rental shops. None of them have taken my advice, and movie attendance is still dropping in that country.

You can argue that setting aside a section of the cinema's snack bar to rent videocassettes isn't really part of the technological environment. However, I think it is — the Philippine cinemas are ignoring the new retailing technology that has outflanked them and that is snaring their customers.

IGNORING THE ECONOMIC ENVIRONMENT

The economic environment is made up of the factors affecting the ability of marketers to provide goods and services and the ability of customers to buy them. They differ from locality to locality, from region to region, and from country to country. Even if you run a small firm that only acts in a local environment — such as a small clothing boutique, for example — your local demand is affected by changes in an entire set of economic environments of which you need to be aware.

This particular environment is probably the easiest one to understand because everybody who is in business knows the basics of supply and demand and reads the newspaper's business pages, which contain lots of economic news. However, many firms have neglected to monitor this environment, with disastrous results. For example, Montgomery Ward was a bigger retailer than Sears before World War II. After the war was over, Sears took over as number one because Ward misjudged the economy. No new Ward retail store was opened in the United States during the years 1945 to 1952. In fact, 27 of their existing stores were closed during those years, and 37 more between 1952 and 1955. All the while, Sears expanded by 118 stores from 1946 to 1954. Sears was right, and Ward was wrong because the U.S. economy grew dramatically during this post–World War II period. Why did Ward cut back during this high growth period?

Sewell Avery took over as Ward's chairman in 1932. Because a depression occurred after World War I, he firmly believed that a depression would occur as soon as World War II was over. He felt that the United States would have difficulties readjusting to a peacetime economy and predicted that "economic conditions are terrorizing beyond what we have known before. We are starting nothing of any size; we are being cautious." His caution led Ward on a downward spiral. Instead of being a leading retailer, ever since the 1960s it's been just a slightly above average size chain with a rather neutral image.

Successful marketers must watch the economic environment and be willing to change strategies. Don't tie yourself to a mistake just because you don't want to admit that you are wrong or because of your principles. Mr. Avery might have been correct about a post–World War II depression, but it wasn't until the late 1950s, after he was forced out, that Ward began to expand again. But you'd think that five years after World War II was over, with continuing economic expansion and no economic collapse, that company leaders would think, "We should reevaluate our strategy." The time was overdue for this rethinking. But it didn't happen for another five years. It probably wouldn't have happened for a much longer period if Mr. Avery hadn't been forced out.[1]

More recently, U.S. toy manufacturer Coleco Industries ignored the worldwide economic environment. It was riding high throughout the early and middle 1980s with its Cabbage Patch Kids dolls and expensive toys with sophisticated electronics. It didn't notice that people's spending power had been eroded in many markets throughout the world. Worldwide demand turned back to cheaper Barbie dolls and the like. Coleco didn't trim its costs soon enough and stuck with its more expensive toy line. The result — in December 1987 it filed a petition from creditors under Chapter 11 of the U.S. bankruptcy code.

IGNORING THE LEGAL ENVIRONMENT

The legal environment is probably the easiest to influence, especially in nations where bribery is institutionalized. Of course, laws vary by city, state, and nation. To obey a law in a foreign country you do business in may mean breaking the law in your home country. This can make marketers paranoid. Even if you don't break the law technically, agreeing to stop doing what you've been doing and pay a penalty to the Federal Trade Commission (FTC) in the United States gives you a lot of bad publicity. The giant retailer Sears did not admit it was using "bait-and-switch" practices in selling its privately labeled sewing machines, but agreed to stop doing it in 1976 or 1977. It usually advertised a sewing machine for an exceptionally low price, such as $39, good for one day only.

In the middle 1960s, when I was living in Washington, D.C., I decided to buy the $39 machine for my first wife. When I got to the store, the clerk told me there was no light on it and my wife would probably sew up her finger. He did all he could to discourage me from buying the machine. He kept pushing a machine that cost around $350, a lot of money in those days. However, I used all my persuasive powers to convince him that I would buy the $39 machine but no other. Eventually, he reluctantly took my $39 plus tax, and I put the machine in the car to show my wife. She didn't like it, of course, because it was Sears's bottom-of-the-line, stripped-down model, so we took it back to the store to get our money back. We had to endure more sales pitches for the $350 model while returning it.

Later, I was told by several young couples we knew in Washington that they had been misled by the ad and had done exactly the same thing as we had done. Over the years, in different cities, I saw the same full-page ad for a Sears sewing machine with a special price good for one day only, for $39, then $49, and then $59. I ignored them. I wasn't surprised when the FTC caught them — I was just surprised that it took them so long. About two months after the FTC announcement was made,

I visited a Sears store that advertised a sewing machine at a low price. The store clerk did not use any "bait-and-switch" tactics on me. Sears was doing what it had promised the FTC it would do.

Sometimes, a firm will admit to wrongdoing. In late 1987, McCall Publishing Company agreed to pay a $400,000 civil penalty to settle charges that it billed people for magazine subscriptions they did not order. According to the FTC, McCall sent sweepstakes entry forms to consumers throughout the United States, then mailed a sample magazine and entered a subscription for everyone who sent in the entry. The subscriptions were begun regardless of whether the customer had checked a box on the form agreeing to the sample magazine, according to the FTC, which charged the publisher with mailing merchandise to consumers without their consent and then trying to collect payment for unordered merchandise.[3]

Getting together with your competitors to fix prices is legal in some nations, but not in the United States and many other western nations. There are many examples of price fixing, and the fines are usually quite high. However, worse than the fines is the adverse publicity resulting from the announcement of the penalties. Your customers hear about it, they lose their trust in you, and turn to your competitors who weren't involved in the price fixing. In 1985, General Cinema Corporation paid a $750,000 fine for illegal movie-bidding practices in Indiana. In 1986, a soft drink bottler it owned paid a $1 million federal fine for conspiring to fix the price of soft drinks in the Washington, D.C., area. And, one year later, a grand jury began investigating it for "possible fixing of box office admission prices in various locations."[4]

The federal government was heavily investigating price fixing in the U.S. soft drink bottling industry in the 1980s. In late 1987, it caught the former sales manager of a Coca-Cola bottler in Athens, Georgia, who pleaded guilty to charges of conspiracy to fix wholesale and discount prices of soft drinks in northern and middle Georgia from 1979 until 1984. The manager faced a maximum penalty of three years in prison and a fine of $100,000. He wasn't working for the bottler anymore, so he would have to pay the fine out of his own pocket.[5]

The previous example is just one of many cases. The federal investigators suspected that Coke and Pepsi *bottlers* have often divided the year up between themselves for special pricing and promotion programs. Using what are called "calendar marketing agreements," retailers agree to promote Coke and sell it at a low price one week, Pepsi the next week, Coke the week after, and so on for the entire year. Testimony at a trial in Charlotte, North Carolina, seemed to indicate that

Seven-Eleven stores in the region had signed agreements with Coke for six months' worth of promotions ($500,000) and with Pepsi for the other six months ($400,000).

It's important to note that the federal jury in this civil suit found that the local Coke bottler conspired with the local Pepsi bottler, not Coca-Cola itself or Pepsi Cola itself. However, Charles Rule, head of the Justice Department's antitrust division said, "At this time, the focus is on the bottlers, but it doesn't appear that these are isolated instances." He wouldn't comment on whether the two giant soft drink companies themselves were the targets of at least 13 ongoing grand-jury investigations.

And so, inquiries into these practices were expected to spread, and as they did spread, the ad publicity resulting from trials might damage local bottlers and national brands alike. From 1985 until early 1988, 13 bottling companies and individuals have been either convicted or charged in federal price-fixing prosecutions.[6]

Sometimes, company managers may not think they have broken a law, and government regulatory agencies may not think so either, but a competitor sues them. When this happens, it may decide to settle matters before they come to trial, to avoid the bad publicity. For example, in the United States, Digital Research, Inc. successfully sold an operating system for first-generation personal computers for many years, then fell on hard times. In the middle 1980s, it hoped to make a comeback with its GEM software which makes the IBM PC act like an Apple Macintosh. However, Apple charged Digital with violating its copyrights on Macintosh software. Digital agreed to stop selling its current version of GEM to avoid a lawsuit (100,000 units had been shipped), and it promised not to sell a new version until Apple approved the prototype.[7]

If you're going to sue, make sure you're going to win. In 1985, Hollywood's Universal Studios's suit against Nintendo backfired. Universal claimed that Nintendo's "Donkey Kong" electronic arcade game infringed on Universal's rights to its "King Kong" motion picture character. Nintendo was exonerated, so the focus shifted to its counterclaims, which sought damages for Universal's interference with Nintendo's licensing program and other matters. Nintendo was awarded $94,400 in lost royalties, $1.1 million in punitive damages, and $1.1 million in attorneys' fees.[8]

IGNORING THE CULTURAL AND
SOCIAL ENVIRONMENT

This particular environment is always changing. Some people say it's the most difficult environment to influence. However, marketers have done good jobs here from time to time by marketing inventions that have changed the way we live. Such examples as electricity, the telephone, air conditioning, the automobile, radio, television, phonograph records, the videocassette recorder, Playboy magazine, photocopying, and even Kleenex tissues's famous slogan from 1920s until the 1950s all come readily to mind. In the 1920s, Kleenex was used just once a day and by females only — to remove makeup from their faces at the end of the day. To promote more use in the United States, Kleenex's famous advertising slogan, "Don't put a cold in your pocket," was born. Women didn't carry handkerchiefs as much after that. My grandmother told me that when she was young, young ladies actually did drop their handkerchiefs to flirt with young gentlemen. Women had to discover a new way to flirt because no self-respecting man would retrieve a dirty tissue dropped by a woman.

But this is a book about marketing *mistakes,* not about marketing *successes.* Playboy Enterprises has been both a success and a failure. In the 1950s, it started a sexual revolution in the United States, and exported it to the rest of the world along with millions of copies of its magazine, *Playboy*. Over time, though, the sexual revolution not only caught up with it but passed it by. Its nude playmates of the month showed pubic hair and genitals only after several competing magazines' centerfolds showed them. Other magazines, much more risqué, began to sell more and more, at Playboy's expense. At its peak in 1972, *Playboy*'s circulation was 7.2 million. In 1987, it was down to 3.6 million. Its Playboy Clubs began to be patronized by fat, older business executives instead of the "swinging singles" set, and most of them have closed, except for a few outside the United States. Its Playboy channel showed heavily censored X-rated movies, while the same uncensored X-rated film could be rented for less than $5 at most neighborhood video stores.

But because it had that old "wicked" image, church and other community groups singled *Playboy* out for censure. The giant convenience store chain, Seven-Eleven, gave in to church pressure and dropped *Playboy* from its stores, greatly affecting its sales, since the average buyer at a Seven-Eleven is a younger male.[9] Many cable TV operators have dropped the Playboy channel as a result of community pressure. In 1988, Playboy Enterprises decided to drop the

Playboy channel and planned to launch a new channel, Night Life, in May 1989, positioning the new venture more as a mainstream cable network. It hoped viewers would *not* associate Night Life and Playboy.

IGNORING YOUR COMPANY'S RESOURCES AND OBJECTIVES

Your company's resources and objectives can be treated as part of the uncontrollable environment, unless you can almost every time convince your bosses to increase your budget for your pet marketing projects. If the company is as marketing oriented as you are, you'll probably win more often than you lose. However, even if you work for a marketing-oriented firm, I've found in my more than 25 years of consulting that most marketing executives are so busy marketing their products and services that they forget about using the same variables in the marketing mix to market "marketing" within their organization. Marketing is, in the final analysis, persuasive communication. How many of you are as successful in selling your ideas to your boss as you are in selling your products and services to your customers? If you're not that successful, then your company's resources and objectives are definitely uncontrollable. Here's an example of the unwanted consequences that followed from not being able to convince others in your organization to be as marketing oriented as you are.

Coca-Cola purchased Columbia Pictures for $750 million in 1982. Coke tried to follow a research-oriented marketing philosophy in the movie business, where instinct and intuition have usually been more effective than logic. Some observers viewed the debate between the parent company and the subsidiary as a battle for Hollywood's soul — casually dressed creative types pitted against MBAs from Coke who refer to motion pictures as "software."

The trouble began shortly after Coke took over. That's when it installed a Coke executive, Peter Sealey, as head of marketing at Columbia. He made everybody there angry by saying that their sales strategies were years behind the times. He began surveying consumers for their opinions about plots and stars. He cut costs drastically, including national tours by stars promoting their movies. Some said that Coke doubled Columbia's production schedule as if it were introducing new products to gain more shelf space at the local supermarket. So there were too many films and not enough in the promotion budget for advertising. And so after some early successes under Coke, Columbia had a string of expensive box office flops, including 1987's $40 million failure, *Ishtar*.

It seems that installing a marketing culture in a subsidiary that traditionally has been production oriented is a difficult thing to do — especially when the subsidiary is a new one. There's always an "us against them" mentality when a company is taken over anyway, and the battle intensifies if the two companies are as markedly different as Coca-Cola and Columbia Pictures.[10]

What to Learn, What Action to Take

You've read examples of what happens when you ignore the uncontrollable environments — three from the competitive environment, three from the technological environment, two from the economic environment, seven from the legal environment, one from the cultural-social environment, and one from the company's resources and objectives. Are there any common threads holding these examples together? Just this: Keep monitoring every environment, so you won't be caught by surprise, and never give up trying to influence them. Many marketers have influenced these environments and have increased profits as a result. Don't let what you learned in your principles of marketing text give you the point of view that it's impossible to change them. You can, and you should if it's to your advantage to do so. If the status quo is to your advantage, use your influence to keep things as they are.

HOW TO LEARN EVEN MORE BY DIGGING DEEPER

Cooper, Arnold C. and Dan Schendel. "Strategic Responses to Technological Threats." *Business Horizons*, (February 1976): 61–69.

Cravens, David W. "Strategic Forces Affecting Marketing Strategy." *Business Horizons*, (September–October 1986): 77–86.

Fueroghne, Dean K. *"But the People in Legal Said . . ."*: *A Guide to Current Legal Issues in Advertising*. Homewood, Ill.: Dow Jones-Irwin, 1988.

Ghemawat, Pankaj. "Sustainable Advantage." *Harvard Business Review*, (September–October 1983): 53–58.

Henion, Karl E. *Ecological Marketing*. Columbus, Ohio: Grid, 1976.

Lazer, William. *Handbook of Demographics for Marketing and Advertising*. Lexington, Mass.: Lexington Books, 1987.

Levitt, Theodore. "Marketing When Things Change." *Harvard Business Review*, (November–December 1977): 107–13.

Michman, Ronald D. *Marketing to Changing Consumer Environments*. New York: Praeger, 1983.

Mitchell, Arnold. *Changing Values and Life Styles*. Menlo Park, Calif.: SRI International, 1981.

Naisbitt, John. *Megatrends: Ten New Directions Transforming Our Lives.* New York: Warner Books, 1982.

Panat, Charles. *Breakthroughs.* Boston: Houghton Mifflin, 1980.

Russell, Cheryl. *One Hundred Predictions for the Baby Boom.* New York: Plenum Publishing, 1987.

Strauss, Lawrence. *Electronic Marketing.* White Plains, N.Y.: Knowledge Industry Publications, 1983.

Thomas, Philip S. "Environmental Scanning: The State of the Art." *Long Range Planning,* (February 1978): 20–28.

Toffler, Alvin. *Future Shock.* New York: Bantam Books, 1970.

___. *The Third Wave.* New York: Bantam Books, 1980.

Welch, Joe L. *Marketing Law.* Tulsa, Okla.: PPC Books, 1980.

White, George R. and Margaret B. W. Graham, "How to Spot a Technological Winner." *Harvard Business Review,* (March–April 1978): 146–52.

Yankelovich, Daniel. *New Rules.* New York: Random House, 1981.

NOTES

1. "Betting on a Depression . . . and What It Costs," *Business Week,* 27 September 1952, pp. 60–66.

2. "Coleco Makes Waves in Hong Kong," *International Herald Tribune,* Hong Kong, 15 July 1988, p. 11.

3. "McCall Agrees to Penalty in Subscriptions Case," *Times,* Chattanooga, 10 December 1987, p. A-3.

4. Jane Fitz Simon, "General Cinema Unit Fined $1 Million for Fixing Prices," *Globe,* Boston, 16 October 1986, p. 65.

5. "This Week in Business: Former Coke Exec Pleads Guilty to Price Fixing," *Business Chronicle,* Atlanta, 23 November 1987, p. 8-A.

6. Andy Pasztor and Larry Reibstein, "Cola Sellers May Have Bottled up Their Competitors," *Wall Street Journal,* 9 December 1987, p. 6

7. Nancy J. Perry, "No Glitter for This GEM," *Fortune,* 11 November 1985, p. 9.

8. William M. Borchard, "On Trademarks: Courts Penalize Trademark Misdeeds," *Advertising Age,* 16 January 1986, p. 34.

9. David Dishneau, "Hef's Daughter Has Bunny Empire Hopping Again," *Chronicle,* San Francisco, 13 May 1988, p. C-3; Jeffrey Zaslow, "As Hutches Vanish, Playboy Bunnies Share the Memories," *Wall Street Journal,* 23 June 1986, pp. 1, 12; Michael J. McCarthy, "Playboy Channel Will Change Name to Help Its Sales," *Wall Street Journal,* 4 August 1988, p. 27.

10. Peter McAlevey, "Coke: Flat in Hollywood," *Newsweek,* 28 October 1985, p. 61.

5

Disasters and Safety — Rumors and Reality

This chapter discusses three main topics: what can happen when you don't plan ahead for disasters; neglecting safety; and how to handle rumors.

NOT PLANNING FOR DISASTERS

You can't anticipate every contingency, but you should make some kind of provision for the worst possible event that could happen — a disaster that can wipe you out. Here are examples that should give you cause for concern.

Insuring against disasters is hard enough, but insuring against unfortunate advertising coincidences is just about impossible. Arkwright-Boston Insurance Company ran an ad that said, "If disaster hit Morton Thiokol, would the policy be worth its salt?" just before the space shuttle exploded. Morton Thiokol, of course, made the main parts of the booster rocket for the space shuttle, and the follow-up investigation centered on the role those rockets played in the disaster.[1]

Some companies — even some industries — can be wiped out by the stroke of a pen. My home town is Laredo, Texas, located on the Mexican border. When I was growing up, Laredoans took a perverse pride in the fact that it was the poorest city in the United States — the metropolitan area with the lowest per capita income. (A few years ago, it gave up its title to McAllen, Texas, another border city.) In spite of the fact that it is such a poor town, its merchants were rich for many, many years because Mexicans would descend on the city in droves, buy tons of clothing, food, and consumer electronics products and take them back into Mexico, after paying the Mexican customs officials a small bribe that served as an unofficial customs duty. Those kinds of U.S. products were a lot cheaper in the United States than in Mexico — and of much better quality — and so merchants in Laredo and other Texas border cities were extremely prosperous in the midst of local poverty. A friend of mine, who owned a small bakery near the bridge between Laredo and Nuevo Laredo, Mexico, became a millionaire — all because of the fact that Mexicans can't buy very good cakes and pastries at home. Until the middle to late 1970s, the rate of exchange was 12.50 pesos to $1. Then, disaster struck. Mexico's economy collapsed. By the late 1980s, the peso had fallen to more than 2,000 pesos to $1. Many merchants in border cities in Texas, Arizona, and California literally went bankrupt overnight.[2]

This tale is not about the stroke of a pen devaluing a currency — it's about the wrong stroke on a computer. On May 29, 1987, a U.S. government computer error caused the immediate closing of the quota on Chinese-made cotton coats, and the U.S. Customs Service immediately embargoed all of this merchandise, worth about $160 million. About 20 importers lost $40 million. One importer said, "I have hundreds of thousands of goods at the docks embargoed. Millions of dollars. If we don't deliver this month, we might as well take the goods and throw them in the garbage. Our industry is so seasonal, the merchandise is worthless later." Here's how the whole thing happened.

Customs officials discovered its computer had failed to log about 3.3 million coats imported from China in 1986. As soon as they discovered the error, they applied the unrecorded units against the 1987 total. The large correction instantly consumed the entire 1987 allotment. The importers found themselves in the middle. Their attorney said, "There's an old African saying that goes: 'When elephants fight, it's the grass that suffers.' These importers are just getting trampled."

Although the importers' trade association lobbied hard, the U.S. government gave the importers only a little relief by shifting some unused quotas into the closed category. But the government has grown impatient with chronic overshipments by China. The embargo I'm talking about here was just one of 27 the United States placed on Chinese textile exports through the first six months of 1987.

Could the importers have suspected something was going to happen? Maybe and maybe not. It depends on whom you listen to. The U.S. Customs Service provides figures to importers. The figures just before the error was discovered showed that a substantial portion of the quota on cotton coats went unused in 1986. By May 29, 1987, only 30 percent of the 1987 allotment of 3.7 million units had been taken. Importers felt pretty secure. Their trade association said they had no way of suspecting the numbers were wrong because competitors don't share information, and so they have to rely on customs statistics in planning their purchases.

But a government official at the U.S. Department of Commerce said, "As prudent businessmen, they should have checked customs figures against those compiled by the Census Bureau." And then a customs official said that census data is computed too slowly for use by importers — "If you're trying to track a quota, you can't use census figures. You have to get that from us." And a congressional aide said, "The fact that the importers were getting erroneous information from customs is not their fault. But they're the ones who suffer." [3]

The U.S. Customs Service has often been inconsistent in classifying imports — so much so that many business executives are so uncertain that they claim they can no longer compete very well in international trade. For example, a Fingerhut Corporation spokesman said a routine shipment of sewing kits was detained in Seattle in 1988. Customs officials classified them as luggage, which carried a duty three times as large as sewing kits. What's more, luggage is subject to very strict import quotas, while sewing kits aren't. Fingerhut said, "The guys at Seattle insisted you could carry lingerie and shaving gear where you were supposed to put your yarn." Fingerhut had to cancel hundreds of orders before New York Customs officials reversed Seattle's decision.

Again, in 1988, when Duncan Hines Muffin Mix ran out of muffin topping, its maker, Procter & Gamble contacted Customs in New York about importing the topping mix from a P & G plant in Canada. After getting the OK, P & G imported the mix. Six weeks later, Customs told P & G the topping mix had been reclassified as sugar, which had a stiff quota. Customs told P & G to return the mix to Canada. P & G appealed. While the appeal was going on, P & G stopped production for over seven weeks. That cost the company over $200,000. Then Customs again reversed itself and said P & G could keep the topping mix and it wouldn't impose the $750,000 penalty it wanted to charge P & G for the mix with a sugar content of $30,000. P & G said, "The enforcement attitude of Customs officials has led to an undue level of fear of enforcement harrassment. We just can't conduct international trade well on this basis." A spokesman for the Joint Industry Group, which represents U.S. businesses in international trade agrees. He said, "The service has developed a bad-cop mentality toward industry. Customs is supposed to stop fraud and illegal activity, not stop imports and exports."[4]

This next example depicts more of a nuisance than a major disaster, but because it's similar to unexpected disasters, I'm including it here.

Canpak, a Philadelphia container company, got a toll-free telephone number in late 1985, hoping it would increase business. The 1986 telephone directory of Eugene and Springfield, Oregon, printed by Pacific Coast Publishing, which came out in August of that year, listed Canpak's 800 number as the one to dial for Oregon State Police road and weather reports. (The numbers were identical, except for the 800 prefix.) After snow hit Oregon's mountain passes in the fall of 1986, Canpak started getting telephone calls asking about Oregon road conditions.

Through the end of 1986, Canpak received at least 600 Oregon calls — more than four times as many as those who called on Canpak business. The directory publisher promised to reimburse Canpak for the wrong telephone calls, but of course the new directory wasn't published until August 1987, and some Oregon newspapers and TV stations added to the confusion by repeating the error. Canpak didn't get a different 800 number because the industrial directory containing its listing had already gone to press. So, it lived with the problem until August 1987.[5]

Product demonstrations are common in stores in less-developed nations than they are in more advanced nations because labor is cheaper in the less-developed nations. Years ago, when labor was cheaper, there were more in-store product demonstrations in the United States. Today, more and more U.S. and Canadian companies are demonstrating their products in public. An executive of Hill & Knowlton, a well-known public relations firm, says, "Consumers are skeptical about advertising, and demonstrations are one way to cut through the criticism and let the consumer experience the product. However, there can be failure and embarrassment if the product isn't tested first." Here are examples of mistakes made when demonstrating products.

In 1987, Gail Wise was hired to demonstrate the strength of Yellobags, a plastic garbage bag. She stood in front of a Dallas grocery store, trying to prove that Yellobags was stronger than two competing brands. She did this by pulling all three bags over the head of a bottle until they broke. During two days at the grocery store, the Yellobags broke about 30 percent of the time. Many potential customers were lost.

In 1986, a sales rep for a novelty drinking glass called on AFG Industries' marketing vice president. (AFG makes and distributes glass.) She told the VP that when ice water was added, the image of a Christmas tree, complete with decorations, would appear on the glass in 15 to 20 seconds. The rep poured the ice water and waited. After two minutes, nothing happened. She didn't make the sale.

In 1987, at a New York trade show, a model was pointing out the features of a Japanese juicer. He plugged it in to demonstrate how it could turn a bunch of carrots into carrot juice, but all he got was the sound of metal rubbing against metal. No juice came out.

The same year at another New York trade show, Mattel Inc. was demonstrating its toy, Slime, which is a green gelatinous plaything. The demonstrator dumped the contents into the hands of the head buyer of a large department store. The Slime, which is supposed to come right off, stuck to the buyer's hand.

At a Philadelphia trade show in 1987, a demonstrator plugged in an Apple PC. Instead of showing what the machine was capable of doing, just a weak green screen appeared. Then it flickered and went totally blank.

Interconnect Planning Corporation flew executives from A&P Food Stores from New Jersey to Oklahoma in 1987 to demonstrate the telephone system it had installed at the Tulsa facility of American Airlines. When they arrived, the receptionist told them, "Just a minute, our phones aren't working. I'll have to walk back to tell them you're here." Then, an American Airlines manager told them that lightning had struck the system that morning, and a backup system had failed. He also told them about what happened when all employees dialed out at exactly the same moment to test the system — it crashed. A&P didn't buy the system.[6]

Allied Roofing and Siding Company of Grand Rapids, Michigan, is in the business of removing snow from roofs. In 1979, the roof of its own building collapsed from too much snow.[7]

Northrop Corporation spent over $700 million to develop and build the F–20 Tigershark fighter plane for the foreign market. It wasn't aimed at the U.S. market because it didn't have the same capabilities of the F–16, F–15, or other higher-cost fighters built for U.S. forces. The first F–20 off the assembly line crashed and burned in Korea on October 13, 1984, killing the company's chief test pilot. As of that date, only two others had been manufactured.

The crash had a serious negative impact on the U.S. company's ability to market the F–20, which cost $11.5 million. More retesting had to be done after the crash, for no buyers were in sight then. On top of that, most foreign governments seem to want planes that are being used by the United States. Defense Secretary Weinberger said that the United States wasn't buying the F–20 because "we have to have planes at least as good as the Soviets." An observer said, "We've been saying all along that this F–20 program is quite iffy. Now, Northrop should rethink the entire program."[8]

Less than four years after the Northrop crash, the first Airbus A–320, a computer-controlled airliner and one of only six delivered, crashed on a demonstration flight at the Paris Air Show on June 26, 1988, killing three people. The black box showed the engines were slow to respond, operating at only 28 percent of their capacity. There was concern that the aircraft's systems were yet to be proven. Europe's Airbus Industrie had invested billions of dollars in the new aircraft, in which six small TV screens replaced the conventional array of instruments. The bad publicity was definitely not needed.[9]

Miami-based Arrow Air had an image of undependable schedules. It had a lot of charter business with the U.S. government and several regularly scheduled commercial flights between Puerto Rico and the U.S. mainland. Then, on December 12, 1985, one of its military charters crashed at Gander, Newfoundland, Canada, killing 248 U.S. soldiers. On February 11, 1986, it declared bankruptcy, accusing the "adverse news media coverage," members of Congress who were "prejudging" the outcome of the investigation of the crash, an "unwarranted announcement" by the Federal Aviation Administration that Arrow was using unauthorized spare parts for its planes, and the suspension of all Arrow charters by the U.S. Air Force for its failure.[10]

In January 1986, the U.S. space shuttle Challenger exploded and crashed, killing all seven astronauts aboard. The National Aeronautics and Space Administration's muddled handling of the disaster turned into a public relations fiasco that almost damaged beyond repair the agency's prestige. Their fumbling was surprising in light of its longtime reputation as one of the "slickest self-promoters" in Washington. Its public relations people did have an emergency P.R. plan, but after years of preoccupation with promoting the shuttle program's 24 previously successful flights, they were caught off guard when the Challenger exploded. Furthermore, six weeks before the explosion, NASA's chief administrator resigned after he was indicted on fraud charges relating to his previous job. The new acting director had been on the job only one week when the explosion occurred. The leadership changeover probably made the situation worse.

The explosion on live TV put NASA on the defensive from the outset. Before the agency could analyze what happened, people — especially the TV networks — were second-guessing them. So, NASA retreated into a shell by drastically restricting the flow of public statements and documents. It even impounded all the weather data collected before, during, and after the launch. During the first two weeks of the investigation, several NASA officials contradicted one another on safety and operating procedures. They became extremely reluctant to release engineering and quality-control records, so reporters got them from less reliable sources — some of these sources leaked information that was damaging to NASA.[11] NASA learned from its mistakes, though. Its P.R. people did a great job on the first Discovery shuttle launch in October 1988.

Because the issue of safety is such a special one, it deserves the following special category. Therefore, I will discuss such examples as the Tylenol tampering, Rely tampons, A. H. Robins' Dalkon Shield, and thalidomide in the next section.

What to Learn, What Action to Take

On pages 80–82 there is a special section discussing in-depth the way Tylenol handled the first and second tampering incidents. Learn from the way Tylenol handled the situation. Don't repeat NASA's mistakes in the wake of the space shuttle disaster. I'll elaborate on other actions to take when I talk about how to handle rumors, another kind of disaster.

TURNING PRODUCT AND SERVICE ASSETS INTO LIABILITIES

Cases That Don't Involve Tampering

Experts tell us the number of product liability suits has climbed sharply throughout the 1980s, along with the total amount of money paid out in damage awards and out-of-court settlements. Jury awards in the United States are commonly in the millions of dollars. Jury Verdict Research Inc. says the number of million-dollar awards quadrupled between 1981 and 1986. Many doctors in Florida decided to retire early because they could no longer afford liability insurance. The issue of safety is an important one.

For example, facing millions of dollars in lawsuits over its badly designed Dalkon Shield IUD (intra-uterine device), which allegedly made its wearers sterile, A. H. Robins filed for bankruptcy in the United States on August 21, 1985, ten years after the controversy began.[12] Similarly, Manville Corporation, which was hit by billions of dollars in asbestos claims, filed for bankruptcy in the United States about the same time.[13]

In 1980, Procter & Gamble removed its Rely tampons from the U.S. market because of government allegations linking it to a sometimes fatal disease called toxic shock syndrome. It used the same Rely technology in its Ultra Pampers disposable diapers. They were introduced in the middle 1980s. P & G claimed the product was safe for baby skin, but many people were worried about the superabsorbency of the new diapers causing toxic shock syndrome in babies with diaper rash and cuts. Others were worried because the gel used in the product is so absorbent, it could "pull out fluids from the body, lowering the threshold for infection." P & G weathered the Ultra Pampers storm, so I'm not citing it as a second mistake.[14]

G. D. Searle & Company announced in early 1986 that it would stop selling its Copper 7 and Tatum T IUDs in the United States because of product liability lawsuits — and the fact that it couldn't buy product liability insurance, despite Planned Parenthood's saying the Copper 7 was "the safest of the IUDs on the market." Searle continued to sell them outside the United States, though.[15]

Merrell Dow Pharmaceuticals made Bendectin, the only prescription drug on the market to help pregnant women suffering from severe nausea. It never lost a case in court accusing it of causing birth defects, but, confronted with legal bills and insurance premiums that exceeded its annual sales, it pulled the drug off the U.S. market in 1983.[16]

In Europe in the late 1950s and early 1960s many pregnant women taking thalidomide, which was prescribed as a sleep inducer, a cough suppressor, a reliever of upset stomachs, and an antidote for morning sickness in pregnancy, later gave birth to deformed babies. The West German manufacturer paid millions of dollars in damages.[17]

Two thousand people in Taiwan were poisoned by polychlorinated biphenyl (PCB) tainted cooking oil in 1979. Between 1979 and 1985, about 160 babies were born to PCB victims. Some were stillborn, others died shortly after birth, and many of the surviving children suffered from abnormalities of lungs, teeth, and skin, and had a weak immunity system that left them susceptible to infection. They were also slow learners. The factory went bankrupt and the owners went to jail. No compensation was ever paid to the victims.[18]

In 1988, a U.S. court held a cigarette manufacturer liable for the cancer-caused death of a long-time smoker, Rose Cipollone. This was the first time a manufacturer had ever lost a case in court. The company, Liggett Group Inc., said it would appeal the verdict.[19] The Liggett Group verdict was the first in the world against a cigarette company. The world didn't have to wait long for the second incident. Just a few weeks later, Sean Carroll, a nonsmoking bus driver from Melbourne, Australia, with lung cancer, received A$65,000 in an out-of-court settlement. He claimed his cancer was caused by passive inhalation of passengers' smoke.[20]

Japan has one of the highest blood donation rates in the world. However, donated blood by law is used only for whole-blood transfusions. The nonprofit Red Cross there doesn't provide blood to commercial companies that manufacture other products, such as the coagulant required by hemophiliacs, and many Japanese doctors operate their own dispensaries. Experts there say doctors prescribe large quantities of blood products for medically questionable purposes. A University of Tokyo Medical School professor said, "The more they use, the more income they can get." As usual, the Japanese government protected this domestic industry — physicians' private practices — from foreign competition. As a result of this situation, 97 percent of the coagulant that Japanese hemophiliacs need is either sold by U.S. companies or made by Japanese companies from U.S. blood.

Unfortunately, U.S. and Japanese companies allegedly continued to sell blood products contaminated with the Acquired Immune Deficiency Syndrome (AIDS) virus for several months after they knew about the contamination and for several months after they began selling a safe, sterilized version of the same blood products in the United States. About 40 percent of Japan's 5,000 hemophiliacs are now believed to be AIDS carriers. As of 1988, forty-six hemophiliacs had died of AIDS. A physician said, "As the number of victims begins to grow, so, too, will the anger." A Red Cross official who thinks the government could have prevented the tragedy said, "I'm very sorry to say so, but I think that's so. The government wants to deny that, but it's a fact."[21]

Union Carbide's leaking gas disaster in Bhopal, India, in December 1984, killed several hundred people. Less than a year later, its plant in Institute, West Virginia, leaked poison gas, injuring six workers and sending 130 local residents to the hospital for treatment.[22]

In 1985, Shiley Inc., recalled 200 of its unimplanted heart valves after a U.S. consumer health group alleged that about 100 people died because the devices broke. The Ralph Nader group said the recall "is too late, and it's not broad enough, because they're not recalling smaller valves, which also fractured. Any cardiac surgeon who implants any of these valves is begging for a malpractice suit."[23]

In 1983, a U.S. firm imported Cabbage Patch and Little Prince dolls from Taiwan. It went bankrupt, and a few months later the former owner requested that Stevedoring Services of America in Long Beach, California, return his storage container. Stevedoring donated the 5,000 dolls inside to 15 hospitals and public service agencies in Los Angeles County. It turned out they reeked of kerosene and may have contained stuffing contaminated with a potentially toxic solvent. Fortunately, all but 12 of the dolls were located and there were no reported injuries.[24]

There are many examples in the United States alone of allegedly unsafe automobiles. Some have been recalled, some haven't. For example, in 1988, the National Traffic Safety Administration began investigating to see if the rear safety belts in Ford Escorts and Mercury Lynxes were defective, after a federal court awarded a teenager $33 million. The person became paralyzed after an Escort he was riding in crashed. At the time I was writing this book, the federal agency was considering a recall of both automobiles.[25] A few years earlier, several U.S. television comedians were telling different versions of essentially the same joke: "Boy, was I worried! I was on the freeway today. Talk about your dangerous situations! I was right behind a Pinto, and tailgating me was an Audi 5000." Of course, Ford Pinto rear gas tanks had a tendency to explode when contacted, while Audi 5000s had a tendency to accelerate suddenly and uncontrollable. (So did some Cadillacs between 1982 and 1988.) The situation worsened to the extent that Audi of America Inc., a unit of Germany's Volkswagen AG, decided to change the name of the Audi 5000 to either Audi 80 or Audi 90, depending on the model.[26] Of course, Ford stopped making the Pinto many years ago. (By the way, the name Pinto means "small penis" in Portuguese slang, so the Pinto had image problems when it was first marketed in Brazil. Ford soon changed its name to Corcel, which is Portuguese for horse.)[27]

So far, I've been talking about unsafe products, but what about unsafe services? In the service category, airlines seem to be making the biggest headlines. If I wanted to document all the airline repair problems I've accumulated in my files, I'd have to write an entire book about that subject alone, so I'll just talk about several U.S. airlines' problems from 1985 to 1988.

The unprecedented FAA inspection of the entire fleets of Texas Air Corporation's Eastern Airlines and Continental Airlines beginning in April 1988 was just the biggest of such inspections. The FAA decided to do this because management and labor were at war with each other. For example, in 1987 Eastern suspended four flight attendants for 30 days without pay for refusing to work on a flight leaving Denver unless their aircraft was de-iced. And in February 1988, it paid $9.5 million in safety rules violations.[28]

Continental Airlines was so embarrassed by its worst-place ranking for so many months in number of complaints lodged with the FAA about all airlines, that it ran this full-page ad under Chairman Frank Lorenzo's signature in several U.S. newspapers in September 1987:

Once people called us The Proud Bird. Lately, they've been calling us other names.

Continental is no stranger to success. As "The Proud Bird," passengers were calling weeks in advance to be sure of getting a seat with us. But recently, while we combined the operations of four airlines, we grew so fast that we made mistakes. Misplaced baggage. Delays. Reservation errors. . . . And a lot of hard-working people at Continental were pretty embarrassed.

It's led us to an intensified commitment to quality. And it's beginning to pay off: Latest reports show Continental's back as one of the top two airlines in on-time arrivals. But we're out to be "America's Best." To get there, we're investing more than $1.25 billion this year alone — to upgrade airport facilities and aircraft and to expand our fleet.

We're continually evaluating and adjusting our flight schedules for better connections and on-time performance. Working to decrease lost baggage — an area where we've already improved 100% in the last six months. . . . But that's just the start.

We think we'll be the talk of the airline industry. And believe me, it won't sound anything like what you've been hearing lately.

Continental and Eastern both improved slightly during 1988 and early 1989, but their monthly FAA ratings weren't consistent. Passenger air miles, revenue, and profit all declined during 1988, and after their machinists union struck in early 1989, Eastern filed for bankruptcy.

The FAA wasn't just picking on Continental and Eastern. It also cited Northwest Airlines for delaying repairs and other safety violations in 1988, but it did not fine them.[29] And it proposed a $766,000 fine against Western Airlines in 1985 for safety violations allegedly discovered in the summer of that year.[30]

In the summer of 1987, Delta Airlines had about ten mishaps within a one-month period — a Delta plane landed on the wrong runway in Boston, two Delta planes had to return to Cincinnati because of equipment failures, two others had to return to Los Angeles because of equipment failures, and a 767 plunged to within 600 feet of the ocean off Los Angeles when the pilot accidentally cut off fuel to both engines. The most serious incidents involved a near collision over the Atlantic Ocean on July 8. The Delta plane was about 60 miles off course when it narrowly missed a Continental plane. News reports indicated that the Delta crew urged the Continental crew not to report it. After the near miss, the same Delta plane strayed into the path of a British Airways jet.[31] You *know* you're in big trouble when Johnny Carson makes jokes about you on his TV show. Delta was the butt of jokes on several Carson programs at that time.

Many of these FAA investigations were inspired by its probe of American Airlines's maintenance policies. Finding too many instances of deferred maintenance, it fined them $1.5 million in 1985. At the time, it was the largest fine ever levied by the FAA. Bob Crandall, chairman of the airline's parent company, said, "All of us were just plain embarrassed by the number of things the FAA found to criticize." When the fine was levied, some air-safety experts viewed American's problems as evidence that maintenance was being strained, or even de-emphasized, in the more competitive environment brought about by deregulation, and the FAA started to increase its scrutiny of all U.S. carriers.[32]

What to Learn, What Action to Take

U.S. firms are at a disadvantage vis-à-vis foreign firms because U.S. product liability law has given foreign manufacturers the advantage. U.S. manufacturers remain liable for their products as long as they are in use. Most foreign marketers don't carry this burden because they only recently entered the U.S. market, and foreigners don't carry heavy insurance burdens in their home nations. An American Textile Machinery Association study reported that foreign manufacturers of machine tools and hardware pay only 1 to 5 percent as much for liability insurance back home. And in Japan and Europe, workmen's compensation pays for workplace injuries — not lawsuit victories. So foreign marketers in vulnerable product categories enjoy lower costs than U.S. marketers.

Given that foreign firms have the advantage, can you learn from what other firms have done to face up to this major problem? I think so. Without some kind of federal legislation putting a limit on product and service liability damages, here's what some firms have done to overcome their vulnerability.

Some firms have abandoned the U.S. market and decided to market their products in foreign countries only. This seems to have worked, but some firms with a strong social conscience, like Merck & Co., the only U.S. manufacturer of the combined measles, mumps, and rubella vaccine, have stayed in business because to leave would endanger the continued supply of this important vaccine in the United States. Merck's attorney said, "A good business executive would not be in this business. The potential liability risk is too high, but Merck is committed to manufacturing vaccines from a social responsibility standpoint." Other firms have decided to stay in the United States for other reasons. The staying power of large firms might give them an opportunity to raise prices once all domestic competitors have quit. But remember the foreign competitors with their much lower insurance premiums.

Other firms have tried to raise their prices to cover their increased insurance costs. Once again, this doesn't work very well if they're in competition with foreign manufacturers.

Most companies are lobbying federal and state governments to change the law. So far, this has met with mixed results. In some no-fault insurance states, such as Massachusetts, auto insurance premiums are sky-high.

FMC Corporation and others are trying "preventive law" programs, which include a legal audit of its businesses. The audit identifies products-services-operations that could set off lawsuits, then either cleans them up or drops them. During the audit, product-development documents that could become evidence in a lawsuit are safeguarded. This means bringing lawyers into the product-development process. They document and justify every decision in advance. Then, they put warnings against every conceivable misuse on their labels. In the final part of the audit, they try to improve the product or to educate customers in its proper use. Sometimes this works, but sometimes it doesn't. Let's face it — preventive law programs can't prove to a jury that a design could not have been improved upon.

Union Carbide has experimented with so-called minitrials in cases involving workmen injured by accidental exposure to toxic chemicals — but this didn't work in Bhopal, India.

Two-thirds of the school districts in the United States have adopted a no-fault insurance program for high school athletes. It costs $1.40 per athlete per year. When a student is severely injured and the family agrees not to sue the manufacturers who have joined the program, the settlement pays all of the athlete's medical and rehabilitation expenses and compensates him or her for the estimated earnings loss over a working lifetime. The system seems to work. From 1981, when the program took effect, until 1986, the families of all 24 athletes seriously injured decided not to sue. By limiting claims only to severe injuries and by barring families from also suing manufacturers, the system seems to have avoided the loopholes that have made automobile insurance so expensive in Massachusetts and other no-fault insurance states.[33]

Disasters Involving Tampering (Actual and Perceived)

Tylenol (twice), Gerber's (three times), Contac, Teldrin, Dietac, Sine-Off, Excedrin, Riunite, Jalisco cheese, imported brie cheese from

France, Girl Scout cookies (twice), salmonella in chicken, Campbell's tomato juice, apples, Chilean grapes, alfatoxins in corn. The list went on and on. For a while in the 1980s, it looked as if nothing was safe to put into your mouth and swallow anymore. Some of these cases involved tampering — others simply became toxic on their own. People didn't know which was which, but they seemed to be more afraid of tampering because that seemed to be the work of "crazy people" whom nobody could trust, not the result of a manufacturing process that somehow went bad.

Which of the above were tampering? Do you remember? This will jog your memory.

Four labels of Italy's Riunite wine — Bianco, Rosato, Lambrusco dell 'Emilia, and Spumante — were withdrawn from store shelves in late 1985 after the U.S. Bureau of Alcohol, Tobacco and Firearms found traces of diethylene glycol, a solvent used in antifreeze. The recall affected 400,000 cases. Speculation at the time was that the glycol may have gotten into the wine from leaky cooling equipment.[34]

In 1985, a food poisoning epidemic killed at least 40 people. It was traced to a cheese manufactured by Jalisco Mexican Products of Los Angeles. Jalisco closed down its cheese making operations, was fined $20,000, and was placed on three years' probation. The president and principal owner of the company was sentenced to 30 days in jail and fined $18,800 for state health and safety code violations.[35]

In February 1986, the U.S. Food and Drug Administration (FDA) recalled several brands of nationally sold imported French brie cheese found to be tainted by a potentially fatal bacteria, Listeria monocytogenes.[36]

In 1987, the main food poisoning scare seemed to be salmonella in chicken. Chicken throughout the United States seemed to be contaminated. Many poultry farms in Arkansas, where a large percentage of U.S. chickens are raised, and in many other states, killed thousands of chickens. People were advised to cook chicken as thoroughly as they cooked pork. Sales fell slightly during the scare, then went back up to normal. The industry didn't mount a public relations campaign.

In 1987, a man called a supermarket in the Boston area, saying he had poisoned several cans of Campbell's tomato juice with strychnine. Within six hours, Campbell employees removed two truckloads of its tomato juice stock from all 84 stores in the New England chain.[37]

Right after the second Tylenol poisoning, a man who called himself "Gary" phoned news media, stores, and SmithKline Beckman Corporation, a pharmaceutical marketer, that he had poisoned three

SmithKline brands — Contac, Teldrin, and Dietac. Sure enough, tampered boxes were found in Houston, San Francisco, and Orlando. The firm recalled some boxes, and sales fell off. Days later, another man called a Houston TV station saying he had tampered with SmithKline's Sine-Off. The FDA and FBI investigated and determined that the Sine-Off incident was just a crank phone call. No Sine-Off recall occurred.[38]

In Seattle, Washington, Excedrin capsules laced with cyanide killed two people in 1986. In 1988, a federal jury convicted Stella Nickell of killing these two people — one of them was her husband. In the meantime, Bristol-Myers recalled all of its Extra Strength Excedrin capsules and lost many sales as a result.[39]

In 1984, the Girl Scouts lost $750,000 in cookie sales when metal straight pins were found in some cookie boxes. In 1986, sales again fell off when metal staples were found in several cookies bought in Illinois.[40]

In 1984, the U.S. Department of Agriculture and the FDA said broken glass had contaminated several bottles in two separate lots of Gerber's baby food packed in glass jars. Gerber recalled hundreds of thousands of jars, and then found there wasn't any glass in the recalled food. In hindsight, Gerber executives felt that consumers were more skeptical of Gerber quality after the recall than before because they felt the problem was larger than originally reported.

Then, in February 1986, shards of glass began to be found once again in Gerber baby food jars in many states. The FDA investigated and said the complaints might have been the result of breakage in shipping. An FDA spokesman said, "We don't really believe that we are talking about a health hazard. It is our belief that the glass fragments the size we are finding do not represent a health hazard. The fragments are very, very small, and the human body can handle it without any problems. Glass slivers up to half an inch long are safe, with the only possible damage being a cut to a lip or gum. I think this is not anything new and is probably something that has been with us since we have used glass." In spite of that statement, food stores began pulling Gerber baby food products in glass jars off their shelves.

Gerber's chairman remembered what happened two years earlier. He decided not to recall any baby food, saying "I think 1984 is a good example of overreaction on our part. We thought by recalling we could reassure consumers, but all that we did was fan the flames." The company blamed the media for helping fuel the panic. "We feel this is a lynch mob. Nobody wants to wait for due process. We're guilty until proven innocent. It's not a Gerber problem. Gerber is the victim. Let's say we give in and recall everything. Who gives in next week?" asked a company spokesman. He also said he believed some customers may have "seeded" jars with glass after they had taken them home in the hope of suing the company later on. Other consumers may have broken glass when they tapped jars on hard surfaces to make them easier to open, he also said.

Gerber strongly believed its products were safe and tamper evident, so it decided not to change its packaging by adding even more tamper-resistant devices, such as shrink wrap around jar lids. It said, "When a person opens a jar, the sound of the vacuum being broken is heard, as well as a small pop from a button in the center of the lid. If the vacuum seal has not been broken, the button will be slightly depressed."

The result? Signs similar to this one at a Tom Thumb store in Dallas began to appear: "For your protection, we suggest that you not buy Gerber baby food until further notice." Gerber's market share fell for a while — then it picked up. It seemed to have weathered the storm. Its competitors, Heinz and Beechnut, did increase their shares for awhile — but eventually, things went back to normal, and they lost share to Gerber. Will Gerber continue its comeback? In September 1988, newspapers reported metal fragments in Gerber jars in east Tennessee. Its products were removed from shelves in the area.[41]

The classic case was, of course, Tylenol capsules. Oh, there were other tampering cases, all right, but Tylenol was the first big one, in 1982. Then, the same thing happened to Tylenol in 1986. In 1982, seven Chicago area residents died after taking Tylenol capsules that were tainted with cyanide. In 1986, a New York woman took a Tylenol capsule tainted with cyanide and died, too. Then, a second poisoned bottle was found at another New York store. What did Tylenol do? They did such a good job, I recommend you follow their example and not Gerber's.

What to Learn, What Action to Take

After the 1982 poisoning, Tylenol recalled 22 million bottles of its capsules. They thought about abandoning capsules and just keeping Tylenol pills on the market, but decided to keep both, after fast but in-depth market research told them this was the best tack to take. It brought out capsules in newly designed triple-sealed tamper-resistant packages, and sent out millions of free coupons. It set up consumer hot lines. In ads a corporate spokesman respectfully asked the public for its continued faith. The recall, new packaging, ad campaign, and coupons worked. Within three months after the poisonings, it had recaptured most of its 35 percent share of the nonprescription pain reliever market.

After the 1986 incident, Jim Burke, Tylenol's chief executive, put together a team of six managers and began a series of crisis management meetings, while another quick, in-depth market research study was being conducted. The atmosphere was contentious at times. Several didn't want to pull the capsules off the market because that was 30 percent of Tylenol's total sales and because 52 percent of their capsule users wanted Tylenol to keep making them and most consumers believed — erroneously — that capsules work faster than tablets. Their research also told them that many people — 36 percent — felt somebody inside a Tylenol plant might be responsible this time. (In the 1982 incident, almost everybody felt somebody outside the company was to blame. Indeed, there were some convictions.) The executives talked about tamperproof packages, but they concluded there never would be a 100 percent tamperproof package, and they worried that their business would collapse if a third incident occurred.

Then, they reviewed their research and noted that most Tylenol users were again ready to buy the brand. On the basis of this, they decided that the best strategy was to make it a capsule problem, not a Tylenol problem. They decided to drop the capsules and to tell the public that capsules could never be completely safe from tampering. Perhaps they sensed after the 1982 poisonings that something like this was going to happen a second time, for in 1984, Tylenol introduced a pill that looked like a capsule, which they called a caplet. By 1986, it accounted for 22 percent of Tylenol sales. So, in "public service-like" TV ads aimed at asking people to give the caplets a try and in hundreds of newspaper and magazine ads, they offered to exchange Tylenol capsules for a coupon good for a free bottle of caplets. It sent more than 100,000 mailgrams to physicians, pharmacists, and hospitals promoting the caplet. This was followed up with 2,500 sales reps — four times larger than their usual sales force — calling on physicians and druggists, and giving them free caplet samples. The overall campaign cost between $100 million and $150 million. (Many marketing experts felt they were trying to stampede such competitors as Excedrin and Anacin into dropping their capsules, too.) It worked a second time. Tylenol kept its market share.[42]

Will there be a third Tylenol incident — there was for Gerber — and if so, how will Tylenol handle it? Only time will tell. In the meantime, learn from Tylenol's responses since they worked. Gerber's response also worked but not nearly as well.

There are many kinds of disasters. They don't have to be physical disasters — they can be mental disasters, too. Here, I'm talking about rumors. Handling damaging rumors is much the same as handling physical disasters. In the next section, you'll learn about the psychology of rumor. This knowledge will also help you whenever your product or service is suddenly deemed unsafe, because a disaster occurs whenever your product or service is perceived by many as unsafe, whether the perception was caused by actual safety problems, tampering, or the malicious spreading of rumors.

GETTING CAUGHT SABOTAGING COMPETITORS AND SPREADING RUMORS

We'll never know if a competitor deliberately put cyanide in Tylenol capsules in the hopes of putting them out of business, or if the poisonings had nothing to do with competition. Let's hope it had nothing to do with competition, and let's hope marketers never stoop that low, especially when human life is at stake. But there are two different kinds of sabotage — physical tampering and the psychological warfare of spreading rumors. Both can put a company out of business if damage control doesn't take place quickly. Forewarned is forearmed. You've got to understand the nature of sabotage if you're going to protect yourself against it. So let's begin talking about this distasteful topic.

Let's discuss physical sabotage first. In warfare, there are three kinds of sabotage. Arson, explosions, and mechanical interference are the most common forms of direct action (active) sabotage. Indirect action (passive) sabotage uses many different nonviolent acts, including encouragement of absenteeism, deliberate slowdowns, deliberate failure to perform preventive maintenance, and purposefully losing important items. Psychological (intangible) sabotage is the closest to rumor. This kind of sabotage tries to cause strikes, panic, and riots through various means, including phony bomb threats, and the like.[43]

When sabotage, both physical and rumor, damages a person or a company, a civil lawsuit is inevitable. If laws are broken as well, criminal penalties can be assessed. Most of the time, it's difficult to find out who is responsible, but when somebody is caught in the act, there is hell to pay. Here are several examples of people caught in the act.

Dow Chemical Company has faced controversy over the years. It made napalm and Agent Orange, and because of this, its consumer products were the target of boycotts during the Vietnam War. They handled the boycotts and the controversy over dioxins with cold, technical rebuttals, insisting on the soundness of their science. They thought that was sufficient. Then, in 1985, they grew weary of confrontation and began an image building campaign with the theme "Dow lets you do great things."

Shortly after this multi-million dollar campaign broke, five members of Greenpeace, the worldwide environmental organization, plugged up the chemical discharge pipes flowing into the Tittabawassee River at one of Dow's plants in its headquarters city, Midland, Michigan, in a protest. Dow had them arrested for trespassing. After the arrests, the results of a routine, voluntary and confidential blood test from one of the protestors, Melissa Ortquist, done while she was in jail, somehow fell into Dow's hands. The test showed she had syphilis. (The test was wrong. Later tests showed she was free of the venereal disease.)

Two Dow employees then began spreading the rumor that she had syphilis. They told their rumor to Midland environmentalist and activist Diane Hebert. Ms. Hebert said, "They were trying to intimidate me. I know of Dow people having bad drinking problems and even sex changes, but I don't go after them individually." She went public with the information.

The county prosecutor found out. Since releasing confidential blood tests is a misdemeanor in Michigan, its office began investigating who released the information to Dow. At first, Dow said the report came from the county health department and that Dow was only trying to locate Ms. Ortquist so she could get treatment. (She had left Midland for her home town in New York after she was released from jail.) When county health officials denied they were the source of the leak, Dow then claimed the report came from one of its own security guards. Newspapers across the nation then picked up the story.

Dow got a lot of negative publicity out of this, and Greenpeace didn't pass up the opportunity to harrass its longtime nemesis with the company's new slogan, "Dow lets you do great things." A Greenpeace spokesman said "The scandal should outweigh Dow's message. Reality means a lot more than advertisements."

Dow responded to all this in a less-than-optimum way. It published a full-page ad in the Midland *Daily News,* but it was addressed only to its own employees, not to the public at large.[44]

In the 1960s, after Ralph Nader's book *Unsafe at Any Speed* first came out and he was relatively unknown, General Motors executives hired a private detective to dig up any dirt they could find on him, to discredit him and his book, which had severely criticized GM's Chevrolet Corvair as an unsafe car. Nader found out, blew the whistle on GM, sued them for a lot of money, and became a household word. The U.S. consumerism movement of the 1960s and 1970s began, I think, out of

GM's error in hiring the private eye. If they had not done this, Nader's book would have made only a small impact, and his influence would not have been nearly as great.[45]

During the 1972 U.S. presidential campaign between incumbent Richard Nixon and Democratic challenger George McGovern, several men were arrested trying to break into the headquarters of the Democratic National Committee. Nobody really knew what they were doing — they could have been looking for Democrat campaign documents, planting incriminating or misleading documents, or bugging the office. The Watergate break-in and subsequent coverup eventually led to Nixon's resignation two years later. In retrospect, breaking into the Watergate offices of the Democrats was very poor judgment, if not just plain stupidity, because Nixon had an insurmountable lead over McGovern when the break-in occurred.

The ultimate sabotage is murder. In 1985, William Starr, president of Starr National Manufacturing Corp., was charged in Memphis with attempting to arrange the murder of a competitor, Larry Levine, president of Kelly Chemical Company, who had accused him of short-weighting packages of de-icing compounds. A Federal Bureau of Investigation spokesman said Starr met with an FBI agent posing as a professional hit man, and offered him $10,000 for the job. The agent accepted, and took a $2,500 down payment. Starr was charged with a violation of the Hobbs Act, which includes a prohibition against the use of force or violence in restraint of interstate commerce. The maximum penalty upon conviction is a $10,000 fine, 20 years in jail, or both.[46]

Now, let's talk about rumors in more depth. The rumors you're about to read were spread either to hurt a competitor, help the spreader's own company, or both. The most prevalent rumors are about financial news (stocks, bonds, etc.), not marketing. For example, here are headlines from 1980 and 1981 in the New York *Times* financial section that have the word "rumor" in them:

- November 13, 1981 — "Grains and Soybeans Rise on Foreign-Sale Rumor."
- June 10, 1981 — "Rumor of Oil Embargo Sends Oil Futures Up."
- May 30, 1981 — "Sugar Prices Sour Again on Rumor of Purchases."
- January 10, 1981 — "Rumor of Hostage Deal Weakens Futures Prices."
- October 18, 1980 — "Hostage Release Rumors Push Gold Futures Down."
- July 23, 1980 — "Precious Metals Rise on Rumors from Iran."
- July 16, 1980 — "Rumors of Rain Send Most Grain Prices Down."
- June 27, 1980 — "Frost Rumors Lift Coffee."

A Chicago Board of Trade spokesman said, "Rumors are part of the information-gathering system." They're built into the system, all right. The chief financial officer of a Chicago commodities firm said, "Rumors generate volume for people who earn commissions, and commissions benefit the whole industry." Indeed, good rumors are good for business, luring speculators into the market. The president of a Chicago trading firm said, "Just enough rumors prove to be true to keep you off step. If there's any truth to them, you're dead if you don't do something. And the smaller the market place, the more prone it is to rumors." For example, he talked about a time at the beginning of his business career in the 1960s when he was a runner delivering orders to egg traders. One day, during a rally in eggs, a trader with a short position in eggs started spreading the rumor that he had heard from "somebody in the know" that eggs cause cancer. Immediately, traders began desperately selling egg contracts.

In the middle and late 1980s, there seemed to be a flurry of rumors in the United States involving key government economic indicators. All you had to do, it seems, was fake a leak of these indicators the day before they were due to be released, and cash in when the market reacts. This kind of rumor spreading is hard to squelch with a quick denial. For example, on September 11, 1986, somebody spread the false rumor that the government's retail sales figures for August would show a buoyant economy, which would put an upward pressure on interest rates. That sent bond prices on a downward spiral, which contributed to the stock market's 86-point drop the same day. Nobody knows if the rumor started as an innocent remark or as an intentional plant to manipulate the market.[47]

By the late 1980s, U.S. financial market rumors became institutionalized and traveled much quicker than ever before with the beginning of such "rumor wire" services as Dow Jones's Professional Investor Report, Reuter Financial Report, Standard & Poor's MarketScope, McGraw-Hill News, Knight-Ridder's Money Center, International Thomson Organization's Technical Data International, and MMS Debt Market Analysis. The proliferation of these "real time" news services have seen to it that rumors flash around the world faster than ever before. A Reuter's executive said, "If a rumor is becoming a market factor, it has to be paid heed to." A MarketScope executive added, "We try not to be a rumor mill, in a sense. But Wall Street acts on these things."[48]

All rumors, whether they're marketing rumors or financial rumors, are much more difficult to deal with than physical sabotage because there's usually no physical evidence to prove or disprove the rumor. It's usually the word of the company against the rumor itself. In the hundreds of seminars I've given, one of the most popular topics is how and why rumors spread and what to do about them. I've heard reports of hundreds of rumors spread in more than 30 countries, but not once have I heard anybody reveal, with proof, who was responsible for starting the rumor. Nobody ever took the blame — instead, every person who was willing to talk said they thought a competitor started the rumor. I'm not going to repeat any of the rumors I've heard in my seminars. I will give you these next examples, though, which have been documented elsewhere in books and news stories.

In 1981, rumors began spreading that Procter & Gamble, the giant U.S. consumer products company, was owned by the Church of Satan. P & G's logo, on its products since the nineteenth century, had an old-fashioned looking drawing of the man-in-the-moon in profile and 13 stars. This was supposed to have satanic overtones. Connected to one another, the stars were supposed to form the number 666, a symbol of the Antichrist. When you hold the logo up to a mirror, the curls in the man's beard also form 666. The man was supposed to be an evil sorcerer. Of course, the man-in-the-moon was a popular decoration in the nineteenth century when the logo was adopted, and the 13 stars represented the 13 original U.S. colonies.

P & G tried to stop the rumors. It set up a toll-free telephone number which people could call for more information. It asked fundamentalist evangelists for help. Jerry Falwell, a popular television evangelist, wrote a letter in June 1982 in which he claimed that P & G had nothing to do with devil worship. He ended by writing, "I urge people everywhere to help put an end to these unfortunate rumors." Billy Graham, another popular evangelist, sent out a letter in July 1982, urging "Christians everywhere to reject these false rumors and to be reminded that it is a sin to bear false witness." That worked for awhile. Then, rumors started again. Finally, in 1985, P & G gave in. It decided to remove its logo from all its products, but it kept the logo on its corporate letterhead and publications.[49]

Did that work? No. I talked about the P & G incident in one of my MBA classes at Arkansas State University in the spring semester of 1987. Next week, one of my students brought me a photocopied sheet of paper that was given to her the same week at the church she attended. Here's what it said, misspellings, capitalizations, underlinings and all:

COMPANY INVOLVED: Proctor and Gamble
PRESIDENT OF PROCTOR AND GAMBLE INTERVIEWED BY PHIL DONAHUE ON NATIONAL TELEVISION

The president of Proctor and Gamble Co. recently appeared on Phil Donahue t.v. show and the subject of which he spoke was his company's support of the Church of Satan.

He stated that a large portion of Proctor and Gamble's profit goes to the Church of Satan, also known as the Devil's Church.

When asked by Phil Donahue if he felt that saying this on television might hurt his business, the president replied, THERE ARE NOT ENOUGH CHRISTIANS IN THE U.S. TO MAKE A DIFFERENCE.

After being contacted by the President of the Church of Satan, Proctor and Gamble's president was notified that if he was going to support the Church of Satan, the company would have to place the emblem/symbol of the church organization on the labels of each Proctor and Gamble product. It is noted that since that time, the symbol of the Church of Satan has been placed on all their labels.

Also . . . recently on the Merv Griffin Show a group of cultists were featured, among them the OWNER of Proctor and Gamble Corporation. He said that as long as the gays and other cults were coming out of the closet, he was doing the same. He said that he had told Satan that if he (Satan) should help him to prosper, then he would give his heart and soul to him when he dies. He gave Satan all the credit for his riches.

PROCTOR AND GAMBLE MANUFACTURES THE FOLLOWING PRODUCTS, AMONG OTHERS;

Cake Mix: Duncan Hines Products
Cleaning: Biz, Bold, Cascade, Cheer, Comet, Dash, Dawn, Downey, Era, Gain, Joy, Mr. Clean, Oxydol, Spic-n-Span, Tide, Top Job, and Ivory Snow
Coffee: Folger's, High Point
Cooking Oil: Crisco, Fluffo, Puritan
Deodorants: Secret, Sure
Diapers: Pampers, Luvs
Haircare: Lilt
Toothpaste: Crest, Gleam
Napkins: Always
Mouthwash: Scope
Lotion: Wondra
Peanut Butter: Jiffy
Shampoos: Head & Shoulders, Pert
Toilet Paper: Charmin
Cold Remedies: Head & Chest, Pepto-Bismol

When in doubt, watch for the SATANIC SYMBOL to be found on the front and/or back of all their products. The actual size is shown at right with the enlarged drawing below. It is a tiny rams horn with three sets of stars placed in such a way that if the stars of each set are joined together they form the number 666, the Devil's number.

Christians should always remember that if they buy any products with this symbol, they are unknowingly supporting the Church of Satan and Devil worship. We suggest that you use what you have on hand, but do not buy any more.

Please feel free to make copies of this and pass them out to anyone you feel should be informed, so that as little business as possible will go to Proctor and Gamble. Then this will easily prove that there are MORE THAN ENOUGH Christians and others who believe in GOD to put a very large dent into his profits.

There are lots of grammatical errors and spelling errors in this 8-1/2" x 11" photocopy my student gave me. Several products' names were misspelled, as was the name Procter & Gamble itself. And Pepto-Bismol isn't a cold remedy. The document itself looked as if it were hastily put together. Still, the rumor persists, even after the logo was removed from all P & G product labels. Perhaps that's why General Motors decided to rethink the Saturn name for its new small-car subsidiary. Focus groups associated Saturn with Satan, and GM didn't want another P & G logo incident on its hands. The focus groups also associated the Saturn name with the U.S. space shuttle program and, indirectly, with the January 1986 deaths of the seven Challenger space shuttle astronauts.[50]

In Illinois and Indiana in 1983, there was a rumor going around that $1 from each case of Stroh's beer sold was going to the Jesse Jackson presidential campaign. In an ad, Stroh Brewery Company offered $25,000 for the identity of the person or persons responsible for beginning the rumor. It denied it was contributing to presidential campaigns, but it didn't mention Jesse Jackson in the ad.[51]

McDonald's was the subject of several rumors. In 1977, its founder, Ray Kroc, was supposed to have appeared on the Phil Donahue Show saying that he supported the Church of Satan. In 1978, rumors hit both McDonald's and Wendy's that their hamburgers had worms in them. I remember the response of one of the U.S. chains. They said they didn't put worms into their hamburgers because worms are more expensive than beef. That was not a statement that was designed to reassure consumers. In the Philippines, Jollibee and Big 20, two hamburger restaurant chains, were both hit several times by the worm rumor in the early 1980s. When I lived in Australia in the 1970s, I heard the rumor several times that McDonald's used kangaroo meat in their hamburgers. And in 1988 in the Philippines, I heard the very same rumor about Kentucky Fried Chicken that I had first heard in the United States in the late 1970s — that its fried chicken was really fried rat meat. In another variation of this same kind of rumor, in Detroit in 1982 Hygrade Ball Park Frankfurters was hit by the rumor that razor blades were found in them.[52]

In 1983, Jockey underwear was the subject of the rumor that tight Jockey shorts cause sterility in men. I remember Johnny Carson making several jokes about it. The nationally syndicated "Dear Abby" advice column ran six letters on the subject in a single column. Abby's comments seemed to indicate she believed the rumor was true. In 1984, the rumor spread to Church's Fried Chicken. Eating it was supposed to make you sterile, according to the rumor.[53]

In the late 1970s, two similar General Foods candies, Cosmic Candy and Pop Rocks, were supposed to make your stomach explode if you ate them and drank a carbonated soft drink at the same time. The rumor spread from the United States to the Philippines because I heard it in both nations. General Foods ran ads in magazines assuring parents that the candies were safe. They also sent form letters to the trade and to school principals and counselors, trying to stifle the rumor.[54]

In the late 1970s, Bubble Yum bubble gum was supposed to have spider eggs inside of it, according to a popular U.S. rumor.[55]

Another rumor involving animal eggs surfaced in the United States. In 1981, several coats imported from Taiwan and on sale at a Kmart store were said to have snake eggs in their pockets. The eggs hatched and killed some customers, according to the rumor. In 1987, I heard the exact same rumor in the Philippines — this time it supposedly happened at Robinson's Department Store in Manila.[56]

I'm going to repeat the same item I talked about in the section titled "Playing by Your Competitor's Rules Instead of Your Own" (in Chapter 3) because it's a very pervasive rumor. In such southeastern Asian nations as Singapore, Malaysia, Indonesia, Thailand, and the Philippines, I've heard the same rumor every year since 1975 — one year, it seems to be about Coca-Cola, and the next year, it seems to be about Pepsi Cola. When Coke and Pepsi executives attend my seminars, they always accuse their rivals of starting the rumors. The rumor: "A few weeks ago, at a bottling plant, they found an employee at the bottom of a big vat of cola syrup." People who hear the rumor usually gag to think that they might have been drinking human blood or worse. Sales dramatically fall for a few weeks for the targeted brand.

In one of the few documented instances in which a marketer started a rumor to damage its competitor and was caught, the subject was cigarettes in World War II in New York City. The cigarette company hired two well-dressed men to ride on New York subway trains during the morning and evening rush hours and talk to each other in loud voices. The conversation went something like this:

> Did you hear what happened in North Carolina last week? The government is
> trying to hush it up so people won't panic. A German submarine landed on
> the coast, and a bunch of commandos got off the boat and started spraying
> poison gas on all the tobacco leaves in Company X's warehouse. Boy, I'm
> glad I don't smoke their cigarettes. People who smoke them will suffer
> permanent brain damage.

Sales of that brand fell dramatically during the rumor campaign.

A rumor that Coca-Cola hasn't tried to do much about has been spread in the United States and Canada since the early 1970s — that Tab, one of its diet soft drinks, really has 80 calories, not just one calorie. It's not a very damaging rumor, so Coke hasn't tried to fight it.[57]

When relatively unknown Congressman John F. Kennedy upset heavily favored incumbent Senator Henry Cabot Lodge in the Massachusetts race many years ago, the Kennedy forces hired "beatniks" to ring doorbells at 3 A.M. in urban areas, passing out Lodge literature. Now is this example rumor or sabotage? It probably has a little of both in it because rumors soon began to spread that many Lodge supporters were "an undesirable element."

Mexico's Corona Beer, the second largest selling imported beer in the United States, suffered when a rumor spread in the summer of 1987 that it was contaminated by urine. Sales fell by 20 percent. (There was also a backlash against it when people started perceiving it as a "yuppie" beer. Also, Miller's Genuine Draft Beer, a new entry, started positioning itself against Corona — successfully.)[58]

What to Learn, What Action to Take

You've read about a lot of rumors in this chapter. You've probably heard most of them. Now, let's see why people spread rumors, when rumors spread the quickest, and what you can do about them:

Why do people spread rumors? Competitors can do it, yes, but there are at least six other reasons why you and other people might spread rumors:

- Verification. Spreading the rumor confirms my view that the world is a rotten place and that I was right all along about that company or product. Hearing the rumor and passing it on substantiates my fears and justifies my antagonistic feelings.
- Boredom remover. It's a diversion, breaking the monotony of everyday life, especially if the event is grotesque, unusual, and surprising — like spider eggs in bubble gum.

- Misery loves company. I'm spreading the rumor because I want to make everybody else feel just as miserable as I feel about what happened.

- Morale booster. When I spread the rumor, I'm important because I'm sharing important news. I'm a loner who craves attention. And this gets rid of my frustrations by cutting the "bad guy" down to size.

- Comfort in ambiguity. There's not really much hard news about this important event, and I'm very interested in what's going on. Therefore, I am comforted when I hear a rumor, and I want to comfort others by telling them the rumor, too.

- Survival in times of crisis and catastrophe. I buy a certain brand of medicine, and I suddenly hear somebody poisoned a batch of my brand. To me, that's a crisis. There's lots of social trauma when many people feel threatened. People want to survive, so any kind of information becomes relevant to them, including rumors.

When do rumors spread the quickest? They seem to spread fastest when they're repulsive and somewhat unbelievable because those qualities attract more attention to them. Rumors spread faster about bigger companies than about small companies and powerful, well-known people than about unknown ordinary people. If they're attributed to an authoritative source — and Phil Donahue, Dear Abby, Ann Landers, Oprah Winfrey, and radio and TV call-in talk show hosts are considered authoritative sources in the United States — they spread faster. If the rumor is about contamination, it definitely will spread quickly.[59]

What can you do about rumors? Remember, time can be your own worst enemy, so you have to act quickly. There are basically two schools of thought — first, do nothing, and second, take action. The "do nothing" advocates say it's best not to call more attention to it. For example, Gallo Wine was *Fortune*'s September 1, 1986, cover story. The article talked about what a great company Gallo is. However, in four short sentences, the magazine reported that Ernest and Julio Gallo's father chased them across a field with a shotgun before killing himself, and that Ernest's son, David, occasionally exhibited "bizarre" behavior. The Gallos pulled all their advertising out of all of Time Inc.'s publications because of those four sentences. However, their well-publicized actions helped to spread the story further. Excerpts from the *Fortune* article spread across the United States in newspapers, and requests for reprints of the article surged. The four sentences they didn't like became highlighted, without the 200 positive ones surrounding them.[60]

The "do nothing" advocates also feel that if you lay low, you won't be as susceptible to new rumors. And of course, if the threat posed by the rumor is low, as the 80-calorie Tab rumor, it's probably wisest to do nothing.

If you decide to take action, experts on rumors recommend three phases. The first is fast action, limited only to local areas affected. If you do this, you should get as much information as possible about it. Using detectives to determine who started the rumor probably won't do any good because the source is probably elusive. Even if your detectives found out, the rumor will already have achieved an existence of its own. You should also give press releases to Better Business Bureaus, leaders, distinguished citizens, important groups, and all media — but that shouldn't be your only response. If you can find out the demographics of the main people spreading the rumors, then go ahead and meet with special interest groups involved, and not just with the spokesmen of these groups — but that shouldn't be your only response, either. Remember, the Jerry Falwell and Billy Graham letters didn't stop the Procter & Gamble Church of Satan rumors.

The second phase is discreet, indirect national action. In this phase, never mention the rumor itself in your public relations campaign. Back in the 1970s when the oil crisis was at its peak, the oil companies didn't talk about high prices and greed issues. Instead, they talked about the positive and constructive measures they were taking to make sure sufficient petroleum products were available to a needy world.

The third phase is fast, all-out national action. There are several things you need to do here. Make sure your people write down the precise wording of the rumor, where it was heard, its target, and so forth. Show the rumor to your competitors, and ask them if they re facing the same problem. It might have spread to the entire industry. If it has, your trade association should take the lead in combatting the rumor — with your all-out support, of course.

Then, see if your sales are affected, and if the morale of your sales reps is affected. Find out how many employee-hours are being spent answering phone calls and mail. Take a quick, accurate survey to see what percentage of the population believes all or part of the rumor. (For instance, when McDonald's was fighting the worms rumor, it found that 69 percent remembered hearing news on radio or TV about the rumor, and 38 percent remembered newspaper stories about the rumor. Only 8 percent decided not to eat at McDonald's because of the rumor, and only 2 percent believed it added worms to its hamburgers. However, 57 percent did pass the rumor on to somebody else.)

Next, if you think you've got a big threat, then begin an all-out action campaign. Here's what you should do:

- Give the facts about the problem to everybody in your firm. Involve the rank and file. Gain their support for your action. Have them form booster clubs. Set up employee rallies. Have your low-level employees available for media interviews.

- Take a quick survey to find out the demographics of your biggest rumor-spreaders, so you'll know what media, geographic regions, and spokesmen to hit the hardest.

- Decide what points to refute, but never deny more than what's in the rumor — why call attention to more things that can hurt you?

- Concentrate on aspects that are unfair, untrue, and unjust (or un-American, un-Canadian, un-British, or whatever nation you're in) — whatever's against people's sense of fair play. Don't play up the theme, "My company is suffering." Nobody cares if you're suffering or not. They care about themselves and how the rumor affects them.

- Some experts think you should call a press conference, while others don't. Those who don't like conferences think you no longer have control over who hears the rumors and facts once the media has the information. I don't think this is a strong enough argument. I share the opinion of those who support press conferences — when the rumor becomes news, it's shared by the whole population, and so the rumormongers will get no more thrill from spreading it. So, get rid of the attraction of spreading harmful rumors by a media campaign that defuses rumor and becomes news in itself.

- Pay opinion leaders, if you have to, to discuss your side of the issues, but don't let the public know you paid them.

- Tell the whole world that you're going to bring lawsuits against all the rumor spreaders.[61]

Even after taking all these actions, you'll probably find the rumor has achieved a life of it own. It'll bounce around from nation to nation for awhile, and then it'll come back to your country to haunt you again. Let's face it — it's an easy dirty trick for your competitors to play on you. It's almost impossible, therefore, to keep rumors from starting in the first pace. Your competitor is forcing you to play by his or her rules, as I said earlier. About all you can do is watch out for rumors and take action before they get out of hand. Make sure you have a great public relations team on call at all times. Train all your employees to be friendly — not just at work, but off the job, too. For example, if a large percentage of your employees get drunk every night, have wild parties, beat up their spouses, and never mow their grass, rumors will soon spread that your company's products or services are just like your employees — and your customers will desert you.

Sometimes, you can preempt them. For instance, if your union is getting ready to go out on strike, you can run an ad before the strike begins telling the public your side of the story, before the union members start spreading rumors about what a lousy employer you are. Electrolux Marketing Inc. ran such an ad in the Manila (Philippines) *Bulletin* in the middle 1980s, just before its union struck, and it was very pleased with the results of the ad.

Finally, remember this — most of you reading this will be subject to a rumor at one time or another. Those that have been reported in the media are probably just a small percentage of the total number spread. Most marketing rumors are aimed at influencing middlemen's attitudes and behavior and aren't reported except to the affected company and to its competitors. Often middlemen try to start price wars by spreading the rumor that your competitor has lowered its prices. Since most of you will be affected by rumors more than once before your business career is over, pull out this book and reread this chapter whenever it happens. Apply the lessons learned and the action plan I suggested. It'll help, but it won't solve your problem. Rumors are probably your hardest problems to resolve.

HOW TO LEARN EVEN MORE BY DIGGING DEEPER

Allport, Gordon W. and Leo Postman. *The Psychology of Rumor*. New York: Henry Holt and Co., 1946.

Bauer, Raymond A. and Dan H. Fenn, Jr. "What Is a Corporate Social Audit?" *Harvard Business Review*, (January–February 1973): 37–48.

Bloom, Paul N. and Stephen A. Greyser. "The Maturity of Consumerism." *Harvard Business Review*, (November–December 1981): 130–39.

Buckner, H. Taylor. "A Theory of Rumor Transmission." *Public Opinion Quarterly*, 29 (1965): 54–70.

Esposito, J. L. and Ralph L. Rosnow. "Corporate Rumors: How They Start and How to Stop Them." *Management Review*, (April 1983): 44–49.

Flynn, Leslie. *Did I Say That?* Wheaton, Ill.: Victor Books, 1986.

Knopf, Terry. *Rumors, Race, and Riots*. New Brunswick, N.J.: Transaction Books, 1975.

Lerbinger, Otto. *Managing Corporate Crises*. Boston: Barrington Press, 1986.

Morgan, Hal and Kerry Tucker. *Rumor*. New York: Penguin Books, 1987.

Myers, Gerald C. and John Holusha. *When It Hits the Fan*. Boston: Houghton Mifflin Company, 1986.

Rosnow, Ralph L. "Psychology of Rumor Reconsidered." *Psychological Bulletin*, 6 (1980): 578–91.

Rosnow, Ralph L. and Gary A. Fine. *Rumor and Gossip*. New York: Elsevier Science Publishing Co., 1976.

Rotbart, Dean. "Anatomy of a Rumor on Wall Street." *Wall Street Journal*, 26 October 1984, p. 1.

Smart, Carolyne and Ilan Vertinsky. "Strategy and the Environment: A Study of

Corporate Responses to Crises." *Strategic Management Journal* 5, no. 3: 199–213.

Shibutani, Tamotsu. *Improvised News*. New York: Irvington Publications, 1966.

NOTES

1.   Cynthia Crossen, "Shop Talk: Ads and Disaster," *Wall Street Journal,* 21 February 1986, p. 21.

2.   Donald W. Hendon, "Shopping Across Borders: The Importance of the Mexican Visitor Market to U.S. Merchants." In *1978 Proceedings: Southwestern Marketing Association,* John E. Swan and Robert C. Haring, eds. (Fayetteville: Southwestern Marketing Association and University of Arkansas, 1978), p. 16.

3.   Steven E. Levingston, "Importers May Lose Shirts in Customs Slip," *Wall Street Journal,* 7 August 1987, p. 2.

4.   Shoba Purushothaman, "Customs Classification Codes Confuse Importers, Who Cry 'Trivial Pursuit'," *Wall Street Journal,* 27 September 1988, p. 38.

5.   Francine Schwadel, "Maybe He Ought to Start Selling Tire Chains and Shovels on the Side," *Wall Street Journal,* 13 January 1987, p. 31.

6.   Kathleen A. Hughes, "If You Show It Off and It Won't Work, You Have a Problem," *Wall Street Journal,* 4 June 1987, pp. 1, 12.

7.   M. Hirsh Goldberg, *The Blunder Book,* (New York: William Morrow, 1984), p. 157.

8.   Roy Harris, Jr., "Northrop's Bid to Market Its F–20 Fighter Is Threatened by Crash of First One Built," *Wall Street Journal,* 14 October 1984, p. 34.

9.   Barry James, "French Pilots Fear a Rush to Judgment in Crash of Airbus," *International Herald-Tribune,* Hong Kong, 30 June 1988, pp. 1, 6.

10.   "Airline in Charter Crash Files for Bankruptcy, Cancels Commercial Flights," *Arkansas Gazette,* Little Rock, 12 February 1986, p. 6–A.

11.   Matt Moffett and Laurie McGinley, "NASA, Once a Master of Publicity, Fumbles in Handling Shuttle Crisis," *Wall Street Journal,* 14 February 1986, p. 21.

12.   Francine Schwadel, "Robins and Plaintiffs Face Uncertain Future," *Wall Street Journal,* 23 August 1985, p. 6; "Business This Week: A. H. Robins Files for Chapter 11," *Business Week,* 2 September 1985, p. 38.

13.   Michael Brody, "When Products Turn into Liabilities," *Fortune,* 3 March 1986, pp. 20–24; Francine Schwadel, "Robins and Plaintiffs Face Uncertain Future," *Wall Street Journal,* 23 August 1985, p. 6.

14.   Francine Schwadel, ibid.; Jolie Solomon, "Superabsorbent Diapers: Marketers Seek Doctors' Support Amid Health Concerns," *Wall Street Journal,* 5 September 1986, p. 17.

15.   "IUDs Taken off Market by Searle: Suits Cited," *Arkansas Gazette,* Little Rock, 1 February 1986, p. 5–A; William B. Glaberson, "Did Searle Close Its Eyes to a Health Hazard?" *Business Week,* 14 October 1985, pp. 120–22; Michael Brody, "When Products Turn into Liabilities," *Fortune,* 3 March 1986, pp. 20–24.

16.   Michael Brody, ibid.

17.   John Lear, "The Unfinished Story of Thalidomide," *Saturday Review,* 1 September 1962, pp. 35–40.

18.   "Deformed Babies for Taiwan's Cooking Oil Tragedy Women," *Straits Times,* Singapore, 28 July 1988, p. 4; "Taiwan Victims of Tainted

Cooking Oil Feel Effects of 1979 PCB-Poisoning," *Wall Street Journal*, 9 August 1988, p. 34.

19. "Impact Called Unclear in U.S. Cigarette Ruling," *International Herald Tribune*, Hong Kong, 15 June 1988, pp. 1–2; Kurt Eichenwald, "U.S. Case May Spur Anti-Smoking Laws," *International Herald Tribune*, Hong Kong, 16 June 1988, p. 3.

20. Russell Grimmer, "Aussie Non-Smoker's Case Opens Pandora's Box," *Straits Times*, Singapore, 26 July 1988, p. 19.

21. Fred Hiatt, "AIDS from U.S. Blood Embitters a Japanese Hemophiliac," *International Herald Tribune*, Hong Kong, 24 June 1988, pp. 1, 6.

22. Barry Meier and Terence Roth, "Union Carbide Plant Lacked New Gear to Detect Leaks," *Wall Street Journal*, 13 August 1985, p. 3.

23. Lee Siegel, "Group Raps Recall," *Sun*, Jonesboro, Ark., 13 October 1985, p. 8.

24. "The Region: 5,000 Gifts That Stink," Los Angeles *Times*, 24 December 1985, part 1, p. 2.

25. Bob Davis, "U.S. Investigates Rear Safety Belts in Escorts, Lynxes," *Wall Street Journal*, 25 August 1988, p. 40; "Escort and Lynx Targets of Probe," *Times*, Chattanooga, Tenn., 25 August 1988, p. A-3.

26. "Audi Is Changing Name of Problem-Plagued 5000," *Wall Street Journal*, 15 April 1987, p. 7; "Cadillac Acceleration Blamed in Five Deaths," *Times*, Chattanooga, Tenn., 24 January 1989, p. A-3.

27. David A. Ricks, *Big Business Blunders*, (Homewood, Ill.: Dow Jones-Irwin, 1983), p. 39.

28. "Eastern Suspends Attendants Who Demanded De-Icing," *Banner*, Cleveland, Tenn., 24 December 1987, p. 28; Laurie McGinley and Andy Pasztor, "Eastern Air Agrees to Pay Civil Penalty of $9.5 Million in Safety-Rules Dispute," *Wall Street Journal*, 11 February 1987, p. 4; Paulette Thomas, Bob Davis and John E. Yang, "Airline Backfire: Texas Air Triggered Investigation of Itself with Shuttle Gambit," *Wall Street Journal*, 15 April 1988, pp. 1, 20.

29. "Northwest Air Safety Policies Inadequate, U.S. Study Says," *News-Free Press*, Chattanooga, 4 March 1988, p. B-2.

30. "Western Airlines May Face FAA Penalty," *Times*, Los Angeles, 21 December 1985, part 1, p. 4.

31. "U.S. Agency May Probe Delta Flight Operations," *International Herald Tribune*, Hong Kong, 16 July 1987, p. 3; Richard Witkin, "Airline Pilot Reportedly Was Asked to Suppress Near Miss Over Atlantic," *International Herald Tribune*, Hong Kong, 13 July 1987, p. 6; "FAA Inquiry of Delta is Set After Two New Mishaps," *International Herald Tribune*, Hong Kong, 17 July 1987, p. 3.

32. Jonathan Dahl, "Equipment Trouble: Airplane Safety Snafus at American Airlines Inspire a Wider Probe," *Wall Street Journal*, 6 November 1985, pp. 1, 19; "FAA Fine Embarrassing, Airline Says," *Arkansas Gazette*, Little Rock, 5 October 1985, p. 9-C.

33. Michael Brody, "When Products Turn into Liabilities," *Fortune*, 3 March 1986, pp. 20–24.

34. "Tuning up with a Little Riunite," *Newsweek*, 11 November 1985; "ABC Starts State Recall of Riunite," *Arkansas Gazette*, Little Rock, 2 November 1985, pp. 1-B, 2-B; Christine Arpe Gang, "Stores Clear Shelves of Tainted Riunite Wines," *Commercial Appeal*, Memphis, Tenn., 2 November 1985, p. C-5.

35. "Jalisco President Sentenced in Sales of Tainted Cheese," *Wall Street Journal*, 23 June 1986, p. 8.

36. "Four Brands of Cheese Recalled," *Arkansas Gazette*, Little Rock, 27 February 1986, p. 5-A.

37. Nancy Jeffrey, "Preparing for the Worst: Firms Set up Plans to Help Deal with Corporate Crises," *Wall Street Journal*, 7 December 1987, p. 29.

38. "Capsule Tests Continuing," *Commercial Appeal*, Memphis, Tenn.: 23 March 1986, p. C-8.

39. Timothy Egan, "Woman Convicted of Killing Two in Excedrin-Tampering Case," *Times*, Chattanooga, Tenn., 10 May 1988, p. A-5.

40. "Staples Found in Girl Scout Cookies," *Arkansas Gazette*, Little Rock, 6 March 1986, p. 6-A.

41. "Gerber Jars Ordered Off Shelves," *Arkansas Gazette*, Little Rock, 22 February 1986, p. 6-A; "Glass in Baby Food Jars No Hazard, FDA Says," *Arkansas Gazette*, Little Rock, 27 February 1986, p. 5-A; "Some Oklahoma Stores Pull Gerber from Shelves as Reports Increase," *Arkansas Gazette*, Little Rock, 28 February 1986, p. 6-A; "Gerber Chairman Defends Decision Not to Recall Its Baby Food Products," *Arkansas Gazette*, Little Rock, 6 March 1986, p. 6-A; John Bussey, "Gerber Takes Risky Stance as Fears Spread About Glass in Baby Food," *Wall Street Journal*, 6 March 1986, p. 21; "Gerber's Baby Food Tested for Metal Fragments," *Times*, Chattanooga, 15 September 1988, p. B-7.

42. Michael Waldholz, "For Tylenol's Manufacturer, the Dilemma is to be Aggressive — but Not Appear Pushy," *Wall Street Journal*, 20 February 1986, p. 21; Bill Powell and Martin Kasindorf, "The Tylenol Rescue," *Newsweek*, 3 March 1986; Skip Wollenberg, "Can Tylenol Survive a Second Scare?" *Sun*, Jonesboro, Ark., 16 February 1986, p. 8; Michael Waldholz and Hank Gilman, "Tylenol Maker to Stop Making Drug Capsules," *Wall Street Journal*, 18 February 1986, p. 31; Jerry E. Bishop and Hank Gilman, "After Tylenol: Most Drug Makers Resist Calls to Abandon Capsules," *Wall Street Journal*, 18 February 1986, p. 31; *Arkansas Gazette*, Little Rock, 20 February 1986, p. 9-A.

43. Ladislas Farago, *War of Wits: The Anatomy of Espionage and Intelligence*, (Westport, Conn.: Greenwood Press, 1976) reprint of the same book published in 1954 by Funk and Wagnalls Co., New York; both on p. 248.

44. David L. Gonzalez and Mary Hager, "How Now, Dow Chemical?" *Newsweek*, 11 November 1985; Dale D. Buss, "If This Is How They're Beginning Their Campaign, How Will It End?" *Wall Street Journal*, 4 October 1985, p. 23; "Dow Publishes Apology for Alleging Greenpeace Protester Had Syphilis," *Arkansas Gazette*, Little Rock, 19 October 1985, p. 6-A.

45. Donald W. Hendon, "Toward a Theory of Consumerism," *Business Horizons*, 18, no. 4 (August 1975): 16–24.

46. James Chisum, "Businessman Charged with Trying to Ice Competitor," *Commercial Appeal*, Memphis, Tenn., 1 April 1985, p. A-1.

47. Jeffrey Zaslow, "Market Mover: Rumors Reagan Died Can Swing Prices," *Wall Street Journal*, 3 October 1986, pp. 1, 8; Paula Dwyer, "The Phony Leaks That Can Move Markets," *Business Week*, 29 September 1986, pp. 40, 41.

48. William Power, "New 'Rumor' Wires Move Stock Prices and Stir Disputes," *Wall Street Journal*, 17 August 1988, pp. 1, 10.

49.   "Business Notes: The Man in the Moon Disappears," *Time*, 6 May 1985, p. 63; "Procter & Gamble's Old Devil Moon," *Newsweek*, 6 May 1985, p. 56; John Bussey, "Wise Guys — and Newspapers — Still Bedevil P & G About Its Infamous Corporate Logo," *Wall Street Journal*, 29 May 1985, p. 33.

50.   "GM to Study New Name for Saturn," *Arkansas Gazette*, Little Rock, 25 February 1987, pp. 1-C, 2-C.

51.   "Stroh Buys Ads to Put Down Rumored Tie to Jesse Jackson," *Free Press*, Detroit, 9 December 1983.

52.   John Reetz, "McDonald's Denies Tale as Just a Can of Worms," *Journal*, Atlanta, 15 November 1978; Gary A. Fine, "The Kentucky Fried Rat," *Journal of the Folklore Institute*, 17 (1980): 222–43; Geofrey Colvin, "Lessons from a Hot Dog Maker's Ordeal," *Fortune*, 7 March 1983, pp. 72–82; Eileen Courter, "Reputation, P.R. Helped Hygrade Survive Hot Dog Hoax," *Adweek*, 4 April 1983, p. 43.

53.   Jim Montgomery, "Did You Know . . . ?" *Wall Street Journal*, 6 February 1979, p. 1.

54.   "Mitchell Busily Defends His Pop Rocks Candy," *Times*, New York, 26 February 1979, p. D-2; "Pop Rocks Go Boom, Boom, Boom," *Newsweek*, 13 June 1977, p. 78.

55.   John E. Cooney, "Bubble Gum Maker Wants to Know How Rumor Started," *Wall Street Journal*, 24 March 1977, p. 1.

56.   Charles Stevens, "Kmart Has a Little Trouble Killing Those Phantom Snakes from Asia," *Wall Street Journal*, 20 November 1981.

57.   Frederick Koenig, *Rumor in the Marketplace*, (Dover, Mass.: Auburn House Publishing Co., 1985), p. 163.

58.   Alix M. Freedman, "Corona Beer Sales are Down Sharply from a Strong 1987," *Wall Street Journal*, 17 August 1988, p. 26.

59.   Adapted from Frederick Koenig's excellent book, *Rumor in the Marketplace*, pp. 22–32.

60.   "Shop Talk: Out of Sight," *Wall Street Journal*, 19 September 1986, p. 23; "Business News Digest: Gallo Withdraws Ads from Time, Inc.," *Arkansas Gazette*, Little Rock, 12 September 1986, p. 1-C.

61.   Adapted from Frederick Koenig, *Rumor in the Marketplace*, pp. 163–73; Terry Clark, "The Concept of a Marketing Crisis," *Journal of the Academy of Marketing Science*, Summer 1988, pp. 43–48.

PART III
MARKETING TOOLS

6
Product or Service — Launching It and Naming It

PRODUCT LAUNCH MISTAKES

Over the years, I've collected many articles in trade journals, academic journals, and books — not only from the United States, but also from many other nations — on why launches of new products and services have failed, in both consumer marketing and industrial marketing. They all continuously give the same reasons, which correspond to my own consulting experience, written about in one of my earlier books, *Battling for Profits*. In this chapter, I've added many, many examples to the list of reasons to give you more in-depth information about this very important set of mistakes that you should avoid at all costs.

TAKING TOO MUCH OR TOO LITTLE TIME TO LAUNCH YOUR PRODUCT OR SERVICE

Some firms take too much time to get the launch off the ground. When this happens, their competitors often find out and try to sabotage the launch and/or try to launch a competing brand. Also, the market may change, and the product or service is no longer relevant. The changing U.S. market was the main reason for Polaroid's Polavision (instant home movies) and RCA's SelectaVision (video discs) failures in the late 1970s and early 1980s. The products became irrelevant in a changed marketplace. Consumers preferred the new technology of the VCR and its spinoffs (video cameras and camcorders) and proliferation of videocassette rentals and sales, and this preference, occurring while Polavision and SelectaVision were under development, doomed these two products.[1]

Other firms rush and take too little time to get the product or service to market, without adequate test-marketing. Here are two similar products — one failed because it wasn't test-marketed and the other succeeded for two reasons — it learned from the previous product's mistakes, and it was test-marketed. Both were sold in the United States. The product that failed was known as "Tingle Pants." Costing $20, it was a black, lycra bikini underwear with a stereo speaker located in the crotch. You had to attach it to the output mode of your stereo, and because of that it was somewhat unwieldy. This disadvantage would have come out in the test market.[2] The test-marketed product that succeeded is Pioneer's modern black leather Bodysonic Surround Sound Chair. Costing $2,000, it put your entire body into close contact with the music from your stereo or radio or with the sound from your TV set. The high-powered amplifiers built into the chair turn sound waves into vibrations that pulse against you.[3]

What to Learn, What Action to Take

What can you do to avoid the mistakes made by Polaroid, RCA, and Tingle Pants? Basically three things. First, before you test-market your product or service, make an accurate sales forecast. Then make sure you test-market it, and finally, monitor the product launch as closely as possible.

GOALS NOT CLEARLY DEFINED

Sometimes, there are conflicts of interest within the company's own operations. A few jealous empire builders will try to sabotage a new product launch to make themselves look good by comparison. Several examples are given in Andrew J. Dubrin's excellent book, *Winning at Office Politics*.[4]

What to Learn, What Action to Take

Solve this problem, first of all, by defining as precisely as possible the market you're trying to reach. Then define what you want to get by going into that market and have some kind of decision-making support team installed in your company at the top management level. This team should be made up of executives from several lines and staff departments to make sure that an overall point of view is maintained.

Let's go back to defining what you want to get when you go into a particular market. I can't tell you what goals or objectives you should set for each target market. That would require detailed knowledge of your specific situation. All I can do here is share with you these general guidelines, which I hope you'll use in establishing your objectives. They've helped me over the years.

First, use general descriptions only to establish benchmarks for change. The rest of the time, be extremely specific. Your objectives should be specific and numerically verifiable. If you can't measure the progress you're making against your objectives, you can't control what is happening, and if you can't count or measure them, you probably don't know what you want, and you should forget about them as goals. Although it will mean a lot of mental exercise, try to state your objectives in quantitative terms that will make them verifiable. For example, instead of saying "I want to improve my sales closing technique," say "I want to reduce rejections to only 20 percent of all sales calls I make." Instead of saying "I want to improve communications with my sales force," say "I will work with each of my sales reps one day per month." See what I mean?

On the other hand, remember that sometimes you can't be that specific. You may not always be able to state your objectives using raw data. When this happens, try to state them in terms of gains, risks, expected values, utility, or other criteria that tell you the degree to which your action has been effective in making the change you wanted.

Your objectives should focus on results, not on activities. For example, don't say, "I want to open five new accounts each month." It's not the number of accounts that's important, it's the results obtained from those accounts that's important. Instead, say "I want to obtain $1,000 in extra profit by opening five new accounts each month." That will make you work harder to achieve your objective.

Make sure everybody in your company understands and accepts the objectives, and make sure everybody is motivated by them as well. They should be high, yet realistic objectives. Some "reaching" is necessary, but if you feel you can't accomplish a goal that's too much out of line, then you won't be motivated enough to try.

Use management by objectives, or MBO. Get the people who are involved in implementing the objectives to participate in setting them. That will make your objectives more realistic and will make people more committed to them.

Rank your objectives from most important to least important. That way, you're following the "exception principle." You're concentrating on bringing the lagging area up to standard, not on the areas that are performing well already.

Be flexible. You may have to trade off the accomplishment of objective A in order to achieve satisfactory results for objective B. Flexibility also means you have to revise your objectives regularly. New opportunities, past failures, unanticipated events, and other changes are always occurring, which means the inflexible company will be at a disadvantage.

Make sure you consider all constraints, including legal, environmental, and competitive restrictions. Don't overlook your financial limits, either.[5]

NEGATIVE THINKING

Negative thinking is the failure to timely identify a good opportunity. For example, Dr. Land, Polaroid's founder, tried to sell the technology for instant photography to Eastman Kodak Company. After being turned down, Land went into business for himself. Kodak also turned down the process of xerography when its investor, Chester Carlson, offered to sell it to them. IBM turned Carlson down twice. An obscure company, Haloid Corporation, bought the technology. It's now known as Xerox Corporation. Going back still more years, the head of Warner Brothers Pictures, Harry M. Warner, was quoted as saying in 1927, "Who the hell wants to hear actors talk?" At least Warners learned from its mistake when it released the first full-length talking picture, "The Jazz Singer." Parker Brothers also learned from its mistake. It turned down the game, Monopoly, at first, and then changed its mind. It introduced the game in the 1930s. It was the firm's biggest success.[6]

What to Learn, What Action to Take

Following these three pieces of advice might keep the negative thinkers in your company from raining on your parade.

First, make sure you have good creative people in your company who specialize in new product and service development. If they have a good track record, the negative bunch won't have an easy target.

Second, while you're still designing your new product or service, begin forecasting its probable demand, and continue to forecast throughout the test market itself.

Third, don't just test the product concept. Make sure a prototype is manufactured before you send it to the test market.

OVERSELLING YOUR NEW PRODUCT OR SERVICE

Overenthusiasm can blind you to market realities. There are two parts to overenthusiastic overselling — you can oversell the project to your boss (or to yourself, if you own the company), then you can oversell the new product or service to your customers. Both of these mistakes can kill you. First, I'll talk about the negative results of overselling to your customers.

For example, in 1975, American Motors Corporation launched the Pacer, another in its line of small cars. It promised fuel economy, but it didn't deliver. It was heavy and clunky, and a gas guzzler. The company took a calculated risk and introduced it, even though it couldn't get the engine on which it had planned. It wanted to put General Motors' Wankel rotary engine in the car, but the Wankel was never produced. So, it used a big, old AMC-designed six-cylinder engine, which added 1,000 pounds and $1,500 to the car, effectively killing it.[7]

In 1985 and 1986, Northeastern Software Inc. was one of the largest mail-order software advertisers in the United States. Its two-page ads in major computer magazines loudly proclaimed it would beat any competitor's advertised price. In its ads it boasted of a very large selection of software. However, it didn't live up to its promises. Many complaints were filed with the Better Business Bureau of Western Connecticut. Eventually, several computer magazines, including *PC World* and *Macworld,* decided not to accept any more ads from Northeastern because of too many complaints — about 20 to 30 per month.

Most complaints were about failure to fill orders and slowness in making refunds. The company didn't specify a shipment period. Federal Trade Commission regulations say that mail-order firms that don't specify a shipment period must send the merchandise within 30 days. If the merchandise isn't available, customers have to be notified within 30 days and offered a refund. Many customers waited for months for their orders to arrive, contacted Northeastern, and then were told the merchandise wasn't available. Many of them didn't get their refunds. One customer received a refund — but the check bounced. In October 1986, Northeastern filed for bankruptcy.[8]

The founder of Avis Rent-a-Car Company wrote a book on entrepreneurship in 1987, *Take a Chance to be First.* The jacket on the hard-cover edition, published first, claimed you would read "hands-on advice from America's number one entrepreneur." The copy was changed in the paperback edition, which calls Mr. Avis simply an "entrepreneur."

Avis explained the reason for the change: "I quickly learned that the braggadocio claim was a definite turnoff for talk-show hosts and members of the press. And since one of the basic tenets of my book is that while everybody makes mistakes, the successful entrepreneur doesn't make the same one twice, I changed the copy for the paperback edition."[9]

Pan American sold 18 jetliners and its air routes from the United States westward across the Pacific to Asian destinations to United Airlines in February 1986 for $750 million. United jumped into that market with great fanfare. It turned United overnight from a token Far East competitor of Northwest Airlines and Japan Airlines into a major player with 80 weekly trans-Pacific and regional flights serving 13 Asian cities. Passengers who were tired of Pan Am's deteriorating service over the Pacific, who perceived Northwest as a penny-pinching airline with mediocre meals, and who didn't like Japanese food welcomed United's entry into the market, especially after reading their glowing ads with heavy promises to be the best carrier to the Orient.

The promises didn't match the reality. During the first year of operation, United developed a reputation for cancelled flights and very late arrivals. Passengers complained about harried air crews, poorly trained ground staff, and endless airport lines. United admitted, "We were very ashamed of our performance." Many customers were lost forever, for word travels fast among travel agents and frequent flyers.

Some of the reasons for United's poor performance included the fact that the 18 planes bought from Pan Am "needed substantially more refurbishment than anticipated. Pan Am did not shortchange on safety. But they had shortchanged on supplies, spare parts, engines. Laying hands on all that was difficult," said a United vice president. Also, the 2,700 Pan Am air and ground employees hired by United needed lengthy retraining courses. Ticketing, maintenance, and other ground operations had to be upgraded. While all this was going on, flights came in late or not at all, leaving frustrated passengers at departure gates.[10]

United's service eventually improved, but it continued to make mistakes. Once, it made an elaborate presentation to a group of Japanese business executives. One of them pointed out that an ad showing a map of Japan didn't include the nation's northernmost island. Another time, it made its in-flight concierges wear white carnations on trips to Asia, unaware that white flowers are a bad-luck symbol to many Orientals. And then there was the time that it nearly got sued for libel when its in-flight magazine ran a story about Australian actor Paul ("Crocodile Dundee") Hogan. He appeared on the cover in outdoor camping gear. The cover caption read, "Paul Hogan Camps It Up for Australia." The word "camp" is an Australian colloquialism for homosexual behavior.[11]

In April 1985, Dragon Airlines was launched by a group of very rich Hong Kong entrepreneurs as the colony's second domestic airline, promising the British colony's air travelers better service than Cathay Pacific, the only Hong Kong–based carrier, and offering them a choice for the first time. The launch was done in the face of two serious obstacles. Archrival Cathay Pacific vowed to defend its Hong Kong turf at all costs. And the Hong Kong government allowed only one domestic airline to fly any given route out of the colony.

At first, Dragonair seemed as if it were overcoming those obstacles, for within 20 months, it was flying to 14 cities in Japan, Thailand, and China and had government authorization to serve 34 other Asian cities. However, it expanded too rapidly, without proper planning, most industry analysts say. Its scheduled routes to three Thai cities were big money-losers from the start, "bleeding the company dry," and probably will never be profitable. Like United, it sought long-distance routes before being capable of flying them, irritating customers in the process. And instead of accepting Cathay Pacific's offer of a cooperative arrangement for flights to China, it decided to fight them, probably because the main stockholder, billionaire Sir Y. K. Pao, had very good relationships with leaders of China's government. He felt these contacts would enable Dragonair to replace Cathay Pacific on the lucrative Beijing and Shanghai routes. This irritated the much larger and older Cathay Pacific, and it set off a bitter struggle that showed no signs of abating by the late 1980s. Dragonair tried to live up to its earlier promises, but couldn't because of these problems.[12]

Between 1981 and 1985, General Electric lost $120 million in its factory automation venture, mainly because it got carried away by intoxicating — and wildly unrealistic — forecasts of the new factory automation industry, dominated by Japan's Fanuc, and GE's place in it. In 1981, it invested $500 million at its old Piney Mountain factory in Charlottesville, Virginia, and predicted that by 1990 it would have 20 percent of a market that many predicted would be worth $25 billion a year. It would get into industrial robots and machine tool controls, becoming in the process "America's factory-of-the-future supermarket, where industry could one-stop-shop for all the computerized gear and automation advice it needed." By late 1985, a GE vice president called the original projections "flaky," and said, "We don't want to pie-in-the-sky forecast where the business is going." General Electric lowered its sights to concentrate on smaller scale two-year and three-year plans for its three reorganized factory automation groups, which were more realistic than their original plans. It no longer dreamt of unseating Fanuc, but planned instead to make money as a niche player. It seemed to be doing better after it realized it couldn't do all it wanted when it began its operation.[13]

In May 1986, Kodak announced its new Ultralife nine-volt lithium battery. After some production problems delayed its actual introduction into the marketplace from autumn 1986 to early 1987, it proudly proclaimed that the new Ultralife had a 10-year shelf life and would last twice as long as its alkaline counterpart. In February 1988, it disclosed that the batteries would not last ten years. It began an expensive recall and put all ads and production "on hold" until it could correct the situation "within a few weeks." That made potential customers suspicious of Ultralife.[14]

Now, here's the other side of the coin. What can happen when you oversell to your boss or to yourself? Many a marketing plan makes glowing promises that are too hard to fulfill simply to get a bigger budget next year. Most of us have done this — you've probably done it. I know I've done it on occasion. That's because marketers are usually optimistic people. We have to be. Most of us began in sales, and sales reps get turned down a lot. If we didn't have thick skin, if we didn't think that the next call would result in a sale, we would have left the business. But you need to temper your natural optimism with realism. For example, Restaurant Trends, an industry research firm in the United States, reported that most people in the industry estimate that about half of all new restaurants fail within one year, and 85 percent close within five years.[15] And yet many people dream of opening their own restaurant, thinking that their homemade recipes, which they enjoy more than the stuff they eat at restaurants in their town, will draw customers like the proverbial better mousetrap.

What to Learn, What Action to Take

What can you do to keep from making the mistake of overselling to your customers? Simply try to improve your standards of ethics and morality. Do this because it's right, because you'll get in trouble (perhaps even with the law) if you get caught, and it's good for your business if it depends on repeat sales.

All this is easier said than done, especially because of a famous study made by John Maloney in the 1960s that almost every good advertising executive has heard about. Maloney claimed that the best ads are those that are not too easily believed, those that have within them the quality of "curious nonbelief," or "too good to be true." You may not believe the claim made in the ad, but you want to try the product or service just to see if it is, in fact, "the best food in town," or "the finest speedboat made." Maloney said believability isn't that important anyway, because people believe what they want to believe, and advertising is too weak to change their minds. So he said, don't be too concerned about making your ads believable. Make sure you don't make illegal claims, he said, but puff up your ads enough to add the "curious nonbelief" factor, and your ads will be more successful.[16] Maloney is correct about "curious nonbelief," but I also think the widespread acceptance of this policy at ad agencies may be contributing to communication mixes that make promises that advertisers can't deliver.

What can you do to keep from making the mistake of overselling to your boss and yourself? Make sure you do a good sales forecasting job. Begin it at the design stage and continue it during the test-market stage, and monitor the launch itself closely and carefully.

INSUFFICIENT RETURN ON INVESTMENT BECAUSE OF SMALL MARKET

Many firms have entered a market only to find that it's a lot smaller than they thought it was. For example, a Virginia firm introduced "Solar Rover" in 1978. It was a solar-powered dog house, designed to keep the pet warm during cold weather. During the day, heat is collected and stored under the house, and during the night, the heat is slowly released into the interior. It cost $800, and it didn't sell nearly as many as the firm thought it would.[17]

A second example is the product marketed under the name Ultrashock and patented in the United States as Electrostatically Enhanced Game. Its first target market was video game arcades, and it was designed to hook up to video games. It did only one thing — at the end of the game, whether you won or lost, you got a shock that made your hair stand straight out. However, by the time the gadget came to market, the video game arcade business had shrunk dramatically. The firm was trying in the mid-1980s to market the machine as a photo booth. The idea: people — usually couples — would go into the booth, get shocked, and then have their photos taken with their hair standing on end. Each photo would have a funny saying at the bottom. That idea didn't work either.[18]

The third example is a classic — the Edsel, which made its debut in the United States in September 1957 and which departed in November

1959. Ford Motor Company lost approximately $200 million on the venture. Part of the mythology of marketing is that the Edsel's failure in the late 1950s was a result of poor market research. That's simply not true. Ford did good market research on the Edsel. For example, the research group did not recommend the name, Edsel, since most people didn't like it. But Ford's management picked the name anyway because founder Henry Ford's son was named Edsel. The trouble was that the market research was stopped too soon, at the insistence of top management. Much of the research was done before its 1957 introduction. When the research was done, there was a strong demand for medium-priced cars. Ford executives felt the trend would continue, so it stopped its research. It shouldn't have, because the market shifted — people wanted lower-priced cars when the medium-priced Edsel was introduced. The market for medium-priced cars was just too small when the Edsel came out.[19]

What to Learn, What Action to Take

What can you learn from these three examples? Here are several hints:

- You've got to know what the competitive boundaries are.
- You've got to know the market's growth rate.
- Make sure you test the concept and the product or service itself. That's the only way you'll generate an accurate forecast when you're designing your product or service.
- Your forecast should be a pessimistic one — the minimum number of a new product that the company is likely to sell. Compare this figure with the investment requirements needed to meet the desired R.O.I. (Your financial people should have already prepared R.O.I. figures at different sales levels.) If the predicted minimum sales level is greater than the minimum sales amount the financial people need to meet the desired R.O.I., then go ahead. If not, either abandon the project or make adjustments in your financial expectations and costs, to match the minimum R.O.I. objectives and sales estimates.
- Make final checks on the size of the overall market when you test-market.

Products or services that are launched without following these five steps are mistakes waiting to happen.

PRODUCT OR SERVICE NOT A GOOD MATCH FOR YOUR COMPANY

Here are five examples from the United States.

Fruit of the Loom, a garment manufacturer that enjoys high name recognition for its underwear, introduced Fruit of the Loom laundry detergent in 1977. It failed and was discontinued in 1981. Industry observers at the time felt it failed mainly because the garment manufacturer did not understand the laundry detergent business.

In 1980, Lucky Stores Inc., then the third largest supermarket chain, bought the 124-unit Sirloin Stockade restaurant chain. In 1982, it sold the unit at a $4.6 million loss. Lucky's president said, "Acquiring that division was a mistake. We simply didn't know how to operate them very well." Its chairman added, "We realized that we just can't do everything right."[20]

In 1967, General Foods Corporation (GF) spent $16 million to acquire Burger Chef Systems, a chain of 700 (mostly franchised) fast-food hamburger restaurants. It quickly expanded to over 1,000 restaurants in just two years. In 1972, it decided to cut back its fast food business and wrote off $83 million. Eventually, it closed or sold all its Burger Chef restaurants. General Food's president admitted the problem was not knowing the restaurant business: "We sent one of our own men, and he just did not know his way around this kind of operation."[21] Eventually, GF applied the lessons it learned from its Burger Chef experience — its Red Lobster restaurant chain has been successful for many years, perhaps because it staffed this chain with experienced restaurant executives.

In 1975, Exxon, the huge oil company, entered the office systems business. It invested over $500 million, but in 1985, it left the business. Most observers felt Exxon never really understood office systems, which was so different from oil.[22]

The retail chain, Banana Republic, launched a travel magazine, *Trips,* in 1988. It had a good mailing list of people who bought its clothes. The magazine lasted less than six months.

What to Learn, What Action to Take

In order to make sure that your new venture is a good match for your company, undertake a strategic analysis of the market early in the product or service development process. If it matches the unique competencies of your company, then you won't face this particular problem.

PRODUCT OR SERVICE NEITHER
NEW NOR DIFFERENT

Service organizations have more of a problem with this one than product marketers. That's because managers of services perceive their offerings as unique, while customers tend to perceive them as homogeneous. After all, these managers think, in a labor-intensive business, the quality of service depends so much upon the people performing the service — the waitresses and cooks at restaurants, the ground personnel and flight attendants working for airlines, and so forth. So they try to hire the best people and train them better than their competitors do. They advertise their service as better, or best, and they actually believe their own advertising.

However, customers don't really think one service is "the better mousetrap" unless it's exceptionally and consistently different from all the others. Most customers don't share the perceptions of service managers concerning quality differences between two competing firms, and because service can be good one day at a restaurant and bad the next — even from the same waiter — customers have more risk and uncertainty in dealing with service firms. The result is they have less brand loyalty for services than they have for, say, their toothpaste.

There's not much need to give examples of services that have failed because they weren't really different from competitors. You know of many in the towns you work and live in — local gasoline stations, dry cleaners, restaurants, insurance brokers, auto repair shops, and other small businesses. When one failed business vacates a premise, there's sure to be another starry-eyed dreamer opening a similar business there in a few months. They come and go. For instance, in Chattanooga, Tennessee, when the San José Mexican Restaurant failed in 1988, Miguel's Mexican Restaurant opened in the same location. I passed by Miguel's almost every day, and I never saw many cars in its parking lot.

What to Learn, What Action to Take

There are seven things you can do to overcome the "me-too" problem that leads to so many failures in the service industry. First, screen your employees before you hire them, and train them better after you hire them. Automobile manufacturers help their dealers by establishing job specifications for service people and by running clinics and training programs on repair procedures. They give the repair personnel step-by-step procedures in manuals.

Change from people to machines if you can. When you do this, you are transferring some service functions to customers, and some customers, especially younger ones, prefer to do it themselves. Banks have done this by stressing automatic teller machines, which provide the same functions as bank tellers. You can insert your credit card into a machine at some airports and purchase tickets at the last minute instead of waiting in a long line to see a ticket agent at the counter. If your target market is mostly older people, you'll find more resistance to this approach, however.

Reduce your customers' perceived risk. For example, beauty shops can offer money-back guarantees, and banks can waive the prepayment penalties on home mortgages. Also, national service organizations have standardized the quality of their service through franchising. Fast-food restaurant franchisers give their operators standardized uniforms, layouts, food products, and selections to maintain uniform quality not only nationwide, but internationally.

Motivate your service personnel to be more productive. Give them attainable sales goals and adequate rewards. If you're large enough, set up a professional customer service department to set standards, monitor performance, and evaluate consumer satisfaction.

Find out what your customers think of you. Take a survey. Chances are, it'll be a big eye-opener. Lastly, position your service as unique.

POOR POSITIONING

Positioning, as we know it today, was first popularized by two ad agency executives in a famous series of articles entitled "The Positioning Era" in *Advertising Age* in the early 1970s.[23] They popularized an advertising technique — "Positioning is what you do to the mind, not what you do to the product or service" — that not only aimed at a particular market segment but was also designed to achieve a desired "position" in the minds of the prospects. Positioning, a new term for an old theory, caught on because the executives dared to predict which then current ad campaigns would succeed and which would fail, and they were right. The campaigns they predicted would succeed were positioning campaigns, and the ones they predicted would fail had no elements of positioning in them. Taking this risk and winning impressed many advertising and marketing executives of that time, and so positioning became an important technique to use in a very fad conscious industry.

Positioning maintains that what is most important is how the brand is ranked in your customer's mind against your competition, not the features and advantages of your product or service. (That's because too many ads are competing for people's attention, and stressing features and advantages won't make your brand stand out.) So, in positioning, your competitors' strengths become as important as your own brand's strengths.

It's also very important to be the first product or service to occupy a gap or position — although that didn't stop Jell-O no-bake cheesecake mix from overtaking Royal's earlier entry from its number one perch, or IBM from overtaking Univac in the computer field. Advocates of positioning say being first gives you great advantages. Just as you know the names of the highest mountain in the world (Everest) but not the second highest, the first person to walk on the moon (Neil Armstrong) but not the second, and your first lover but not your second, so, too, is the first brand to occupy a gap in the memory bank called your mind forever burned into your consciousness. Because customer's minds don't have that much room for too many brands, IBM, Xerox, Hertz, General Electric, and Coca-Cola have great advantages over Wang, Savin, National, Westinghouse, and Royal Crown.

So much for the theory of positioning. There are many examples of good and bad positioning in trade journals. For example, Volkswagen used positioning when it advertised its Beetle in the United States as an ugly but practical car, and won. When it abandoned positioning, it lost. American Motors made the same mistake when it abandoned positioning its Ramblers as economy cars and began introducing new models that were gas guzzlers.

What to Learn, What Action to Take

I think advocates of positioning go too far. The strongest advocates tell us that you don't have to be creative in your advertising — all you have to do is find the right position and continue hammering away at your target customers so that you own this position, just as Nyquil continues to remind Americans that it's the nighttime cold remedy. The most successful advertisers use positioning and creativity in their ads, and so you should not use positioning as your only advertising technique. Talking about advantages (and even features) is important, too. An ad that combines creativity and positioning is more likely to stand out in the midst of the advertising clutter than is an ad that has just one of these important elements in it.

So, if you decide to use positioning, what must you do? First, find out by doing research what position you and your competitors now occupy. Multi-dimensional scaling, or MDS, is the statistical technique most widely used to determine this. It will also give you guidelines as to which position you should occupy. Second, write your positioning statement with great care. That statement should be based on the MDS research you did. Third, spend enough to overcome the clutter. That's the only way you'll get your target audience to notice your positioning message. Don't give up if positioning doesn't work immediately, for the technique takes a long period of time to be effective. For example, it took Marlboro cigarettes many years of "wild west/cowboy image" advertising to achieve its sales leadership.

Let's talk about MDS. You can use the MDS subroutine in a basic statistical software package, such as SPSS–X. Here's an example of an early MDS study, done for a new kind of paper towel launched in the middle 1970s. The company was trying to position it as a substitute for a cloth towel or rag. From Figure 1 can you tell if it was successful in its positioning or not?

The study involved 600 people. Each person evaluated 9 different products used in the bathroom on 16 attributes such as soft when dry,

FIGURE 1 — MDS Map: New Industrial Bathroom Cleaner

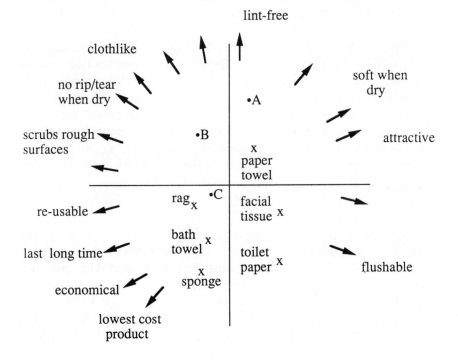

lint-free, flushable, and so forth. The attributes are the 16 arrows, or vectors, in the drawing, and the 9 products are the dots and x's, including a bath towel, toilet paper, and brands A, B, and C. Brand A was the new product, and brands B and C were its competitors, already on the market. Now, $600 \times 9 \times 16 = 86,400$ pieces of data. Without the use of a computer, it would have taken months, perhaps years, to analyze all this data. It took just a short period of time for the computer to analyze the data and make the drawing. The computer program positioned each attribute as a vector in a particular two-dimensional space, and it simultaneously projected each attribute so that the projections reproduced the original data.

A marketing manager studying this drawing would be interested in how people perceived Brand A vis-à-vis its competitors, what characteristics the respondents — especially the housewives — thought were important, what attributes go together, and how different groups of people perceive different products.

Let's look at the flushable vector first, on the bottom right side. The computer shows you on this two-dimensional space how each product correlates with each dimension. Which of the nine kinds of cleaners had the highest correlation with flushable? Toilet paper did. Which of the six products (not the three unnamed brands) correlated best with lint-free? The paper towel did. Which one correlated worst? Toilet paper. See how this works?

Well, all that may be very nice, but how can the marketing manager use this information? Think about what happens to two products that are similar. Where will they be on this two-dimensional space? Close together or far apart? The answer is close together. Different products, of course, will be far apart. Now, which brands are similar to which attributes? Brands A and B are similar to the paper towel. Brand C is similar to bath towels, rags, and sponges. That means Product A could not be positioned as a substitute for a cloth towel or rag without changing the product characteristics, because most people were perceiving it more as a paper towel. Brand C already occupied the cloth towel/rag position.

Here's what else the drawing tells you. Which attributes go together? Reusable and lasts a long time go together, don't they? Which attributes are completely different, polar opposites in other words? You an tell that flushable is the polar opposite of clothlike. What about attractive and reusable? Do they go together? No. What does this mean? Well, it seems that highly attractive products aren't very reusable, in terms of perception. Therefore, if you say in your ads that you're attractive and reusable, people won't believe you — just as many people won't believe you when you say you have the highest quality and the lowest price.

I didn't show you all the computer-generated drawings in this old study. Other drawings were made when the computer was told to change the lengths of vectors to show how important each attribute was in distinguishing between brands. And a very important drawing superimposed respondents' preferences on the two-dimensional space to show gaps, which, of course, is so central to good positioning.

NO REAL BENEFIT DELIVERED

If your target market doesn't perceive (and actually receive) important benefits, you won't succeed. If you are a committed follower of positioning, you won't think this is an important mistake, but it did turn up again and again in the literature on new product and service failures and in my consulting. The first five examples are from the United States, and the sixth is from Australia.

The "Two Potato Clock" was introduced in 1984. A digital clock, priced between $12 and $20, it ran off the energy generated by two electrodes placed in any slightly acidic medium, a potato, for example, or beer, or oranges. It sold poorly. People who buy digital clocks prefer to plug them into the wall — that's a lot simpler.[24]

Skunkguard stinks! It really does! When you crack open a one-inch capsule, you get a liquid, concentrated essence of skunk, all over you and anybody near you. Selling at $15 an ounce, it is aimed at women who want to protect themselves from rapists. The idea is to make the woman so repulsive, the attacker runs away. The skunk odor clings to the attacker like lint, making it relatively easy for the police to sniff him out.

The benefit — getting rid of an attacker and helping to identify him — wasn't worth the cost to most women. The cost? Her clothes. An enclosed neutralizing agency can remove the smell from her skin, but not from her clothes. And there's the cost of unscheduled capsule-bustings. Most women didn't want to take a chance, and so the product has sold very, very poorly since it was introduced in 1985.[25]

Burger King spent $40 million in 1985 and 1986 in its ads, featuring a nerdy-looking character named Herb. (Nobody ever knew his last name.) He was supposed to be the only person in the United States who never tasted a Whopper Burger. For months, in a classic "teaser" campaign, Burger King talked about him, but they never showed him. Herb finally showed himself in Burger King ads that ran in the January 1986 Super Bowl. After that, he visited several Burger King restaurants.

Customers who spotted him won $5,000. Video Storyboard Tests Inc., which surveys customers to gauge the memorability of TV commercials, ranked Burger King ads third just before the Herb campaign and sixth during the campaign. The ads annoyed or bored many customers, and, worse, they failed to increase customer traffic, probably because they focused on Herb, and not on how good Burger King sandwiches are.[26]

The United States Mint, a federal government agency responsible for coining and printing the nation's money, brought out the Susan B. Anthony $1 coin in July 1979. It was designed to replace the $1 bill. The treasury would save $50 million a year in printing and processing costs if Americans used the new coin instead of the $1 bill. In the spring of 1980, it gave up trying to get Americans to switch from the $1 bill to the "Suzy." By then, it had coined 840 million "Suzys," and 525 million were still in federal vaults, uncirculated and untouched.

What happened? Observers said no real benefit was delivered to the public. To be more specific, it was too similar to a quarter, and people didn't like that. Its small size meant people didn't take it seriously. People had a choice of using the $1 bill or the $1 coin because the government didn't withdraw $1 bills from circulation. If it had forced people to use the $1 coin, it might have succeeded. Many people thought the "Suzy" was ugly, and many subconsciously equated the coin with two relatively unpopular causes, the Equal Rights Amendment to the U.S. Constitution and the feminist movement. About the only time and place the $1 coin was popular was for a brief time in 1985 in San Francisco. It enjoyed a certain vogue in the city's sex parlors. Customers would enter a booth, drop the "Suzy" into a slot, and the curtain would rise to permit a few moments of conversation with a naked woman on the other side of the glassed-in booth.[27]

It seems the U.S. Mint didn't learn from its "Suzy" fiasco. In 1987, it launched its American Eagle gold coins, positioning them as an investment. However, the Mint couldn't supply anybody with brochures on the coin for a long time because of three problems: It couldn't match the coin's gold color in the brochure for several months, bureaucrats decided to change a sentence in the brochure after they were already set in their final production galleys, and foreign language translation errors occurred. As a result, this important selling tool was over six months late.[28]

In 1988, the Australian government introduced a $2 coin. It also didn't deliver any real benefit to consumers. It was very much the same story as the "Suzy" — it was so small it resembled one cent and two cent coins, and Aussies didn't accept their new coin, either.[29]

What to Learn, What Action to Take

Don't make the mistake that Burger King, the U.S. and Australian Mints, the Two-Potato Clock, and Skunkguard did. Find out what benefits your target market wants. Production-oriented executives will ask the wrong questions in their market research, though. They'll focus on the features of the product or service by asking people questions about what features they want. And then, they'll concentrate on the features and show why these features offer customers advantages over competing offerings. Instead, focus on what benefits your customers want. If you're marketing post-hole diggers, don't focus on how sturdy the tool is — focus on the hole. Customers don't care about the digger — they care about what the digger will do for them.

Once you've found out what benefits your target market wants, make sure your entire marketing mix is aimed at delivering those benefits to them at a profit.

POOR SUPPORT FROM YOUR MIDDLEMEN

Don't forget you have two sets of customers — your middlemen and your final consumers. Holly Farms Corporation is a large Memphis-based chicken marketer. In 1987, after a full year of test-marketing and discussions with final consumers indicated its new roasted chicken would be a success, it spent $20 million building a new plant in North Carolina just for the new product, and started a national rollout. However, it failed so dismally that the company halted the planned expansion so it could reconsider its marketing strategy.

Final consumers liked the fully cooked chicken because it was a modern, more convenient alternative to raw chicken. However, grocers didn't like it because of its short shelf life. Holly Farms said the chicken could last on the shelf for 18 days, but to err on the side of caution, it marked the last sale date 14 days after the chicken was roasted. But it took up to nine days to get the chicken from North Carolina to grocery stores, and that didn't give grocers much lead time. To avoid getting stuck with an outdated inventory, many waited until they ran out before reordering. On the other hand, shelf life isn't a factor in the case of raw chicken because it sells in large volume and is gone in the first few days after delivery. Poultry department personnel know from experience how much to stock.

Because most final consumers and most supermarket executives who tried the product called the taste "outstanding," Holly Farms decided not to give up. At the time I wrote this book, it was trying to lengthen the shelf life by 5 to 10 days by packing the chickens in nitrogen instead of air and by delivering them separately from its raw poultry. It was also developing a program to educate meat managers in supermarkets. It was shifting a large percentage of its promotion from TV and radio to grocery stores in the form of coupons, demonstrations, contests for meat managers, and other promotional gimmicks. Maybe it'll succeed the second time. After all, smart companies learn from mistakes — that's the whole point of this book.[30]

What to Learn, What Action to Take

Avoid the kind of mistake Holly Farms made. Never forget how important your middlemen are. Choose them wisely. You need push (middlemen support) as well as pull (final consumer support) to be successful in marketing. Make sure you reward your middlemen so they'll be more likely to push your product or service. Test the product or service concept with middlemen to see if they'll stock and support it even before you market-test it in the field. Pay close attention to any middlemen resistance that develops.

SOLVING A NONEXISTENT (OR UNIMPORTANT) PROBLEM

Poor market research can kill you here. You've got to make sure you ask all the important questions, not just most of them. And don't ask questions that aren't important.

For example, when Dow Chemical Company introduced Dowtherm 209 in the U.S. market in the 1960s, it had great hopes for this new kind of antifreeze-coolant. Aimed at the maintenance supervisors of large fleets of diesel trucks, it told its customers that they would no longer suffer any down time if they used Dowtherm 209 because if it ever leaked into the crankcase, it would do no harm. Other antifreeze-coolants would damage the engine when they leaked. One of Dow's ads said, "We're not even ashamed to tell you it costs twice as much as conventional antifreeze-coolants." The trouble was, conventional antifreeze-coolants hardly ever leaked into the crankcase, so as far as the maintenance supervisors at the big truck fleets were concerned, they were paying twice as much money to solve a nonexistent problem. Dow did a poor job of research, in hindsight. They neglected to find out how often antifreeze-coolants leaked into the crankcases of diesel trucks. The product sold poorly.

Here's a second example. R. J. Reynolds Tobacco Company introduced Real cigarettes in 1977. One executive boasted, "Through sophisticated market research techniques, we have included the consumer and his thoughts and reactions in every step of this product's development. We think Real will be the most successful new brand introduction in the recent history of the cigarette business." Despite the research and heavy ad support, Real was withdrawn from the U.S. market in 1980. What went wrong?

Because research indicated that smokers didn't want flavorings or additives in their cigarettes, Reynolds positioned Real as a natural cigarette. Its ad copy included phrases like "nothing artificial added" and "all natural." But this time, the market researchers asked too many questions. Until they were asked the question about flavorings and additives, smokers really didn't care whether cigarettes were natural or not. So, Reynolds constructed a selling proposition that was based on a nonproblem.[31] The company didn't learn from its mistakes. In 1989, it withdrew its smokeless cigarette brand, Premier (with its four-page instruction manual), from the U.S. market after only five months. It lost over $300 million.

What to Learn, What Action to Take

How do you make sure you ask all the important questions and yet not too many questions? How do you know if you're getting good market research or poor market research? Follow these guidelines:

- Hire a market research firm that has a good reputation in your industry.
- A good market research firm helps you anticipate problems, not just react to problems.
- It keeps up with trends in the marketplace and with the latest research techniques.
- It's so good, it even gives "how-to" seminars through a profit center subsidiary.
- It can find the information you need at a reasonable cost within a reasonable period of time.
- Its reports are succinct and relevant to your decision making.
- It challenges you to think, to raise your level of creativity.
- It doesn't try to sell you research you don't need.
- It doesn't try to overimpress you with oversophisticated statistical techniques you don't really need.

Get proposals from several market research firms before choosing the one you'll use. Don't expect the firm to include the questionnaire they'll be using, or any professional advice. That'll come after the study is done, so don't look for a "free lunch." Market researchers don't want to have anything to do with those kinds of clients.

Suppose you ask several market research firms for proposals. How can you evaluate them? These guidelines can help:

- Does the proposal indicate that they understand my industry and my problems?
- Will the output be useful to me when I make my decisions?
- Is the research design sound?
- Does it make logical sense?
- Who are the people who are going to do the research?
- How much experience do they have?
- How are the interviewers going to be supervised?
- What kind of facilities do they have?
- Will they turn in the report in time for it to be useful to me?
- Will they rush to meet my deadline, or will they allow enough time to do a thorough job?
- What kind of statistical techniques do they propose?
- What kind of software will they use?
- How much will the whole job cost me?
- Am I protected against unexpected cost overruns?[32]

But even well-known market research firms with excellent reputations make mistakes on occasion — expensive ones, too, as the Dowtherm, Real, and Premier examples show. So don't rely on survey research alone. Go out in the field and test-market your product or service. Use an experimental design, with matched experimental and control groups. One study reported that the average market test in the United States used three test areas, lasted about ten months, tested different levels of one or more marketing mix variables (especially advertising), and used both store audits and consumer surveys to measure the effects of the different marketing mixes.[33]

When you pick your test market cities, follow these guidelines:

- Their demographics should reflect those of the target market as a whole.
- They shouldn't be overtested, so the jaded boredom factor won't set in.
- Each market should be self-contained, without any dependence on a neighboring area, to avoid media spillover or buying from wholesalers outside of the market area.

- They shouldn't be too big or too small. In the United States, the population of the central city in the area should be between 75,000 and 300,000, although this criterion is violated more often than any other.

- They shouldn't be dominated by any one industry, nationality, or racial group, nor should there be high unemployment or seasonal layoffs.

- The cities shouldn't have an unusual historical development in the product category you're interested in. For example, don't pick a market where the brand that dominates has very low market shares everywhere else.

- Don't overlook the climate.

Dow Chemical Company tested a new lubricant for outboard motors in both Michigan and Florida. The lubricant was successful in Florida during all four seasons. It was successful in Michigan during the summer, but the following spring, Dow discovered that it had congealed, allowing the outboard motors, idle all winter, to rust. The problem didn't occur in Florida, where the motors were in year-round use.[34]

NOT DOING MARKET RESEARCH, DOING POOR MARKET RESEARCH, OR IGNORING ITS FINDINGS

Many firms at least pay lip service to market research. They pay for it, read the report, and then go ahead and do whatever they wanted to do in the first place. Some can't tell good research from bad research. Sometimes, a company won't do research at all. Sometimes this works. Time Inc., the largest magazine publishing company in the United States, didn't test-market many of its magazines before launching them. Most of them succeeded. But *TV-Cable Week,* which it launched in 1983, collapsed after just 25 weeks of publication and $47 million of losses. According to reports, corporate Vice President Kelso Sutton made the costly no-test decision, then wondered aloud why no tests had been conducted prior to launch.[35]

What to Learn, What Action to Take

I think it's dangerous to launch a new product or service without doing any research. It's easy to learn from the *TV-Cable Week* example — simply do market research, and use its findings. Don't ignore them. It's harder to tell good research from poor research, especially since marketing managers don't usually come from the ranks of market research — they don't have any special expertise in this area. Follow the guidelines for picking good market research firms and evaluating their research proposals.

POOR SALES FORECASTING

After you get the market research report, you've got to do something with it. You've got to forecast sales. As I mentioned earlier in this chapter, most marketers are overly optimistic, and so sales forecasts are quite often overly optimistic, as GE's forecast for its factory automation venture was.

What to Learn, What Action to Take

Here are several actions you can take to make your forecasts more accurate:

- Ask for three forecasts — an optimistic one, a pessimistic one, and a most likely one. You'll feel more secure by looking at these three sets of figures.

- Look at the forecasters' past record of accuracy. How far off are they? Are they consistently high? Consistently low? It's easy to make allowances for past errors if you can see some overall pattern in the past.

- Use only those sales forecasting techniques that use the data you have access to and that your personnel understand well.

- How quickly do you need the forecast? If you want it very fast and you're going to do it by hand, forget about regression analysis — it will take you too much time. On the other hand, a regression software package doesn't take that much time to generate a forecast.

- The better marketers I know use several sales forecasting methods. Each method is used as a check on the other. This way they have more confidence in the final forecast.

- Don't set the final forecast in concrete. Re-evaluate it periodically, and be flexible enough to change it when conditions demand that you do.

- If you use your sales reps to generate a forecast, don't use their estimates as quotas. They'll purposely understate the amount they think will sell in order to get a lower quota.

- Ask yourself, "Are the assumptions underlying the forecast sound or not?" If they're not sound, it's GIGO — garbage in, garbage out.

- Read a good book on sales forecasting such as *Forecasting Methods* by Chisholm and Whitaker, published by Irwin, or get a good software package. Core Analytic, a software manufacturer, has two — Autocast and 4Cast/2 — and there are several other good ones around.

NOT ANTICIPATING YOUR COMPETITORS' STRONG RESPONSE TO YOUR LAUNCH

Marketers will try to disrupt each other's test markets and actual product launches, and most of the time their reactions are stronger than you might expect.

A few years ago, General Mills test-marketed in the United States Crisp 'N Tender, a liquid batter coating for chicken. It didn't anticipate how strongly General Foods would protect its Shake 'N Bake brand, which had a commanding 90 percent market share in that product category. General Foods introduced its own liquid, Batter 'N Bake and fought Crisp 'N Tender every step of the way. Outgunned, General Mills withdrew Crisp 'N Tender. Shortly afterward, General Foods withdrew Batter 'N Bake so it wouldn't cannibalize Shake 'N Bake. It didn't have any reason to keep Batter 'N Bake on the market after Crisp 'N Tender withdrew.

This kind of a battle is common in the packaged goods business. For example, the Ralston Purina Company has the reputation of doing all it can to sabotage a competitor's test market. As soon as it finds out about a test-market or a product launch, it immediately inaugurates deals, sends out free samples, and mails thousands of coupons to the test-market area. Be careful when you compete against Ralston Purina in the United States. Forewarned is forearmed.[36]

In 1975, Calgon learned that Procter & Gamble was testing Bounce, a product designed to be used in clothes dryers to eliminate static cling. It rolled its Cling Free into markets throughout the United States before Bounce was out of tests.[37]

What to Learn, What Action to Take

How do you overcome this problem of shortsightedness? For one thing, don't be overoptimistic. Be pessimistic instead, and look at the worst-case scenario. Expect a competitor to come in and try to drive you out of the market before you gain a foothold, but if you position your new product or service uniquely enough, your competitors' attacks won't affect you as much. Also, monitor your launch, and make sure all your sales reps are on the alert for rumors and other signs that indicate your competitors are about ready to jump in. Finally, don't allocate all your funds to the launch itself. Hold a certain percentage in reserve, and use it to make a counterattack when necessary.

CHANGES IN THE ENVIRONMENT YOU DIDN'T ANTICIPATE

The Walt Disney Studio was tremendously successful in the 1940s, 1950s, and 1960s, making family-oriented films and cartoons. Then, the U.S. market changed, and Disney didn't change with the market. Moviegoers avoided G-rated motion pictures like the plague. The Disney studios were losing money whenever they launched a new film, and their executives were perplexed. How could they make anything but a G-rated film? It was unthinkable! If they made a PG–13 or R rated film, it feared that its reputation would suffer — and that would affect attendance at its immensely successful amusement parks in California, Florida, and Japan.

They solved their problem by bringing in new management from rival Paramount Studios. The new team simply launched a subsidiary, Touchstone Films, and made sure the general public did not learn of the connection between Touchstone and Disney for the first few years. It worked. It turned out a long line of successes, including *Splash!,* and attendance at Disneyland, Disney World, Epcot Center, and Tokyo Disneyland is still growing.

What to Learn, What Action to Take

Fortunately, the Disney-Touchstone example had a happy ending. Too many companies launch a new product or service only to find that the market has changed dramatically since it first began the development process. I've given examples of these launch failures before — Polavision and SelectaVision, Real and Premier cigarettes, the Edsel, and many others — almost all launch failures occur for several reasons, not just one. How could these failures have been avoided? Do a good job of sales forecasting, but don't stop there. You need to carefully monitor your environment through the design, test, launch, and maturation phases of development by designing a proper environmental sensor system.

POOR QUALITY

In other words, the product or service just didn't work as in these examples from the U.S. market.

Lexicon, introduced in 1979, promised to translate languages electronically for $225 plus $65 for each language cassette. However, it wasn't that good. All translations were word-for-word renderings. There were no verb conjugations, no idiomatic constructions, no grammar.[38] It wasn't a success.

Software users complain often and loudly about programing errors. Software makers say their programers make as many as 50 mistakes per 1,000 lines of instructions in early drafts of a program. The bugs that aren't caught are usually minor spelling mistakes. However, often there are very serious uncaught errors. In September 1985, Lotus had to send out thousands of diskettes to repair a version of its Symphony program that frequently ate up data. The James A. Cummings Construction Company sued Lotus for $254,000, charging that faults in a Lotus software program caused it to underbid a contract. Cummings alleged that Symphony's spreadsheets failed to properly add the planned $254,000 estimate for general and administrative costs, resulting in a loss in completing the contract. Vernon Kidd was using his computerized radiation-therapy machine to alleviate his skin cancer in 1986, when a defect in the machine's software caused the machine to burn him with radiation 80 times more potent than the prescribed dose. He died. Some early copies of Microsoft's Multiplan spreadsheet program caused information to disappear when a user tried to print it out. Lotus's Jazz software package crashed or shut down when the user tried to insert files from Microsoft's Multiplan software package.[39]

To add insult to injury, some software manufacturers charge customers to fix its software errors. For example, Tandy Corporation's TRS–80 Model 4 computers made before August 1987 can't handle dates after December 31, 1987, in their operating system. The U.S. company knew about the problem since 1983, and it sold more than 400,000 of them. Typing in 1988 dates makes the computer stop. To solve the problem, the owner had to buy a $39 software program from Radio Shack stores or lie to the computer. This made a lot of consumers angry. By the way, the new version of its Model 4 computers won't work after 1999.[40]

International Business Machines launched its first personal computer, the PCjr, in late 1983, In March 1985, it stopped making them. It missed the important 1983 Christmas season because of last-minute quality problems. Complaints began almost immediately about its limited memory, awkward rubberized keyboards with keys that looked like Chiclets chewing gum, and high price. Business users didn't like the fact that it had only one disk drive, instead of the two needed to run most business programs. Sufficient memory to run many of them was a very expensive addition. After first denying there were problems, IBM decided to make changes in the summer of 1984 — it changed the keyboard, cut the price, expanded the memory, and eased credit terms to dealers. Nothing worked. IBM learned from its mistake, though. Its later PCs sold much better, perhaps because they were better designed.[41]

In 1983, a British firm introduced Beauty Bronze UVA Sunbed and Sunroof into the U.S. market. It sold for around $2,700. Users discovered that dials didn't work, parts were missing, instructions were vague and incomplete, and smoke poured out of the connections between the Sunroof and its base.[42]

Hammacher Schlemmer & Co. sold La Valtromplina Nut and Bean Roaster in 1984 for $70. It was unsteady on its legs, liable to burn the hand of the user, and produced roasted coffee beans and nuts that were consistently burnt.[43]

In 1978, Snell Division of Booz Allen Hamilton developed a nonliquid temporary hair coloring that consumers used by inserting a block of sold hair dye into a special comb. The reason it didn't work was simple — on hot days when people perspired, any hair dye excessively applied ran down their necks and foreheads. Snell didn't test its dye under conditions in which people perspire.[44] But in 1988 in the Philippines, a Japanese firm, Bigen, introduced its Speedy Hair Color in a tube with a specially designed comb. Bigen learned from Snell's mistake. (The local distributor told me he heard that Bigen read about Snell's failure, still thought the idea was a good one, and decided to introduce an improved version of the product. That's really learning from mistakes!) To dye your hair, you squeeze the Speedy tube's contents onto the comb and comb your hair with it until your hair is well covered by cream. After five minutes, you shampoo your hair, and it's dyed — without later running down your neck and forehead.

In 1981, a New Jersey firm introduced a wrist camera called Wristmatic at $40. It took poor pictures, jammed, and fell apart. Needless to say, it didn't sell.[45]

Pussyfoot, introduced in 1979, was a sloppily glued together acrylic cat feeder that was easy for humans but hard on cats. The $10 food dispenser's lid had a tendency to hit the cat on the nose when eating.[46]

Easyseat cost $35 when it was introduced in 1982. It was supposed to be a more comfortable bicycle seat, consisting of two seats, one for each buttock. However, it was extremely uncomfortable, "plunging users into agony in their nether regions."[47]

Federal Express introduced its new ZapMail in 1984 with a lot of publicity. It was a service that sent letters via couriers and city-to-city facsimile machines. It guaranteed next-day delivery anywhere in the United States. In 1986, it threw in the towel, with a $340 million pretax writeoff against 1986 earnings. The product quality just wasn't good enough for its customers. For example, it was difficult to reprint light original documents. The fax machines often broke down. The slightest disturbance on a telephone line (the vehicle used to transmit the fax signal) would interrupt the transmission. Many high-volume customers found out shortly after signing up for the ZapMail service that it was cheaper to install its own system, and dropped out. After all, ZapMail users had to buy their own fax machines in order to become ZapMail customers, so the infrastructure was already there. It seems that Federal Express had greatly overestimated the size of the market for the quality of service it was offering. It bravely made statements saying it would try again at a later date. Maybe it will. I'll bet it won't.[48]

The next example occurred in Singapore in 1988, at a big exhibition of Apple software, hardware, and peripherals. Visitors received a free software package, Interferon, which was an anti-virus "vaccine" program. (A virus is a self-replicating program that attacks the computer's memory and storage system by scrambling, erasing, and destroying the information stored.) The trouble is, the anti-virus software itself had a virus.[49]

In 1988 the Royal Australian Mint's brand new $10 note had a plastic hologram of Captain James Cook in a bubble at the top left corner. Whenever the note was mishandled or rubbed, though, the hologram disappeared. The government withdrew the plastic note the very next day after it was introduced.[50]

What to Learn, What Action to Take

What can you do about products and services that don't work? Find out what's wrong by testing each product and service thoroughly before introducing them to your ultimate market. Testing should be done in the laboratory first, where unanticipated side effects can be detected. But don't stop there. Do a field test-market, to iron out the distribution bugs and other problems you're sure to encounter in the real world. And don't forget to buy liability insurance, if you can. It's a good investment.

THE WRONG NAME

Picking the right name for a company, product, or service is a major decision. Years ago, companies often derived their names from their founders (Chrysler) or their location (Lloyd's of London), and products were named for their makers (Heinz). (I've never been able to figure out where Japan Airlines' Nikko Hotels International came up with the name Hotel Beijing-Toronto for their hotel in the Chinese capital, though.) Today, names can't be chosen that casually. There are over 12,000 items in an average U.S. supermarket. Over 25,000 trademarks are registered with the U.S. Patent Office every year. The major mistakes in choosing the wrong name for companies, products, and services fall into the following categories.

REPLACING A GOOD CORPORATE NAME WITH STRINGS OF LETTERS

This means giving up years of goodwill. It takes much time and money to make consumers aware of a handfull of meaningless letters. I think the U.S. corporations now known as CPC, GAF, TRW, SCM, and USM made mistakes when they changed their names. Only long-standing, well-entrenched companies with high visibility and enormous advertising budgets are successful here. Radio Corporation of America made a successful change to RCA many years ago. More recently, United States Steel successfully changed to USX Corporation, but many firms would have been better off staying with their old names. In fact, you can also lose years of built-up goodwill by failing to revitalize your old name with a fresh visual image. American Trust Company almost made this mistake when they bought Wells Fargo Bank. They were thinking about dropping or combining the names, but then discovered through market research the tremendous equity in the Western imagery associated with Wells Fargo, which still uses stagecoaches in its logo.[51]

NOT REPLACING YOUR OLD NAME WITH A NEW NAME WHEN CONDITIONS WARRANT

This can be equally disastrous. The American Institute of Decision Sciences, a professional association that was more widely known by its acronym, AIDS, changed its name to the Decision Sciences Institute in 1986. The same year, AID Insurance Company Mutual changed its name to the Allied Group. The Iowa-based company got its new name in a contest open to its employees and policyholders. In 1985, the southern California firm, A.i.d.s. Ambulance Service, whose name meant "Attitude. Integrity. Dependability. Service," changed its name to AME when its drivers were taunted and harrassed by people who assumed that the ambulances were for AIDS victims only. One injured man refused to get into an A.i.d.s. ambulance because he was afraid he would catch the fatal disease by doing so. But Dep Corp., which has been making Ayds diet candies in the United States since the late 1930s, hasn't changed the name of its flagship product. The chairman said, "Obviously, our product does not give anyone AIDS. But with a name like Ayds, we'll have to do some remarketing. We are looking at all aspects of the problem — and that includes the name. So far, sales of Ayds have generally held steady."[52]

Of course, AIDS is a serious medical problem. Other products have names that were very good at one time, but over time, the name lost some of its effectiveness. For example, in the late 1950s, Sputnik was picked as a brand name for several products in different parts of the world, to tie in with the world's first artificial satellite, launched in October 1957. How many consumers remember Sputnik today? A U.S. cereal enjoying good sales in the late 1980s is Pac-Man Cereal, named after the video game. Video games aren't as popular as they once were. Will Pac-Man Cereal continue its popularity as did Baby Ruth Candy Bars in the United States (named either after then President Taft's daughter, Ruth, or after Babe Ruth, the famous professional baseball player, in the early years of the twentieth century) or Pavlova desserts in Australia (named after the famous Russian ballerina who has been dead many years)? Or will it die a fast death as Billy Beer did in the United States in the late 1970s? (Billy Beer was named after then President Jimmy Carter's beer drinking brother, Billy Carter.) There's a precedent. Pink Panther cereal, named after a then popular U.S. cartoon character, is no longer around.[53]

NOT CHECKING THE MEANING OF THE NAME IN EVERY NATION (OR REGION) IN WHICH YOU MARKET YOUR PRODUCT OR SERVICE

This can often be disastrous, as well. In Quebec, the French-speaking province of Canada, Hunt-Wesson's Big John brand was literally translated into Gros Jos — then, after the product introduction, it found out that "gros jos" in Quebec is slang for "big breasts." Chevrolet's Nova automobile was exported to several Latin American markets with poor success. One reason was that "no va" in Spanish means "doesn't go." Mexicans used to laugh at the Chevrolet Nova whose engine didn't run.[54]

NOT CHECKING THE MEANING OF THE NAME IN YOUR OWN COUNTRY

You'd think it would be easier to check the meaning of the word you choose for your brand or corporate name in the country you live in, wouldn't you? Most companies do, but some companies don't. When Houston Natural Gas Corporation and Internorth Inc. merged, they decided to rename the company so there would be no bruised egos at the company whose name came out second or whose name disappeared. So the giant pipeline company hired a consultant specializing in naming products, services, and corporations. The consultant decided Enteron Corporation was the best name, and that's what the company was named. Neither the company nor the consultant seemed to be bothered by the dictionary definition of "enteron" — the alimentary canal, the digestive tract from start to finish. The company said, "The dictionary definition describes a very efficient pipeline which is vital to life and which provides nourishment. In a subtle sort of way, that's an accurate description." Furthermore, most residents of the United States, other than physicians, don't know what "enteron" means anyway.[55]

On the other hand, when UAL, Inc., the holding company that owns hotels, car rental services, and United Airlines, changed its name to Allegis Corporation, it tried to explain to the U.S. public what "allegis" meant. Most observers think it did a poor job, but the corporation continued to hold on to its Allegis name for about two years. It didn't change the names of its airline, hotels, and other corporate holdings. Eventually, in 1988, it changed its corporate name back to UAL Inc.

PLACING FUTURE LIMITATIONS ON YOU WITH TOO SPECIFIC A NAME

Having too specific of a name can tie you too long to a smaller market and keep you from expanding. For example, Liquid Plum'r is used to clean out clogged drains. It's hard for the U.S. marketer to extend its product line under that name. I mentioned this in one of my seminars and asked the participants to brainstorm some ideas for new products or services under the Liquid Plum'r brand name. Nobody could come up with anything that would work. One person said Liquid Plum'r might be a good name for laxatives, but the only response was heavy laughter.

Allegheny Airlines learned through market research that people thought of it as a regional airline, even though it was larger than many airlines that people perceived as nationwide in scope. So, the Pittsburgh-based airline changed its name to USAir, which communicated very readily to the public its national reach.

ALLOWING COMPANY POLITICS INSTEAD OF THE MARKET TO SELECT YOUR NAME

This is a big mistake. Nestlé, a huge Switzerland-based conglomerate, almost made a fatal mistake in the 1960s when it introduced its freeze-dried coffee into the U.S. market. Its corporate policy was to emphasize the Nestlé and Nescafé brand names world-wide and headquarters was going to name its new U.S. entry Nescafé Gold. However, Nescafé instant coffee was having great difficulty competing with Maxwell House's instant coffee brands and enjoyed only small market shares. The U.S. division did its own market research and found that it would be best to de-emphasize the Nestlé and Nescafé names, especially since Maxwell House already had the first freeze-dried coffee on the market, Maxim, and Nestlé was going to have to play catch-up. It argued strongly for the adoption of the name Taster's Choice, which had little association with the Nestlé and Nescafé names. Swiss headquarters reluctantly went along with the request. Taster's Choice clobbered Maxim in the marketplace and quickly became number one in freeze-dried sales.

A similar example occurred about the same time when the company then known as Standard Brands decided to replace its poorly selling Chase and Sanborn coffee brand in the northern California market with a different brand name. It was going to be the same coffee under a different name. The new products manager, based in New York City, tested four names — Bright Moment, Gleason's, Putnam's Inn, and Sutter's Gold — in a focus group in San Francisco. Before the test results were known, he decided to test the same four names in a similar focus group in New York City, even though Standard Brands had no intention of introducing the brand in the east, where Chase and Sanborn had strong market shares. He received the New York results before the California results, and Putnam's Inn was the favorite of the New York respondents. He decided on the basis of the New York results to name the product Putnam's Inn and told his choice to many people at Standard Brands. Then, the California results came in, and none of the four names were liked by the western respondents. To an easterner, "inn" connotes the warm and friendly ambience of a ski lodge with its roaring fireplace and good camaraderie. To a westerner, "inn" has the connotation of a short-time cheap hotel. Only gays liked Bright Moment, Gleason's sounded like a private label, and Sutter's Gold brought forth images of bitter mining camp coffee. Instead of starting over with new names as he should have, he didn't want to lose face, so he stuck with Putnam's Inn. The launch was a disaster.

The moral behind these two examples is this — do a lot of good market research before picking a brand name. Don't allow your personal preferences to interfere with the preferences of your consumers. Nestlé's Swiss bosses deferred to the U.S. consumer, but Standard Brands's new product manager did not. One succeeded, and the other failed.[56]

NOT USING A DISTINCTIVE ENOUGH NAME

This can be a mistake, but sometimes it's alright. For example, a car battery named Reliable isn't bad, but Diehard communicates the high quality of the product much more effectively and imaginatively. Kodak is a very distinctive name. So is Disney. But in Japan, Fuji isn't distinctive, and in the United States, neither is Universal Studios or Standard Oil. On the other hand, in Chinese-speaking nations, rational sounding names are often used, and they seem to be better accepted there than in western nations. For example, in Kaohsiung, Taiwan, Republic of China, there is a "Very Good Barber Shop." In Taipei, one of the leading hotels is the Brother Hotel. Several brands are called "Typical."[57]

PICKING A NAME THAT'S TOO HARD TO PRONOUNCE AND SPELL

Sometimes a distinctive name shouldn't be used if it's hard to pronounce and spell. Nestlé's is a distinctive name, but it has the letter "l" in it. There is no letter "l" in the Japanese language, and the Japanese have difficulty pronouncing that name. Siemens, a large German corporation, admits its name is frequently misspelled abroad.

PICKING A NAME THAT'S TOO DISTINCTIVE

Don't use a distinctive name if it's too distinctive. For example, Dr Pepper is a delicious soft drink whose flavor is very hard to describe and duplicate. (Coca-Cola tried to duplicate its taste with its Mr. PiBB and failed, in my opinion.) People who have never tried it before are usually turned off by its name, which sounds like a chili-flavored medicine instead of (in my opinion) the most delicious soft drink in the world. Many critics have attributed its slow growth outside of its native southern United States to its name. On the other hand, Hershey's Whatchamacallits candy bar, which tastes like peanut brittle, did not seem to share this problem, even though it's as distinctive a name as Dr Pepper.[58]

PICKING A NAME THAT INSULTS OR IRRITATES CONSUMERS

Some names have insulted or irritated specific markets. Yves St. Laurent's very expensive Opium perfume isn't purchased by many

Americans of Chinese descent in the United States because they still remember that opium was forced upon their culture by outsiders.[59]

COINING WORDS THAT DON'T MEAN ANYTHING TO NAME YOUR PRODUCT OR SERVICE

People respond best to names they understand quickly. Many marketers have violated this principle by coining brand-new words that don't mean anything. Standard Oil Corporation of New Jersey spent millions educating consumers about its new name, Exxon Corporation, for example. Here's another mistake they made. They said they wanted one name that could be used everywhere, including internationally. They were already using Enco as their gasoline brand name in many states in the United States where they couldn't use their Esso name, and they were using Esso abroad. In the Enco states, they had already educated the motoring public that Enco meant Energy Company. However, they decided not to use Enco internationally because it had a negative connotation in Japan. After spending millions of dollars changing Enco and Esso to Exxon, they decided to keep the Esso name in international markets after all. Apple Computer didn't have to spend that much when it introduced its Macintosh computer in the United States, because most members of its target audience know that Macintosh is a kind of apple.[60]

What to Learn, What Action to Take

I've summarized the main lessons from these mistakes into the following important guidelines:

- Think twice before you give up years of goodwill to change your name — but don't hesitate to change your name when conditions in the environment make it necessary.
- Check for unpleasant meanings both domestically and in foreign markets. If the name offends or insults important markets, it's probably best not to use it.
- Remember that too specific a name will tie you to a smaller market and prevent future expansion.
- Never let company politics decide your name. Always make sure the market picks the name.
- Make sure your name is distinctive, but don't use it if it's hard to pronounce and spell or if it's too distinctive in a negative sense.
- Get professional help. There are many companies who specialize in picking names. There are several software packages you can use, including Applied Systems and Technologies's "TrAid Names," and Salinon Corporation's "Namer,"

both from the United States, and Watts Computer Software's "Nomifax," from the United Kingdom.

HOW TO LEARN EVEN MORE BY DIGGING DEEPER

Adams, James L. *Conceptual Blockbusting,* 2d ed. New York: W. W. Norton and Co., 1980.

Alford, C. L. and J. Barry Mason. "Generating New Product Ideas." *Journal of Advertising Research,* (December 1975): 27–32.

Beveridge, J. M. and E. J. Velton. *Positioning to Win.* Radnor, Penna.: Chilton Book Co. 1982.

Bobrow, Edwin E. and Dennis W. Shafer. *Pioneering New Products.* Homewood, Ill.: Dow Jones-Irwin, 1986.

Calantone, Robert and Robert G. Cooper. "New Product Scenarios: Prospects for Success." *Journal of Marketing,* (Spring 1981): 48–60.

Charmasson, Henri. *The Name Is the Game.* Homewood, Ill.: Dow Jones-Irwin, 1987.

Chay, Richard F. "How to Improve Your Chances for Test Market Success." *Marketing News,* 6 January 1984, sec. 1: 12–13.

Cooper, Robert G. "Identifying Industrial New Product Success: Project NewProd." *Industrial Marketing Management,* 8 (1979): 124–35.

Crawford, C. Merle. "Marketing Research and the New Product Failure Rate." *Journal of Marketing,* (April 1977): 55–61.

___. "Product Development: Today's Most Common Mistakes." *University of Michigan Business Review,* (January 1977): 1–6.

___. "Evaluating New Products: A System, Not an Act." *Business Horizons,* (November–December 1986): 48–55.

Drucker, Peter F. *Innovation and Entrepreneurship.* New York: Harper & Row, 1986.

Forecasting Sales. Business Policy Study No. 106, New York: National Industrial Conference Board, 1963.

Gilly, Mary C. and Richard W. Hansen. "Consumer Complaint Handling as a Strategic Marketing Tool." *Journal of Consumer Marketing,* (Fall 1985): 5–16.

Gonik, Jacob. "Tie Salesmen's Bonuses to Their Forecasts." *Harvard Business Review,* (May–June 1978): 116–23.

Guerts, Michael and James Reinmuth. "New Product Sales Forecasting without Past Data." *European Journal of Operational Research,* 4 (1980): 84–94.

Hisrich, Robert D. and Michael P. Peters. *Marketing Decisions for New and Mature Products.* Columbus, Ohio: Charles E. Merrill, 1984.

Kerin, Roger A., Michael G. Harvey and James T. Rothe. "Cannibalism and New Product Development." *Business Horizons,* (October 1978): 25–31.

Kotler, Philip and Murali K. Mantrala. "Flawed Products: Consumer Responses and Marketer Strategies." *Journal of Consumer Marketing,* (Summer 1985): 27–36.

Jones, John P. *What's in a Name: Advertising and the Concept of Brands.* Lexington, Mass.: Lexington Books, 1986.

Keil, John M. *The Creative Mystique.* New York: John Wiley and Sons, 1985.

___. *How to Zig in a Zagging World.* New York: John Wiley and Sons, 1988.

More, Roger A. "Timing of Market Research in New Industrial Product Situations." *Journal of Marketing,* (Fall 1984): 84–94.

Nierenberg, Gerald I. *The Art of Creative Thinking*. Santa Barbara, Calif.: Cornerstone Books, 1982.
Osborn, Alex F. *Applied Imagination,* 3rd ed. New York: Scribner's, 1963.
Parnes, Sidney J. and Harold F. Harding. *Source Book for Creative Thinking*. New York: Scribner's, 1962.
Ries, Al and Jack Trout. *Positioning*. New York: McGraw-Hill, 1980.
Quinn, James Brian. "Managing Innovation: Controlled Chaos." *Harvard Business Review,* (May–June 1985): 73–84.
Takeuchi, Hirotaka and Ikujiro Nonaka. "The New Product Development Game." *Harvard Business Review.* (January–February 1986): 137–46.

NOTES

1. Louis A. Fanelli, "Trouble Ahead for Polavision?" *Advertising Age*, 2 January 1979, p. 2, and "RCA Sinks Its Video Disc Operation," *Marketing and Media Decisions,* May 1984, p. 56.

2. *Gadget: The Newsletter for Grown-Up Kids,* February, 1981.

3. Suzanne Woolley, "Sound Systems That Hit You with Good Vibrations," *Business Week,* 22 February 1988, p. 170.

4. Andrew J. Dubrin, *Winning at Office Politics,* (New York: Ballantine Books, 1980).

5. Synthesized from Howard W. Carlisle, *Management: Concepts and Situations,* (Chicago: SRA-Science Research Associates, 1976), p. 598; Edgar F. Huse and Randall S. Schuler, *Management,* 2d ed. (St. Paul, Minn.: West Publishing Co., 1982), pp. 123–25; George S. Odiorne, *Management Decisions by Objectives,* (Englewood Cliffs, N.J.: Prentice-Hall, 1969), pp. 27, 33, 34, 123–25.

6. M. Hirsh Goldberg, *The Blunder Book,* (New York: William Morrow and Co., 1984), pp. 151, 155.

7. Amanda Bennett, "Pregnant Roller Skate and Other Disasters," *Wall Street Journal,* 19 November 1986, p. 24.

8. Hank Gilman, "Your Money Matters: Software by Mail Frustrates Firm and Its Clients," *Wall Street Journal,* 4 November 1986, p. 35.

9. William Matthew, "Shop Talk: He Used to Brag a Lot About His Role as Number Two," *Wall Street Journal,* 5 January 1988, p. 27; Warren Avis, *Take a Chance to be First,* (New York: Macmillan, 1986; and McGraw-Hill, 1987).

10. "Venture Nightmare for United," *Arkansas Gazette,* Little Rock, 31 August 1986, p. D-5; Susan Heller Anderson, "G'day!" *United* 31, no. 6 (June 1986), pp. 36–38, 40.

11. Judith Valentine, "Flying High: Airline Market Grows Rapidly in Pacific Basin Despite Complex Rules," *Wall Street Journal,* 26 February 1988, pp. 1, 9.

12. John Berthelsen, "Bumpy Start by Dragonair is Blamed on the Asian Carrier's Miscalculations," *Wall Street Journal,* 19 May 1987, p. 23.

13. Peter Petre, "How GE Bobbled the Factory of the Future," *Fortune,* 11 November 1985, pp. 52–54, 58, 62–63.

14. Clare Ansberry, "Kodak Ten-Year Battery Has Flaw: Black & Decker Halts Sale of Items," *Wall Street Journal,* 22 February 1988, p. 30.

15. John R. Dorfman, "Your Money Matters: Investors Enticed by Restaurant Ventures Find That Success is Rarely on the Menu," *Wall Street Journal,* 25 February 1988, p. 29.

16.   John C. Maloney, "Is Advertising Believability Really Important?" *Journal of Marketing,* (October 1963), pp. 1–8.

17.   *Gadget,* op. cit., September 1978.

18.   Cynthia Crossen, "If Two Really Funny Guys Start to Talk, Anything Can Happen," *Wall Street Journal,* 10 January 1986, p. 13.

19.   William H. Reynolds, "The Edsel Ten Years Later," *Business Horizons,* (Fall 1967), pp. 39–46.

20.   Ellen Paris, "Know Your Real Strength," *Forbes,* 9 May 1983, p. 71.

21.   "The Bigger They Are . . ." *Forbes,* 15 February 1972, p. 21.

22.   Richard B. Schmitt and Laurie P. Cohen, "Exxon's Flop in Field of Office Gear Shows Diversification Perils," *Wall Street Journal,* 3 September 1985, pp. 1, 17.

23.   Series of articles in *Advertising Age,* 24 April, 1 May, and 8 May, 1972.

24.   *Gadget,* op. cit., July 1984.

25.   Clare Ansberry, "Technology Marches On: Doctor Strives to Make People Repulsive," *Wall Street Journal,* 11 September 1985, p. 35.

26.   Ronald Alsop, "Marketing: Burger King Hypes Herb Ads, But Many People Are Fed Up," *Wall Street Journal,* 23 January 1986, p. 31.

27.   Bob Greene, "Heads You Lose, Tails You Lose," *Esquire,* April 1981, pp. 12, 14; Trevor Armbrister, "The Case of the Two Bit Dollar," *Reader's Digest,* January 1980, pp. 128–30; and John Flinn, "Suzies Queued in U.S. Vaults Are Frisco Conversation Pieces," *Commercial Appeal,* Memphis, Tenn., 5 August 1985, p. C-4.

28.   Kevin G. Salwen, Alan Freeman, Janet Guyon and Michael Siconolfi, "Shop Talk: Phantom Fliers," *Wall Street Journal,* 29 June 1987, p. 25.

29.   "The User-Friendly Coin," *Straits Times,* Singapore, 26 July 1988, p. 17.

30.   Arthur Buckler, "Holly Farms' Marketing Error: The Chicken That Laid an Egg," *Wall Street Journal,* 9 February 1988, p. 44; "MAP Roasteds Are Road Ready," *Packaging Digest,* January 1989, pp. 38–41ff.

31.   Stanley E. Cohen, "The Real Fiasco," *Advertising Age,* 7 July 1980, p. 16.

32.   Adapted primarily from J. Donald Weinrauch, *The Marketing Problem Solver,* (New York: John Wiley and Sons, 1987), pp. 62, 76, 77.

33.   V. B. Churchill, Jr., "New Product Test Marketing — an Overview of the Current Scene," Midwest Conference on Successful New Marketing Research Techniques, March 3, 1971.

34.   *Dun's Review,* June 1967, p. 45.

35.   Tim Metz, "What Went Wrong at TV-Cable Week?" *Wall Street Journal,* 10 March 1986, p. 13; Jonathan Alter, "Taking a Bath on TV-Cable," *Newsweek,* 17 March 1986, p. 74.

36.   J. Donald Weinrauch, *The Marketing Problem Solver,* (New York: John Wiley and Sons, 1987), p. 81.

37.   Sally Scanlon, "Test Marketing 1976: Calling the Shots More Closely," *Sales and Marketing Management,* 10 May 1976, pp. 43–48.

38.   *Gadget,* op. cit., April 1979.

39.   Michael Rogers, "Software Makers Battle the Bugs," *Fortune,* 17 February 1986, p. 83; "Firm Sues Lotus, Claiming Software Fault Led to Loss," *Wall Street Journal,* 30 July 1986, p. 12; Bob Davis, "Costly Bugs: As Complexity Rises, Tiny Flaws in Software Pose a Growing Threat," *Wall Street Journal,* 28 January 1987, pp. 1, 9; Dennis Kneale, "Buyer Beware: Software Plagued by Poor Quality and Poor Service," *Wall Street Journal,* 2 October 1985, p. 33.

40.   William M. Bulkeley, "Sad but True: Thousands of People are Lying to Personal Computers," *Wall Street Journal*, 21 January 1988, p. 33.

41.   Kim Foltz, "The PCjr's Sudden Death," *Newsweek*, 1 April 1985, p. 65; Dennis Kneale and John Marcom, Jr., "IBM's Surprise Decision to Retire PCjr Triggers Wave of Speculation on Fallout," *Wall Street Journal*, 21 March 1985, p. 8.

42.   *Gadget*, op. cit., December 1983.

43.   *Gadget*, op. cit., August 1984.

44.   Roger Recklefs, "Success Comes Hard in the Tricky Business of Creating Products," *Wall Street Journal*, 23 August 1978, pp. 1, 27.

45.   *Gadget*, op. cit., August 1981.

46.   *Gadget*, op. cit., January 1980.

47.   *Gadget*, op. cit., January 1983.

48.   Timothy K. Smith, "Federal Express Will Scuttle ZapMail, Sets $190 Million Write-Off; Stock Soars," *Wall Street Journal*, 30 September 1986, p. 2; Brian Starfire, "Human Carriers Still Preferred to Electronic Mail," *Arkansas Gazette*, Little Rock, 3 October 1986, pp. 1-C, 2-C; "The Zapping of Federal Express," *Newsweek*, 13 October 1986, p. 57.

49.   Romen Bose, "Apple's Free Anti-Virus Program May be Infected," *Straits Times*, Singapore, 30 June 1988, pp. 44.

50.   "The User-Friendly Coin," op. cit., 26 July 1988, p. 17.

51.   Tom O'Neill, "Avoid the Ten Great Naming Blunders," *Marketing News*, 12 September 1986, p. 72.

52.   "Business News Digest: AID Insurance Changes Its Name," *Arkansas Gazette*, Little Rock, 11 February 1986, p. C-1; *Sentinel*, Orlando, Fla., 17 November 1985; "American Topics," *International Herald-Tribune*, Hong Kong, 8 July 1987, p. 3.

53.   Donald W. Hendon, *Battling for Profits: How to Win Big on the Marketing Battlefield*, 2d ed. (Jonesboro, AR.: Business Consultants International and Singapore: Executive Data Centre, 1987), pp. 293, 296.

54.   David A. Ricks, *Big Business Blunders*, (Homewood, Ill.: Richard D. Irwin, 1983).

55.   Cynthia Crossen, "Shop Talk: Digest This," *Wall Street Journal*, 4 March 1986, p. 29.

56.   Donald W. Hendon, "Bradford's Inn Coffee," (Boston: Intercollegiate Case Clearing House, Harvard University, 1974).

57.   *Battling for Profits*, p. 293.

58.   *Battling for Profits*, p. 296.

59.   Ibid.

60.   Tom O'Neill, "Avoid the Ten Great Naming Blunders," *Marketing News*, 12 September 1986, p. 72.

7
Pricing

Marketing executives often make mistakes in the area of pricing. Two major mistakes are being too greedy when setting prices and not knowing how to make price concessions.

GREED IN SETTING PRICES

The media is full of stories like these that would drive a public relations executive crazy. In 1986, Exxon Corporation had to pay more than $2 billion to several states in the United States for overcharging oil consumers.[1] In 1985, Atlantic Richfield offered to pay the U.S. Department of Energy $225 million to settle government claims that it violated oil price controls in effect from the early 1970s until January 1981.[2] In 1985, the U.S. government charged General Electric, the fourth largest defense contractor, with defrauding the government of $800,000 in illegal labor costs.[3] After looking at the results of a 1985 congressional audit, a congressman accused General Dynamics Corp. and Westinghouse Electric Corp., two large defense contractors, of plotting to overcharge the U.S. Air Force for tools to repair a jet radar system.[4] When Rockwell International pleaded guilty in 1985 to 20 counts of false billings amounting to $290,000 on spare parts work, the Pentagon temporarily suspended it from receiving new contracts. Rockwell agreed to pay the U.S. government $1.2 million and barred six employees from work on federal contracts.[5] In 1988, a major investigation of bribery at the Pentagon centered on allegations that Defense Department procurement officials accepted payoffs from contractors in exchange for advance confidential information on government contracts. United States federal agents seized files at the Pentagon and in the offices of 15 companies, including McDonnell

Douglas, Northrop, United Technologies, and Unisys.[6] The brokerage and investment house then known as E. F. Hutton pleaded guilty in 1985 to 2,000 counts of mail and wire fraud in a scheme the U.S. Justice Department said involved daily overdrafts that sometimes totaled $250 million. The company pleaded guilty to abusing the system for clearing checks from July 1980 to February 1982. Its vice chairman, Thomas P. Lynch, and two other senior company executives resigned. Ten lower-level officials were reprimanded, and some were required to give as much as $50,000 each to charity.[7] In 1985, the U.S. Securities and Exchange Commission sued First Jersey Securities and Robert Brennan, its chairman and founder, charging them with illegally profiting from stock-price manipulation from November 1982 to January 1983. It was the second time in six years that the SEC charged them with fraudulent practices.[8] The U.S. Treasury Department and other government agencies were also busy in 1985. They charged six banks with failure to report large cash transactions — Bank of New England, Bank of America, Chase Manhattan, Manufacturers Hanover Trust, Chemical Bank, and Irving Trust Company. They were fined several million dollars.[9] Again in 1985, the attorney general in Massachusetts filed an antitrust suit against three supermarket chains — Stop & Shop, First National, and Waldbaum — charging them with conspiring to fix prices in western Massachusetts on grocery, meat, and dairy items that formerly were sold under double-value coupons. The suit alleged that the three chains conspired to eliminate the coupons, effectively fixing prices "at artificial and noncompetitive levels." Stop & Shop and Waldbaum were indicted in 1984 in Connecticut on similar price-fixing charges. They pleaded no contest and paid $275,000 each in fines.[10] And in 1989, Panasonic Corp. agreed to pay consumers $16 million to avert U.S. government charges that it fixed prices on electronics products sold in 1988.[11]

Then, of course, there was the Ivan Boesky inside trading scandal. In 1986, Boesky paid $100 million in penalties and illegal profits from trading on insider information. In 1988, the SEC filed insider trader charges against the investment firm Drexel Burnham Lambert and Michael Milken, the head of its junk bond trading unit. The same year, it filed a civil complaint against Stephen S. K. Wang, a junior analyst at Morgan Stanley, with an illegal insider trading scheme with Hong Kong business executive Fred C. Lee. The same year, advance copies of *Business Week* were used in illegal stock purchases. The list goes on and on.[12]

Yes, being too greedy can hurt you. Overcharging is much older than the stereotypical butcher with the heavy thumb. You can get away with it some of the time, but, as Lincoln said, "You can't fool all of the people all of the time." When you get caught, your customers find it hard to trust you any more, and many of them desert you. During the 1980s, so many firms got caught with "a heavy thumb" that many customers in the United States found it difficult to trust any company at all. The companies mentioned in the previous two paragraphs are just the tip of the iceberg.

What to Learn, What Action to Take

First of all, you've got to know that price is the most overused element in the marketing mix. There are three reasons for this. It's likely so many firms get greedy on matters of price because they realize that final consumers don't really know the prices of items they had bought recently and/or can't estimate accurately the prices of several highly advertised products. Other evaluative criteria are often more important to final consumers.[13] If marketing managers think final consumers don't know that much about price, then they may be tempted at times to overcharge some consumers. Prices rise and fall, based on marketing executives' perception of consumers' price knowledge. This is one important reason why price is so often used by marketing managers.

There are two other important reasons. Of the four elements in the marketing mix — price, promotion, product, and channels of distribution — price is the easiest and quickest one to change. Marketing managers are hired to produce results. Whenever sales go down, they must do something, at least to live up to their own image as decision makers — and to justify their high salaries to their bosses. When the crunch comes, what's the first thing that comes to mind? What's available to put out the fire fast? Price, of course! So, it's often overused. This is why you see price wars erupting so often.

The final reason for the overuse of price in the marketing mix is that purchasing managers who work for middlemen are always looking for the best price deal from a manufacturer. Therefore, sales reps and sales managers tend to think first about price reductions when they find it hard to make a sale. Price seems to be what purchasing managers talk about first, so it occupies a primary place in the minds of sales reps and sales managers. As a result, they put pressure on marketing managers to come up with more and more price deals. But the more you give deals, the more likely it is your competitors will match them, and that leads to price wars!

The second thing you need to know about in order to properly set prices is what you can learn from the famous PIMS studies. Started in the

1970s by the Harvard Business School and the Marketing Science Institute, PIMS wanted to determine what was the impact on profit of marketing strategies — hence, the name, Profit Impact of Marketing Strategies. It had such an important impact, that PIMS became an ongoing project, operated as a profit center by Harvard and the MSI. The PIMS investigators found companies showing market-share gains usually outperformed their competitors in three ways:

- There were more new products developed and added to the line by the share-gaining companies.
- When their product quality increased compared to that of their competitors, they gained in market share.
- If they increased their market expenditures faster than the rate of market growth, they increased their market share. But what kinds of marketing expenditures?
    - More sales-force expenditures led to gains in both industrial and consumer markets.
    - More advertising expenditures led to gains mostly in consumer markets, but not so much in industrial markets.
    - More sales promotion expenditures led to gains in both markets.
    - The only exception to increased expenditures occurred in the area of price. If you cut your prices more deeply than your competitors, you didn't achieve significant gains in market share.[14] So, overusing price is counterproductive.

Be wary when your sales reps tell you that they can't sell your product because your competitors have lowered their prices. Watch out for price wars started by your customers. They can and sometimes will lie to you. (See "Ignoring the Competitive Environment" in Chapter 4.)

When your sales fall, find out why before you blindly cut your prices. Other elements in the marketing mix may be at fault. Or if your market share is steady and sales are down, it's probable that you and your competitors are adversely affected by some uncontrollable environmental variable. If you find out that lowering your prices will help, please remember that you shouldn't drop your price too soon, before it's necessary. On the other hand, you can't wait for the problem to resolve itself — you'll have to take some kind of action. Good executives will know when to lower their prices.

Make sure you realize that price wars are extremely dangerous. Do everything you can not to get caught in one. I wouldn't advise you to start a price war. If your competitors cut their prices, don't automatically retaliate by cutting your prices, too. Perhaps you can launch a counterattack by hitting your competitors instead in one of their weak spots — service, product quality, advertising creativity, sales promotions, and so forth. Doing this might stop a price war before it gets too serious. You can tell you're in a price war if several of these early warning signs are present:

- The product is no longer differentiated. It's now a "commodity" in the eyes of the middlemen and final consumers.
- Somebody in the industry is making "excessive" profits, and many of the competitors know this.
- There is excess capacity in the industry.
- One of your competitors has a much lower cost structure than anybody else. It will probably be this firm that starts the price war.
- There is at least one slow, weak competitor that can be hurt the most. Most competitors know who this is. Perhaps the war will begin to get rid of this weakling and take over its market share.
- The market is a mature one. Prices are usually cut toward the end of the market maturity stage of the product life cycle.
- One of your competitors has heavy financial resources behind it, which enables that firm to weather the price war without too much difficulty.
- One of your competitors wants to "buy" a position in the marketplace and feels the cost is no object.
- There is a belief that "order" will replace chaos later, and so the firm that begins the war won't fear any long-term consequences. Neither will the firms that enthusiastically enter the war later on.
- There are many price-sensitive customers (middlemen as well as final consumers) who are quick to react to a price cut.
- One of the firms strongly believes it can shut out or drive out one of the other firms in the industry and wants to try it.
- The market is large enough to fight over.
- There is a general belief that a price cut may expand the total market for everybody.[15]

If you do decide to lower your prices and start a price war, follow these rules. Before you lower your price, remember that you may be starting a price war. Ask yourself, "Do I really want to do that?" If the answer is yes, then go all out — lower your prices significantly. Make them noticeably different from before. Be a leader — don't play follow-the-leader. For maximum impact, make sure you lower your prices before anybody else does. Catch your competitors unaware, so make sure there's no warning signals out.

Don't just lower your prices. Make sure you coordinate your lower price with other elements in your marketing mix. Specifically, you'll have to make sure the entire trade knows of your price reduction. To do this, you'll have to make your reps quickly visit or phone all their accounts, especially their key accounts. All key accounts — yours and those of your competitors — should be visited within one week of your price reduction.

Pay special attention to your competitors' key accounts. Before you lower your price, get together with your sales reps and come up with a special plan for each one, combining all elements of the marketing mix. That way, you can immediately attack your competitors at their most vulnerable point — their higher prices. Make sure you quickly visit each of these accounts. Keep calling on them. They won't come to you. If you don't contact them, they'll eventually hear about your lower prices, and they'll just get on the phone and contact your competitors and tell them, "What are you going to do about their price cuts? I'd like to keep doing business with you, and I will if you cut your prices, too." That's why you'll need to put together a sales pitch that offers more than just a lower price.

You've got to be able to predict if your competitors will be able to match your lower prices — and if so, for how long they'll be able to do it. You've got to make sure you can outlast them. That means you need to do a lot of homework before you launch your price war. Use your marketing intelligence-gathering facilities to find out your competitors' costs. (See my discussion of security in Chapter 3 for hints.) Make sure you don't guess wrong, or you could be making a fatal mistake.

To keep from losing too much money in the price war you must first visit your vendors. Use your buying power to force down prices of items you buy before you launch the price war. Supermarket chains do this all the time, but industrial marketers sometimes forget about doing this. Second, look for market segments that aren't so price sensitive in geographic areas that are far away from the region where your price war is. See if you can sell more to them at your normal (or even higher) prices. Third, it will help if the rest of your product line is profitable. Sell more items in other profitable lines so you can use the profits from them to finance your price war.

Remember that a price war has a strong built-in momentum, especially because price is the easiest and quickest variable in the marketing mix to change. It'll be very hard to stop it — unless you have a commanding market share. The U.S. Postal Service has no trouble raising its prices, does it? But if you don't have a commanding share, there's not much you can do by yourself to end it, especially if you do business in nations such as the United States whose laws forbid collusion and price fixing. If your country has no such laws, get together with several of your competitors. Once you get together a group that has at least a 60 or 70 percent market share, you'll be able to stop the price war — the rest of the competitors will find it in their best interest to go along with you, for if they don't, it's easy for you to ruin them.

On the other hand, you've got to remember that smaller competitors have a lot of leverage over larger firms. It's like the story of David and Goliath in the Bible. David was smaller, yet quicker and more flexible than Goliath, and David won. It's a little more complicated in the world of marketing, though — there are a few more reasons why Davids sometimes beat Goliaths. Her's an example I learned about from a consulting job I did.

The product category was high-volume consumer packaged goods, of which 250,000 cases were sold each month. Product A had an 80 percent market share, and it sold 200,000 cases every month throughout the geographically large country. Its distribution was widespread, and it had no unusual geographic concentrations or gaps. Its major competitor, Product B, had a 10 percent market share, with monthly sales of 25,000 cases spread evenly throughout the same country.

Product B decided to launch a price war. It dropped its price by $5 per case and began selling at cost. Its parent company, a large and very profitable multinational consumer products firm, was prepared to subsidize Product B for at least a year in its price war. Product A's multinational parent company was equally large and profitable, but it decided it wouldn't match the $5 per case price reduction. Why not? At its monthly volume of 200,000 cases, the price war would have cost Product A $1 million per month, and it would only cost Product B $125,000 per month. Instead, Product A spent $125,000 per month on coupons, sales promotions, advertising, and new product introductions. Product B increased its market share to 15 percent after four months, mostly at the expense of minor competitors, and then stopped the price war. Product A, which lost 2 percent of its share, stopped its counterattack then, and things settled down to the normal level of competition in the industry.

Now, Product A could have launched a price counterattack on product B if the latter's sales were concentrated in a small geographic area, because the price war would have only occurred in a small part of the country, not throughout the country. But Product B was sold everywhere that Product A was sold, so Product A didn't have that option.

Learn from this example. If you're a big firm, don't feel smug and superior. Smaller firms can sometimes attack you, and you won't be able to retaliate in kind.

Once the price war is over, what's the best way to raise your prices? Never raise your prices when the economy is bad. Look for signs of a boom. Raise your prices when your customers are in a buying mood, not when they're retrenching. Shoot when the ducks are flying — don't waste your bullets on an empty sky.

Here's where it's not always best to be the leader. Don't be the first to raise prices — unless you're the biggest player in the marketplace. Wait for others to raise their prices, and go along with them. If you wait a few weeks in order to try and get extra business with your lower prices, you'll probably find your strategy is not a good one. That's because your competitors' sales reps will be telling their customers, "All prices in the industry are going up. We're not the only ones." Customers will be hearing this from so many of your competitors, they'll believe it. When you come in with your low-price story, they'll be reluctant to switch vendors in the short run — unless you hit them with other attractive elements in your marketing mix, not just price. Furthermore, when you finally do raise your prices, your customers will think you've raised them twice — and your competitors' sales reps will make certain they think that. You'll lose all credibility with the trade if that happens.

How much and how often should you raise your prices? Not too much — tie your price increases to the inflation rate. If your price increases are relatively small and frequent, your customers will eventually notice that most price increases are coming from just one vendor — you. I think you should follow industry norms.

To ease the pain, move something else down at the same time you raise your prices. Or talk about passing on your savings in production costs to them in the future. Tell them about the smaller lots they can buy to keep their cash payments level. Improve your service. Give them different buying options. If your sales reps come in with a different series of options, they're in a negotiating position with your customers. Never put your sales reps in the position where they have to say, "Take it or leave it," to your customers. Giving them a range of options will move the arguments away from your main point of weakness — your price increase. Never forget about easing their pain by increasing their options when you raise your prices.

Float a trial balloon to your customers. Have your sales reps tell them a price rise will happen soon, to get them used to the idea. Always let them think the price rise is going to be more than it actually turns out to be. When they find the rise is less than you thought it would be, they'll be relieved.

It's a good idea to tell your key accounts ahead of time about the price rise. Let them stock up at the old price. You might even want to find ways of giving them a little more time than your other customers — call it a special allowance or rebate — but make sure they know it's only a temporary rebate, or they'll expect it to last forever.

If your customers keep fighting you on the price increase, then ad up all your cost increases since your last price increase. Show them as percentages against the previous period. Don't fake the figures. In fact, bring along photocopies of some of your bills this period and last period to prove you're not lying. Then, if you can, show your customer that your price increase is less than the sum total of all your own increases — for example, maybe you've improved your productivity and lowered your production costs. Add up all your cost increases and tell your customer, "This is what I would have had to have charged you if I hadn't improved my productivity. But because I did improve it, and because I'm sensitive to your needs, I've absorbed a fair share of my cost increases. I'm passing on only some of them to you." Of course, you can't make use of this guideline if you didn't improve your productivity since your last price increase.[16]

Even if price-fixing and collusion is legal in the nation you do business in, it's probably best not to do it. Your customers will resent it when they find out — and most of the time, they will find out. Of course, never do it if it's illegal. Not only are you subject to fines and perhaps even jail terms, it's also terrible public relations. Your business is bound to suffer, at least in the short term.

NOT KNOWING HOW TO MAKE PRICE CONCESSIONS

In my seminar, "How You Can Negotiate and Win," I give the executive participants seven different ways of giving away $100 worth of concessions and ask them to pick both their favorite way and the way they dislike the most. One way is giving away the same amount of money each time a concession opportunity presents itself until the $100 is given away. Another is an escalating pattern, and there's also a de-escalating pattern. One gives the $100 away only at the very end of the negotiation, while another gives the $100 away at the very beginning. In one pattern, more than $100 is given away, so you have to take back some concessions. And so forth.

I've found that there are big differences in preferences and dislikes among people of different nations. For example, Brazilians, South Africans, and the people of the United States all liked one particular pattern, while Canadians, Australians, New Zealanders, Taiwanese, and Thais like a different pattern. A third group made up of nationals from

Hong Kong, Singapore, Malaysia, Indonesia, Philippines, India, and Kenya liked a third pattern. Almost every nationality disliked the same patterns, so there was more agreement there. I've reported the specific results in my book, *How to Negotiate Worldwide,* published in 1989 by Gower and Wiley.[17]

This seminar has generated consulting opportunities for me, and I've been able to observe firsthand how my clients and the people they negotiate with make price concessions. Most of them make the same mistakes over and over, no matter from which nation of origin. Because I'm not at liberty to reveal precisely what kind of mistakes specific companies make, however, and because there are very few published case studies on how business executives concede, I won't be able to provide any specific examples. You'll have to take my word for it that many errors are made when price concessions are made, whether it's by sellers lowering their asking prices or by buyers increasing their offers. So, I'll just move on to the do's and don'ts of concession making.

What to Learn, What Action to Take

Give yourself enough room by starting off with a high offer if you're selling or with a low offer if you're buying. Never reveal your bottom line too early.

Get the other person (TOP) to open up first while you keep your objectives, needs, and demands hidden. This gives you an early advantage over TOP.

Don't ever be the first to concede on a major issue. It's okay to concede first on a minor issue, though — especially if TOP thinks your concession was a major one.

Be a good actor by showing pain whenever you make a concession. Never make a concession with a smile. Make TOP think your concession hurts you — that way, TOP will think your concession was, indeed, a major one.

Make TOP work hard for every concession you make. That way, they'll appreciate them even more.

Use trade-offs to your advantage. Always get something every time you make a concession. Remember that saying, "I'll think about it," is a concession, because it raises TOP's expectations. Instead, say, "What will you give me if I consider it?"

Concede slowly. As much as possible, don't concede at all, if it can be avoided.

Say "no" often. The trouble with "no," though, is that most people can't take a "no" very well, and you might lose momentum early in the negotiation. Therefore, time this negative response precisely so as not to turn TOP away completely.

On the other hand, you should remember that saying "no" is quite often just a negotiating ploy. Test TOP to see if the "no" is genuine or not. Never take no for an answer. Remember too, that sometimes, their "no" is done just to ask you for help without losing face.

Don't be afraid to take concessions back if you haven't signed the contract yet. Anything goes until both signatures are on the contract. Be careful about using this technique too often, though. Taking back concessions could give TOP the impression you're undependable. You've got to choose the right situation in which to do it. It might be acceptable to do so when TOP reneges on a promise, for instance, but Asians don't like it at all because taking something back means losing face.

Keep a record of your concessions and those of TOP to see if there's a pattern. Study them so you can more appropriately respond to TOP's future moves.

Constantly keep TOP's expectations low by not giving in too often, too soon, or too much.

HOW TO LEARN EVEN MORE BY DIGGING DEEPER

Curry, David J. "Measuring Price and Quality Competition." *Journal of Marketing,* (Spring 1985): 106–17.

Kaikati, Jack G. "Marketing Without Exchange of Money." *Harvard Business Review,* (November–December 1982): 72–74.

Monroe, Kent B. *Pricing: Making Profitable Decisions.* New York: McGraw-Hill Book Co., 1979.

Nagle, Thomas. "Pricing as Creative Marketing." *Business Horizons,* (July–August 1983): 14–19.

Nimer, Daniel A. "Pricing for Profitable Sale Has a Lot to Do with Perception," *Sales Management,* 19 May 1975: 13–14.

Oxenfeldt, Alfred R. "A Decision-Making Structure for Price Decisions." *Journal of Marketing,* (January 1973): 48–53.

Rao, Vithala. "Pricing Research in Marketing: The State of the Art." *Journal of Business,* (January 1984): 39–60.

Ross, Elliot B. "Making Money with Pro Active Pricing." *Harvard Business Review,* (November–December 1984): 145–55.

Tellis, Gerald J. "Beyond the Many Faces of Price: An Integration of Pricing Strategies." *Journal of Marketing,* (October 1986): 146–60.

NOTES

1.   *Arkansas Gazette,* Little Rock, 28 February 1986, pp. 1-C, 2-C.

2.   Denise Gellene, "Arco Offers to Settle Claims for $225 Million," *Times,* Los Angeles, 24 December 1985, part IV, p. 2.

3.   "The Pentagon Stings an Industrial Giant," *Newsweek,* 8 April 1985, p. 58.

4.   Norman Black, "Congressman Accuses Firms of Billing Plot," *Sun,* Jonesboro, Ark., 22 September 1985, p. 12.

5.   Tim Carrington, "Pentagon Imposes Temporary Ban on Rockwell Jobs," *Wall Street Journal,* 1 November 1985, p. 2.

6.   Philip Shenon, "Procurement Officials at Pentagon Are Focus of Bribes Investigation," *International Herald Tribune,* Hong Kong, 17 June 1988, p. 2.

7.   Lawrence Kilman, "Fewer Listening to E. F. Hutton," *Commercial-Appeal,* Memphis, Tenn., 4 May 1983, p. B-4; Andy Pasztor, "Hutton Memos Show Approval of Overdrafts," *Wall Street Journal,* 1 July 1985, p. 3; Scott McMurray, "Battered Broker: E. F. Hutton Appears Headed for Long Siege in Bank-Draft Scheme," *Wall Street Journal,* 12 July 1985, pp. 1, 14; Andy Pasztor and Scott McMurray, "Hutton's Vice Chairman, Two Others Agree to Step Down Following Check Probe," *Wall Street Journal,* 6 September 1985; Dexter Hutchins, "Post-Hutton Lessons in How to Manage Corporate Cash," *Fortune,* 11 November 1985, p. 134.

8.   Scott McMurray, "First Jersey and Chairman Brennan Again Sued by SEC on Fraud Charges," *Wall Street Journal,* 1 November 1985, p. 2.

9.   "Bankers Indicted in Scheme," *Arkansas Gazette,* Little Rock, 16 October 1985, p. 6-A; "Top Bank Draws $4.75 Million Fine," *Arkansas Gazette,* Little Rock, 22 January 1986; Leon E. Wynter and Philip L. Zweig, "Banks in New York Fined Over Currency Violations," *Asian Wall Street Journal,* 20 June 1985, p. 7.

10.   "Massachusetts Sues Three Supermarket Chains, Alleging Price Fixing," *Wall Street Journal,* 10 October 1985, p. 27.

11.   Ann Hagedorn, "Panasonic to Pay Rebates to Avoid Antitrust Charges," *Wall Street Journal,* 19 January 1989, pp. B-1, B-6.

12.   Kurt Eichenwald and James Sterngold, "Fall of a Wall Street Trainee," *International Herald Tribune,* Hong Kong, 29 June 1988, pp. 1, 20; John M. Doyle, "SEC Accuses Drexel Burnham of Fraud and Other Violations," *Times,* Chattanooga, Tenn., 8 September 1988, p. F-4.

13.   George Haines, "A Study of Why People Purchase New Products," in *Science, Technology, and Marketing,* ed. R. M. Haas (Chicago: American Marketing Association, 1966), pp. 665–85, 693; Gregory P. Stone, "City Shoppers and Urban Identification," *American Journal of Sociology,* (July 1954), pp. 36–45; "Colonial Study," *Progressive Grocer,* (January 1964); Robert Dietrich, "Poor Price-Quiz Scores Give Shoppers No Cause for Pride," *Progressive Grocer,* (January 1977), p. 33; F. E. Brown, "Who Perceives Supermarket Prices Most Validly," *Journal of Marketing Research,* (February 1971), pp. 110–13; Elihu Katz and Paul F. Lazarsfeld, *Personal Influence,* (New York: Free Press in Glencoe, 1955); Irving S. White, "The Perception of Value in Products," in *On Knowing the Consumer,* ed. Joseph Newman (New York: John Wiley and Sons, 1966), pp. 90–106, especially pp. 92–93; William D. Wells and Leonard A. LoScuito, "Direct Observation of Purchasing Behavior," *Journal of Marketing Research,* (August 1966), pp. 227–33; L. K. Anderson, J. R. Taylor and R. J. Holloway, "The Consumer and His Alternatives," *Journal of Marketing Research,* (August 1966), p. 64; Kent B. Monroe, "Buyer's Subjective Perceptions of Price," *Journal of Marketing Research,* (February 1973), pp. 70–80; Andre Gabor and Clive W. J. Granger, "Price Sensitivity of the Consumer," *Journal of Advertising*

Research, (December 1964), pp. 40–44; Benson P. Shapiro, "Price Reliance: Existence and Sources," *Journal of Marketing Research,* (August 1973), pp. 286–94; Richard S. Cimball and Adrienne M. Webdale, "Effects of Price Information on Consumer-Rated Quality," presented at 1973 meeting of American Psychological Association in New Orleans; Jacob Jacoby and Jerry C. Olson, "Consumer Response to Price," *Purdue Papers in Consumer Psychology,* No. 157, 1976.

14.   Sidney Schoeffler, Robert D. Buzzell and Donald F. Heany, "Impact of Strategic Planning on Profit Performance," *Harvard Business Review,* (March–April 1974), pp. 137–45; Robert D. Buzzell, Bradley T. Gale and Ralph G. M. Sultan, "Market Share — A Key to Profitability," *Harvard Business Review,* (January–February 1975), pp. 97–106; Ralph E. Winter, "Corporate Strategists Giving New Emphasis to Market Share, Rank," *Wall Street Journal,* 3 February 1978, pp. 1, 21; Robert D. Buzzell and Frederik D. Wiersema, "Successful Share-Building Strategies," *Harvard Business Review,* (January–February 1981), pp. 135–44.

15.   Donald W. Hendon, *Battling for Profits,* 2d ed. (Jonesboro, AR: Business Consultants International and Singapore: Executive Data Centre, 1987), pp. 215–16.

16.   John Winkler, *Pricing for Results,* (New York: Facts-On-File Publications, 1984), pp. 126–30.

17.   Donald W. Hendon and Rebecca A. Hendon, *How to Negotiate Worldwide,* (London: Gower Publishing Co., 1989), forthcoming.

8

Channels of Distribution

CHOOSING THE WRONG MIDDLEMAN OR SUPPLIER

Setting up a long-term mutually profitable relationship between a supplier and distributor is difficult, and the decision to sign a contract with a distributor or supplier is one of the most important decisions that marketers ever make. Once the decision is made, there are long-term consequences for both parties. However, the mutual obligations, while sometimes burdensome, must not be allowed to overcome the synergistic benefits — or else the relationship will break down in bitter acrimony.

In a way, it's very much like a marriage. We all try to choose our spouses as best we can, but we sometimes let emotion get the better of us. The wedding day is a happy one. But it's only after the day-to-day reality of living with the other person sinks in that we know if we've made the right choice or not. Distributors and suppliers, of course, pick each other rationally and not emotionally, so there is less likelihood of a divorce.

On the other hand, the goals of the two partners are sometimes diametrically opposed. For example, a manufacturer may want the retailer to sell the product at the lowest possible price, but the retailer wants to sell it at the highest possible price. Only if both sides make sufficient profit — in the short term as well as the long term — will the distribution marriage work. In my consulting, I always stress that to my clients.

I also tell them that human beings change a little bit each day, and couples are fortunate if they change in the same direction — the marriage lasts and stays happy. If they change in different directions, they'll get divorced. In today's business world, the environment is always changing — new markets open, old ones close, new laws are passed, and so forth.

The only constant in business is change. Distributors and suppliers need to predict changes accurately and move in the same direction, for a good relationship today can turn into a terrible relationship tomorrow, especially in a dynamic environment.[1]

Sometimes, a distributor will make a mistake and choose a supplier that is nothing but trouble. If the supplier has most of the power in the relationship — as most franchisers have compared to franchise holders — it may be hard to get out of the relationship. However, most distributors will simply stop buying products from the supplier and switch to somebody else. I think suppliers have more problems at times choosing the right distributor. True, they can always choose to sell to somebody else, but if they decide to bypass distributors and build a direct selling organization from scratch, they must realize that this alternative means a lot of research and hard work. Here's what happened when a manufacturer picked the wrong way to distribute its products.

The U.S. company then known as Smith Kline and French was best known in the late 1960s and early 1970s for its best-selling Contac cold remedy capsule. It decided to market a low-priced cosmetics line. It hired one of the hottest creative ad agencies of the day, Wells Rich and Greene, to promote it. It named its line Love Cosmetics. Mary Wells, head of the agency, told the press, "We chose Love because that name will never become outdated."[2] Everything pointed to success for the new venture, but only a few years later, in the mid-1970s, Smith Kline and French sold the Love name to Chattem, Inc., which couldn't make it successful, either.

Love's major mistake, I feel, was its choice of distribution channels. Smith Kline and French's sales force called mainly on pharmacies and drug chains, where Contac enjoyed almost 100 percent distribution, good shelf space, and heavy sales volume. Cosmetics were sold in drug stores, sure, but at that time 40 percent of all cosmetics were sold in department stores. Its sales force didn't call on department stores. Smith Kline and French had three options:

- It could use its own sales force and have representatives call on both drug and department stores. However, that option would dilute their sales reps' effectiveness in drug stores, and sales of Contac might suffer.
- It could hire a special sales force to call on department stores only, leaving its present sales force calling on drugs stores only. That would be more expensive.
- It could ignore department stores and 40 percent of the market, and sell Love only in drug stores with its present sales force.

They chose the third alternative, reasoning that lower-priced cosmetics would sell better in drug stores than department stores. They were wrong, of course. It was a mistake to ignore such a large percentage of the market. And its drug store sales force spread itself a little thin in drug stores anyway, because the reps had to learn to deal with cosmetics personnel, and not deal strictly with over-the-counter medicine buyers as before.

What to Learn, What Action to Take

Put yourself in the other person's place. If you're a supplier, know what your distributors want. If you're a distributor, know what your suppliers want. Both checklists, "How Suppliers Should Choose (and Later Evaluate) Distributors" and "How Distributors Should Chose (and Later Evaluate) Suppliers," will help both sides.

How Suppliers Should Choose (and Later Evaluate) Distributors:

- Is the distributor adequately financed? What's its financial position? This includes accounts receivable, cash position, debts, inventories, fixed assets, payment records, current ratio, acid-test ratio, total liabilities to net worth, and trends in these areas over the years. Does it pay its bills on time? Does it have the ability to discount its bills?

- Does the firm have adequate business experience? What's its sales management, financial control, recordkeeping, warehousing, and inventory control like?

- How well established is the firm? Is it a one-person operation? If so, how old is the owner? What territory does the owner actually cover with his or her sales reps? Any plans for succession when the owner retires?

- Does the firm have the ability to grow? Does it want to grow?

- What is its annual inventory turnover? Will it tell you its annual sales figures for the last five years?

- What's the quality of the distributor's sales force? How aggressive is it? How able are its sales reps? How many reps are there? How well trained are they? Any objections to you helping out with training them?

- What's the firm's historical trend of sales volume as measured against the performance requirements established by your regional sales manager? What's its ability to get new business?

- What's its market share or penetration in the area you're interested in?

- Does the firm cover the territory you want covered? Any overlap with any other distributors you use?

- Will it be content in some areas with less desirable customers to avoid overlapping into the area of your other distributors?

- How many of the important prospects in the firm's territory does it sell to? How many of them are missing from its customer list?
- Is the firm willing to carry a full line of products to service all customer needs? Does it carry competing product lines? If so, will that cause a problem? Or will those products add to the prestige of your products? Do these products complement or supplement yours and help facilitate your sales?
- Does the distributor have adequate product knowledge, technical and otherwise? If not, can it get it? Is it willing to train its sales reps in this area?
- What's its attitude? Does it really want to handle your line, or is the company going after your line because of present shortages? Do you think you'll be dropped after the shortages ease?
- Is the distributor willing to carry adequate stocks?
- What are the firm's equipment and facilities like? Is there enough warehouse space, properly laid out, to enable it to carry adequate stocks of your line? Are there convenient sidings or truck approaches to its warehouse? Does the firm receive goods at convenient hours?
- How many office employees does it have? Other indicators of size?
- What's the quality of its service to its own customers?
- Is it willing to perform post-sale service?
- What are the company's service facilities like? Will it keep an adequate inventory for service?
- What kind of trade contacts does it have? What kind of reputation and standing does it have with the trade? (I mean here other manufacturers, middlemen, and customers.) How long has it been in business?
- What's the company's on-time delivery record?
- Are the firm's price policies compatible with yours? Does it maintain stable prices, or does it initiate price wars?
- What's its attitude toward the various allowances and cooperative promotional efforts you offer?[3]

How Distributors Should Choose (and Later Evaluate) Suppliers:

- Is the new item a better product than one or more of those you now carry? What are the comparative values per pound or gram? Sales potential?
- How many competitive products are sold locally? How many other distributors are there in the same trading area? Is the new item established in terms of local user acceptance?
- Will the new item add sufficient profit and volume to justify your carrying it? What kinds of merchandising and promotional allowances will the producer give us? Will that be sufficient?
- Will the new item cannibalize our old ones? Which items are more profitable to us — the cannibalized old ones or the new ones?
- How compatible is the new item with what we now carry?

- Does the new item fill an honest consumer need or want?
- Has this need been verified by consumer research?
- Is there introductory promotional effort strong enough to get sufficient customers to try it?
- What happened to the product in test markets? How are other distributors doing with it?
- Will the producer support the new item with enough national, local, regional, and cooperative advertising and promotion to keep it moving at a profitable rate?
- Will the producer provide me with technical assistance? Does it conduct training schools? Other kinds of sales cooperation?
- What is the product's shelf life?
- How much inventory will we have to carry?
- Are there any shelf stacking difficulties from the package? Is it compatible with our warehouse's physical handling system? Is the packaging attractive?
- What will the producer do about slowly moving stock? Damaged goods?
- Is the product guaranteed?
- Is the suggested selling price competitive?
- Is the quota the producer gave us realistic and challenging?
- What is the manufacturer's reputation in terms of local user acceptance? In terms of the image of the company and the brand name? This has to do both with final consumers and in past dealings with us. In regard to past dealings, what's the producer's reputation for speed, consistency, and reliability in deliveries? Does the firm have a clear, settled, consistent, printed policy in dealing with its distributors? What's its financial rating? Factory capacity? Access to raw materials? Existing sales volume?[4]

HOW TO LEARN EVEN MORE BY DIGGING DEEPER

Adler, Lee. "Symbiotic Marketing." *Harvard Business Review,* (November–December 1966): 59–71.

Gaskie, John F. "The Theory of Power and Conflict in Channels of Distribution," *Journal of Marketing,* (Summer 1984): 9–29.

Hlavacek, James D. and Tommy J. McCuistion. "Industrial Distributors — When, Who, and How." *Harvard Business Review,* (March–April 1983): 96–101.

"How Just-in-Time Inventories Combat Foreign Competition." *Business Week,* (14 May 1984): 234–36.

Lynagh, Peter M. and Richard S. Poist. "Managing Physical Distribution/Marketing Interface Activities: Cooperation or Conflict?" *Transportation Journal,* (Spring 1984): 36–43.

The M.A.C. Group. *Distribution: A Competitive Weapon.* Cambridge, Mass.: M.A.C. Group, 1985.

Narus, James A. and James C. Anderson. "Contributing as a Distributor to Partnerships with Manufacturers." *Business Horizons,* (September–October 1987): 34–42.

Pearson, Michael M. "Ten Distribution Myths." *Business Horizons*, (May–June 1981): 17–23.
Varadarajan, P. "Rajan" and Daniel Rajaratnam. "Symbiotic Marketing Revisited." *Journal of Marketing*, (January 1986): 7–17.

NOTES

1.   Donald W. Hendon, "The Distribution Marriage," *World Executive's Digest*, (November 1987), p. 6.
2.   "Advertising: Drug Store Love-In," *Time*, 14 March 1969, p. 93.
3.   Synthesized from Ralph S. Alexander, James S. Cross and Richard M. Hill, *Industrial Marketing*, 3rd ed. (Homewood, Ill.: Richard D. Irwin, 1967), pp. 271–75; B. Charles Aames and James D. Hlavacek, *Managerial Marketing for Industrial Firms*, (New York: Random House Business Division, 1984), p. 241; Harper W. Boyd, Jr., and William F. Massy, *Marketing Management*, (New York: Harcourt Brace Jovanovich, 1972), pp. 385–86; Louis H. Brendel, "Where to Find and How to Choose Your Industrial Distributors," *Sales Management*, 15 September 1951, pp. 128–32; John M. Brion, *Marketing Through the Wholesaler/Distribution Channel*, (Chicago: American Marketing Association, 1965), p. 34–37; Jack E. Bryer, "Finding and Hiring Good Manufacturers Reps," *Industrial Marketing*, (January 1964), p. 93; William T. Diamond, *Distribution Channels for Industrial Goods*, (Columbus: Bureau of Business Research, Ohio State University, 1963); H. Robert Dodge, *Industrial Marketing*, (New York: McGraw-Hill, 1970), pp. 245–49; "How Jordan Found 50 Good Manufacturers Reps," *Industrial Marketing*, (October 1965), p. 110; Ferdinand F. Mauser, *Modern Marketing Management*, (New York: McGraw-Hill, 1961), p. 338; Robert M. Pegram, *Selecting and Evaluating Distributors: Business Policy Study No. 116*, (New York: The Conference Board, 1965), pp. 21–91; Bert Rosenbloom, *Marketing Channels*, (Chicago: Dryden Press, 1983), pp. 184–89; J. Taylor Sims, J. Robert Foster, and Arch G. Woodside, *Marketing Channels*, (New York: Harper & Row, 1977), pp. 143–44; Frederick E. Webster, "The Role of the Industrial Distributor in Marketing Strategy," *Journal of Marketing*, (July 1976), pp. 10–16.
4.   Synthesized from J. Taylor Sims, J. Robert Foster and Arch G. Woodside, *Marketing Channels*, (New York: Harper & Row, 1977), pp. 155–56; James Cooke, "How a Food Retailer Looks at New Products," in *New Product Development*, ed. J. O. Eastlack, Jr., Marketing for Executives Series, Number 13 (Chicago: American Marketing Association, 1968), pp. 21–24; Ralph M. Alexander, James S. Cross and Richard M. Hill, *Industrial Marketing*, 3rd ed. (Homewood, Ill.: Richard D. Irwin, 1967), pp. 277–79; Louis H. Brendel, "Where to Find and How to Choose Your Industrial Distributors," *Sales Management*, 15 September 1951, pp. 128–32.

9
Advertising

The most common mistake in advertising is using the wrong appeal. There are many ways to mess up here.

MISUSING FEAR APPEALS

Fear appeals are one possible advertising ploy, but they can misfire. Here are examples of what can go wrong when you use fear appeals the wrong way.

In the 1960s, PSA Airlines, then operating in California only, used safety as its theme. It wanted its customers to know its pilots cared greatly about safety and would not fly an unsafe plane. Thinking this message would reassure its passengers, it ran ads in which its pilots said, "We're scared, too." Its pilots were supposedly so scared of flying that they took extra care to make certain their plane was safe before it took off. This completely backfired. The target audience wasn't reassured — in fact, many of them deserted PSA for other airlines that didn't have such "chicken" pilots. Passengers in the 1960s wanted brave pilots, not fearful pilots.

Schlitz used to be the second largest beer in the United States. It changed its formula slightly and alienated much of its target market, and then it did something that scared a lot of those who remained loyal. It ran a series of TV commercials that were parodies of laundry detergent ads familiar to most viewers. The detergent ads showed a well-dressed man in a laundromat telling a housewife, "I'm going to take away your brand. . . ." Before he can say, "and replace it, free, with my brand. Try it for a week and then tell me which brand gives you a better wash," the housewife says, "Oh, no, you're not going to take away my brand."

The Schlitz ads had a meek and milk looking man talking to various people, telling them "I'm going to take your Schlitz away . . ." Before the meek looking man could finish by saying, "and replace it, free, with my brand. Taste my brand and tell me which one you like better," the people protested, often in a threatening way, and raved about how wonderful Schlitz was. The meek looking man never got anybody in the ads to try his beer.

Probably the ad in this series which threatened and offended most people involved a tough looking black prize-fighter who looked and sounded like the then heavyweight champion, Muhammad Ali, who threatened to beat up the meek looking white man if he tried to take his Schlitz away. This notorious series of ill-fated ads became known in the industry as the "Drink Schlitz or I'll kill you" campaign. Market share of the brand fell during this campaign.

Burger King tried a variation on the same approach in June 1985. To let Americans know it changed its Whopper sandwich for the better, it used a smooth talking, well-dressed executive to tell several celebrities of the change. One of them, Mr. T, shook his fist and jabbed his finger at the camera before tasting the Whopper. After he tasted it, he said, "Okay, fool, it's good. I'll let you live." That offended many people, too.[1]

In 1985, a U.S. TV commercial for Champion Batteries tried to show the battery's virtues by seeing how long a driver could wait before starting his car while a speeding train approached. They pulled the ad after many complaints.[2]

In the summer of 1988, Eclipse Laboratories began a series of magazine ads in the United States for its Skin Cancer Garde Sunblock Lotion showing people dressed in black gazing into an open casket. The headline read, "Here's how you can look with a healthy tan." Several dermatologists became concerned that these scare tactics are misleading. One dermatologist said the ad was deceptive "because the chances of death from skin cancer are infinitesimally small," and that the ad wasn't "a very tasteful way of communicating about cancer." And in the spring of 1988, Michael Max's leather stores in New York City ran an ad showing a corpse dressed in leather with a tag on her toe with the store's name. The headline read, "Another fashion victim." Many readers complained.

What to Learn, What Action to Take

Segment your market psychographically. Fear works best with people who are low in anxiety and high in self-esteem, who can cope, aren't interested in the topic of fear itself, and think they aren't very vulnerable. Fear is good in establishing new market segments, more effective than with old ones. A moderate fear appeal is better than a heavy or low fear appeal. A "social fear" appeal is better than a "physical fear" appeal, which is why ads for deodorants and mouthwash seem to work pretty well. Don't use fear if the source isn't perceived as credible. If you do, though, be sure to cite independent sources, such as test agencies. Finally, nobody knows which medium is best for fear appeals.[3]

MISUSING SEX APPEALS

In the section on sexism, I discussed what can happen when sexism becomes an issue to your customers. Evelyn Arroyo of Hoboken, New Jersey, didn't follow the guidelines you learned about there. Instead, she tried to use her sex appeal when she ran for election to the school board in her hometown in 1986. Then 21, the beautiful former model and teacher's assistant at a day-care center posed for an ad wearing an off-the-shoulder evening gown and a seductive smile. The copy said, "Everyone knows the Hoboken Public School System is one of the worst in the state. Now, all the politicians promise reform. That's what we get, promises, promises (not even Arpege). For a new approach, vote Evelyn Arroyo." She said, "The politicians aren't supporting me, so I figured the only way I could win was use my natural assets." She lost by a wide margin.[4] On the other hand, a pornographic movie star, Cicciolina (Ilona Staller), won election to the Italian Parliament in a campaign in which she repeatedly exposed her breasts.

What to Learn, What Action to Take

If you're going to use sex in your ads, be careful because it's easy to offend a large part of your target audience. Basically, males like it more than females, and younger people like it more than older people. Race, income, and education levels make no difference, though.

CHANGING THEMES TOO OFTEN

J&B Scotch used to be the largest-selling scotch whiskey in the United States. Its advertising was straightforward, and for years, you could count on seeing J&B's crossword puzzle in Friday's *Wall Street Journal*. Then, it decided to change tactics. In 1980, it began to use the slogan, "it whispers," alongside dreamy pictures of Scottish castles and lakes. The ads were meant to suggest the smooth taste of J&B. It was too subtle. Dewar's knocked the brand into second place.

In 1985, J&B dropped its whispering campaign. The new campaign featured toy soldiers in red coats toting J&B bottles as they troop off to battle. The ads talked about pride, tradition, and conviction, with the punchline slogan, "Scotch of great character." The ad agency felt that images of stately soldiers and longer, descriptive copy would better communicate J&B's British heritage and craftsmanship. Sales continued to slide, and so it switched ad agencies just 15 months after the "great character" campaign began. The new agency, a small creative shop, said it would focus on quality, style, and fashionability.[5]

What to Learn, What Action to Take

Advertisers are often very impatient for results. They won't wait long for a campaign to prove itself. Some kinds of campaigns, especially positioning, take a long time to work. It took several years for Marlboro to re-establish itself as a very masculine man's cigarette. (It used to be a woman's cigarette with a red filter.) It went from men with inverted tattoos to Julie London's sultry style of singing to American cowboys, but it wasn't until it added the theme music from the movie, "The Magnificent Seven," to the cowboy scenes that the long-term campaign really caught on. Where would Marlboro be today if the Philip Morris Company had been overly impatient for the masculinity campaign to finally prove itself?

Be like Philip Morris — don't be overly impatient. Don't change for the sake of change. Don't cut down one of the giants of the forest just to rearrange your advertising landscape. You may be bored with your campaign, but your target audience may not be, and who are you trying to please — yourself, or your target audience?

HELPING YOUR COMPETITOR
WHEN YOU ADVERTISE

Here are two ads that helped competitors more than the advertisers.

Back in the middle 1960s in the United States, every time Chase & Sanborn coffee ran a televised ad, it helped its archrival, Maxwell House coffee, instead. Posttests showed that people remembered and liked C & S's ads, but most of them thought they were Maxwell House's. Still more testing indicated that C & S had a neutral image for so many years that very few people remembered its name.

In 1985 in the United States, Pepsi ran a humorous ad set 400 years in the future. An archaeologist held up several items, including a guitar, baseball, and Coke bottle. Although the professor claimed not to know what the function of the Coke bottle was, since only Pepsi-Cola was sold in the twenty-fourth century, he held the Coke bottle high at the end, as King Arthur might have brandished Excalibur, with stirring music in the background. What the viewer remembered was the empty bottle of Coke, not Pepsi.[6]

What to Learn, What Action to Take

In most nations, you can't mention your competitors in your ads, though you can in the United States. Many U.S. advertisers won't mention their competitors, thinking, "Why should I give them free publicity?" Others won't do it because they don't want a lawsuit on their hands.

The advertising business is very fad conscious. The first few ads that start a bandwagon get noticed, and the rest don't because they're too similar. When U.S. advertisers were first allowed to name their competitors, the target audience really noticed. After awhile, the novelty wore off, and today it's just another tried and true technique that's probably not noticed by viewers zipping and zapping TV commercials with their remote controls and VCRs. I personally feel that it's not good to name your competitors — why give them free publicity, unless:

- They're better known than you are. You have more to gain than they have.
- You are perceived as vastly superior to your competitor by the majority of your target audience after the ad has run.
- You're absolutely certain of your facts. You don't want an embarrassing lawsuit later on.
- You pretest your ads very carefully before you run them.

NEGLECTING PSYCHOGRAPHICS

In the 1960s, marketers were looking for something more than demographics to describe their target audience. They came up with a technique of measuring lifestyles known as psychographics. Your lifestyle refers to your pattern of living in the world as expressed in your activities, interests, and opinions (AIOs). To discover people's psychographic profiles, you have to ask them how strongly they agree or disagree with statements such as the following. My children are the most important thing in my life (child oriented), and I like to try new and different things (new brand tryer).

The questionnaire is quite lengthy, sometimes running to more than 100 statements, but it can be answered quickly. The information is then analyzed on a computer to find distinctive psychographic groups, such as liberals, conservatives, swingers, family-oriented groups, and so forth.

When marketing executives prepare their marketing plans, they look for relationships between their brand and psychographic groups. After aiming their brand at a relevant group, the ad agency's copywriter can create advertising that's more congruent with the symbols in the target group's lifestyle.

In 1975 in the United States, Dr Pepper, the unusual fruity and delicious soft drink, began calling itself "the most original soft drink ever in the whole wide world." Sales soared. It had illusions of catching up with Coke and Pepsi after it passed 7-Up in sales, and so in 1980, it tried to become a drink for the masses with its "Be a Pepper, too" ad campaign. Sales dropped, and psychographic research done later showed why.

In 1982, its ad agency did its first psychographic research and found that Dr Pepper drinkers were "inner-directed" people, who should "live life in accordance with their own personal values and not try to meet other people's expectations. They view themselves as original, even a little crazy, and look for interesting experiences." The "Be a Pepper, too" ads catered to "outer-directed belongers, who follow the latest trends and seek peer approval" — the typical Coke and Pepsi drinkers.

But Dr Pepper continued the "Be a Pepper, too" campaign, and sales continued to stagnate. In 1985, though, it finally switched to "inner-directed" ads which appear to be wild and crazy. One featured a cranky Godzilla who demolished whole city blocks after drinking the contents of a cola tanker truck. He settled down after drinking Dr Pepper inside a water tower. It continued its "out-of-the-ordinary" theme in 1986 and 1987, then switched to a "Just what the Doctor ordered" theme in 1988. It can't go too far in its fight against Coke and Pepsi, though — many of its bottlers also bottle Coke or Pepsi.[7]

What to Learn, What Action to Take

Never forget how important psychographics are. Never forget to do psychographic research. And once you have the findings, don't ignore them — use them in your ad copy. Dr Pepper didn't for while, and its sales suffered as a result. Don't let that happen to you.

THE WRONG KIND OF SYNCHRONICITY

In 1985 in the United States, both Estee Lauder and Lincoln-Mercury Division of Ford used the identical theme song, "You Are So

Beautiful to Me," in its ads — one for a perfume and one for a station wagon. The same thing might happen to Sunkist Raisins and American Express, both of whom were using the old rock song, "My Girl," in its American TV ads in early 1989. Neither advertiser knew of the other's plans.[8]

Some of you may not think this is a mistake. I think it's a minor mistake myself, but a mistake nevertheless. I feel ads should be as different as possible in order to stand out. That's the best assurance they'll be remembered. And suppose some women didn't like the station wagon ad — when they heard the same song in the Estee Lauder ad later, they might decide not to buy the perfume because of that deep-seated feeling of dislike for the station wagon ad.

What to Learn, What Action to Take

If you agree with my logic, do your best to be unique. Don't blindly copy currently fashionable ads. They won't stand out, and people won't remember them. Make your ads memorable by being unique.

ADVERTISING BLUNDERS AIMED AT THE HISPANIC MARKET

The Hispanic market in the United States is large and diversified. By the late 1980s, there were over 18 million Hispanics and they enjoyed purchasing power of over $70 billion.[9] Although over 40 percent were born in the United States, most have retained their subcultural identities and remained Spanish speaking. Many Hispanic ad agencies have sprung up since the 1970s to help marketers who don't know much about this important market segment, are careless, and are confused. Mainstream marketers are beginning to cater more and more to this market. Many mistakes have been made in the process, and they can be broken down into three categories — translation errors, cultural misunderstandings, and failing to differentiate among the four (possibly five) major Hispanic subgroups.

ERRORS IN THE MEANING OF SPANISH TRANSLATIONS

Bilingual Hispanics have strong preferences for the Spanish language because they feel it's their "own" language and because 43 percent of Hispanics speak only Spanish or just enough English to get by.

Therefore, it's important to properly translate English into Spanish. Here are three translation errors:

- "Budweiser, the King of Beers" couldn't literally translate itself into Spanish without making a grammatical error. *Cerveza* (beer) is a feminine noun. How can a female be king? Budweiser would have to be the queen of beers.

- Coors Beer talked about its water with this incorrect translation — "la agua." It should be "*el* agua," for agua is masculine and requires a masculine adjective, *el,* not the feminine adjective, *la.* This may not seem important, but many Hispanics noticed it and thought Coors did not care about the Hispanic market.

- Frank Perdue of Perdue Chickens used this slogan in English: "It takes a tough man to make a tender chicken." The Spanish ad said, "It takes a sexually excited man to make a chick sensual."[10]

MISUNDERSTANDING HISPANIC CULTURE

Nine Lives Cat Food wouldn't go over well with Hispanic audiences, because in Spanish folk culture, cats have only seven lives.[11]

In the early 1980s, a Christmas ad for a beer showing the beer next to a plate of tacos and enchiladas wasn't well received because Mexicans don't eat tacos and enchiladas at Christmas. That's a time when they go out of their way to make everything special, including food.

About the same time, another beer ad featured a macho looking Hispanic man with his arm around an Hispanic woman. He had a beer in one hand and a taco in another. Hispanics felt that the ad was saying that all an Hispanic male wants is sex, drink, and food, and were offended by it.[12]

Coors beer's theme, "taste the high country," positioned the Colorado Rockies as the place where the best beer is brewed because the best natural ingredients are found there. However, Hispanics couldn't understand the slogan because they couldn't relate to the high country-mountain lifestyle found in Colorado. So after several weeks, the campaign had to be modified to suggest to Hispanics that they can take beer from the high country and bring it to their own high country — wherever that may be.

A televised ad for a phone company that aired on the East Coast had the wife telling her husband, "Run downstairs and phone Mary. Tell her we'll be a little late." They made two big errors here — no Hispanic wife dares to order her husband to run anywhere, and Hispanics generally do not phone to say they will be late.[13]

NOT DIFFERENTIATING AMONG
HISPANIC SUBGROUPS

While all Hispanics share the same "general" language and a similar Spanish-speaking mother-country cultural background, there are four major subgroups, each with their own idiosyncracies — Hispanics of Mexican descent, of Puerto Rican descent, of Cuban descent, and all others from Spain, Central, and South America. (Many people, including myself — and I'm part Mexican and fluent in Spanish — feel that California Hispanics are quite different from Texas Hispanics. There are subtle differences in attitudes, dress, and slang expressions of which you need to be aware.) Don't think you can use the same ad copy for all four (or five) groups all the time. They use different words for the same thing — for example, brown sugar is called *azucar negra* in New York, *azucar prieta* in Miami, *azucar morena* in South Texas, and *azucar pardo* elsewhere. Here are two examples of mistakes made when appropriate Spanish words have a negative or vulgar connotation for a specific subgroup:

In its New York City ads, an insecticide company promised to kill all bugs. The correct Spanish dictionary words, *bichos,* was not appropriate, for Puerto Ricans use *bichos* to refer to male genitals.

In Miami, a bread maker talked about its loaf of bread as *un bollo de pan,* but in Cuban slang, that means female genitals.[14]

Finally, some ads can contain very subtle nonverbal details that one subgroup will like and another will dislike. For example, a beer company filmed an ad using San Antonio's famous Paseo del Rio (or Riverwalk). Hispanics in California liked the ad because of its Spanish flavor. However, the Mexican-Americans in San Antonio didn't like it much because they felt only Anglo tourists go to the Riverwalk, not Chicanos. It's too "touristy" for them as well as for Anglo residents of San Antonio. I know. I used to live there. Most San Antonio residents, including myself, usually go to the Riverwalk only when entertaining out-of-town visitors.

What to Learn, What Action to Take

If you're not Hispanic, you'll probably make all three mistakes — translation, cultural misunderstandings, and not differentiating among different subgroups. Non-Hispanics can avoid these mistakes by following these recommendations.

When you're marketing to the important Hispanic market, be open-minded, inquisitive, and willing to learn.

Bring in representatives from each of the major Hispanic subgroups when you're developing your strategy and tactics. I'd recommend having a Texas Hispanic as well as a California Hispanic. But remember — even professional translators disagree on what's a good translation, how creative you can be, and so forth. So expect differences of opinion.[15]

To avoid translation errors, stay away from words with multiple meanings or idioms. Use "reverse translation" — that is, translate the English into Spanish; then translate the Spanish back into English; finally compare the first English version with the second version. If they're the same, fine. But often they won't be. Also, look up and follow the ten rules for writing translatable English that Brislin, Lonner, and Thorndike talked about, including simple and short sentences, and avoiding metaphors, colloquialisms, and vagueness.[16]

Don't insist on literal translations — try instead for "decentered translations." This means making English and Spanish forms natural-sounding conceptual equivalents, not mere lexical equivalents. This makes the translation more accurate and less artificial.[17]

Pretest your ads even more thoroughly than you do for your English-speaking market. You can't rely on your past experience in mainstream marketing or on your intuition — you will make mistakes, so pretest very thoroughly.[18]

ERRORS IN USING CELEBRITIES IN YOUR MARKETING MIX

The old A.I.D.A. formula you learned about when you studied advertising said you've got to get the audience's attention first. Once you've got that, then, the receivers of the ad would become interested in the product, then desire it, then take some kind of action. Many marketers use celebrities to get people's attention because they are already well known. Marketing Evaluations, Inc., a U.S. research firm, has been selling its Performer Q rating service for years — that's probably why Bill Cosby appears in so many ads, and why Kate Jackson seems to get one TV series after another — they both usually get high Q scores.

On the other hand, psychologists tell us about the "sleeper effect."[19] This means that after awhile, people can't remember from whom they heard about the product or service — from Bill Cosby or from their neighbors or friends. Advertisers who believe strongly in the sleeper effect often don't use celebrities to save money.

If you use well-known figures in your ads, make sure you don't make these next five mistakes.

USING SPOKESMEN WHO ARE TOO GOOD

Watch out for "video vampires" — spokesmen who are too good. People remember these celebrities, but they don't remember which product or service they were advertising. Here are three examples from the United States:

- Can you remember which product the late Orson Welles was talking about in the early 1980s when he said, "We will sell no wine before its time?" Most people did *not* remember he was talking about Paul Masson wines. Vinters International's chief executive said, "The product was secondary to the man."
- A few years earlier, in the 1960s and 1970s, football star Joe Namath said he wore panty hose. People remembered Namath, but not the product's name.
- In the 1970s and 1980s, Ricardo Montalban kept talking about "rich Corinthian leather," and most people remembered him and his accent, but not Chrysler, the automobile manufacturer that sponsored the ad.[20]

USING CELEBRITIES WHO ARE CONTROVERSIAL

Don't use celebrities who have been controversial in the past. Dreyer's Grand Ice Cream's televised advertising campaign in the western United States stresses an "unbelievable" claim that its low-calorie brand tastes as good as its regular ice cream. It has used "unbelievable" people to endorse Dreyer's "unbelievable" claim, including a Scotsman who claimed to have seen the Loch Ness monster and a woman who said she has had several encounters with UFOs (unidentified flying objects, or flying saucers).

In 1987, it used John Ehrlichman, the former aide to Richard Nixon during the Watergate scandal of the early 1970s, as one of its "unbelievable" people. However, viewers objected because he had been convicted of perjury in a case that went against deeply held U.S. values. Dreyer stopped running the ad immediately. A spokesman said, "It wasn't necessarily the number, it was the intensity of their comments that disturbed our management the most." Pulling Mr. Ehrlichman was probably the right thing to do. Dreyer's didn't drop the whole campaign, though. The spokesman said it generated sales 50 to 70 percent above projections.[21]

NOT CHECKING INTO A CELEBRITY'S PAST
BEFORE YOU USE HIM OR HER

Hindsight is easier to use than foresight. Dreyer knew John Ehrlichman was controversial before it used him. It's much harder to follow this next principle: Don't use celebrities who become controversial after they endorse your product, either. In 1989, Pepsi dropped pop singer Madonna from its ads after receiving complaints from religious organizations. And two stars of the ABC television series *Moonlighting* were dropped because of what they did and said after they made their respective endorsements.

Bruce Willis became the spokesman for Seagram's Golden Wine Cooler in the United States. Then, in December 1987, the *National Enquirer* magazine ran a story alleging that he had sought help for a drinking problem. He was dropped shortly afterward.[22]

Willis' costar, Cybill Shepherd, was used by the Beef Industry Council/National Live Stock and Meat Board to persuade people in the United States to eat more beef. She appeared in a few ads in early 1987, saying "I'm not sure I trust people who don't eat hamburgers." Then, *Family Circle* magazine quoted her saying that one of her beauty secrets is avoiding "red meat." The meat people dropped Shepherd, but kept James Garner, its other spokesman who does eat red meat. They dropped him later when he developed heart trouble. Of course, this delighted the pork producers association, which was using Peggy Fleming at this time to promote "the other white meat," pork.[23]

Two other famous examples occurred in the late 1970s. E. R. Squibb Company was using tennis star Billie Jean King in its U.S. ads, and then dropped her after she disclosed she had a lesbian affair with a former secretary. And Ivory Snow detergent changed its packaging after it was revealed that the young mother on its box was Marilyn Chambers, the U.S. pornography film star.

An executive at a leading ad agency had this to say: "It's better for a pitchman to die than to be caught alive in a scandal. When the person personifying your brand gets in trouble, the brand indirectly gets in trouble, too." Referring to the Bruce Willis scandal, another ad agency executive said, "Bruce's image and the brand are really linked. So the problem will be to start from ground zero to find a whole new image for Seagram's Golden Wine Cooler."[24]

Some controversies aren't too important. For example, Absolut vodka tied in with David Cameron, a well-known fashion designer, in an ad that appeared in several fashion magazines in February 1988. The ad featured a model wearing Cameron's silvery tank top and appears to be a rendition of the Absolut vodka label. While the magazines were still on the newsstands, David Cameron filed for protection from creditors under Chapter 11 of the Bankruptcy Code. An executive at the ad agency that created the ad said, "The ad has nothing to do with Cameron's business or merchandise. It's just that he's a fabulous artist. We plan to continue the ad. He's a very talented young man." I agree. Many people heard about Bruce Willis, Cybill Shepherd, James Garner, and Billie Jean King, and almost everybody knows about John Ehrlichman's role in the Watergate scandal. But how many people who saw the Absolut ad know that David Cameron went bankrupt, and if they did, how many would care? Very few, I think.[25]

NOT COVERING ALL BETS WHEN YOU USE SPORTS CELEBRITIES

Be careful when you use sports celebrities, because you can't predict the future. Donnay, the Belgian tennis racket maker, increased its worldwide market after Swedish tennis star Bjorn Borg, who dominated tennis in the late 1970s and early 1980s appeared in its ads. After Borg retired in 1981, the firm suffered heavy losses. It went bankrupt in 1988. Observers said its sales fell because Donnay couldn't replace Borg with another tennis star.[26] In the late 1950s, Sweden's Ingemar Johansson knocked out World Heavyweight Champion Floyd Patterson and became champion himself. Patterson was given a rematch. Schick Razor Blades used Johansson in a U.S. campaign that began just a few weeks before the rematch touting its blades of "Swedish Stainless Steel." The campaign was planned to run for several weeks thereafter — that's how certain Schick was that Johansson would beat Patterson again. Instead, Patterson knocked out Johansson, and an embarrassed Schick immediately cancelled its campaign.

In the 1980s, U.S. advertisers seem to have learned from this famous error. Just before the Super Bowl, I've seen many ads with quarterbacks from both teams in national ads — never a quarterback from just one team. Miller Brewing Company, which uses ex-athletes in its Miller Lite Beer ads, interviews former teammates and others before signing the ex-jocks to contracts. But in September 1988, advertisers in Canada, Japan, Finland, and Italy made the same mistake Schick made with Ingemar Johansson. A Canadian courier service, outboard motor company, and American Express Canada; Japan's Kyodo Oil Company and Mazda Motor Company; Valio, a Finnish dairy association; and the Italian sportswear company, Diadora, were all using the world's fastest man, Canada's Ben Johnson, in their ads. That month, Johnson won a gold medal in the Seoul Olympics — then was disqualified for using steroids. All these firms immediately stopped all ads with Johnson.[27]

PUTTING ALL YOUR EGGS IN ONE BASKET BY NAMING YOUR PRODUCT OR SERVICE AFTER A CELEBRITY

Let's take this one step further. Instead of just using celebrities in ads, some products are named after celebrities, and this can be especially dangerous. (Included in my definition of celebrities are Disney and other cartoon characters, which have been successful for many years. Also included are television programs, such as Dynasty, Bonanza, and Miami Vice.) Here are five examples, all from the United States:

Although Gloria Vanderbilt was successful with jeans and perfumes named after her, fancy chocolates and a frozen tofu dessert under her name did poorly and were dropped. Bill Blass chocolates and the Reggie (Jackson) candy bar were also flops.[28]

Dynasty, a popular evening soap opera, has licensed many products, including $10,000 Dynasty furs, $1,000 Dynasty evening dresses, $15 Dynasty pantyhose, $150 Dynasty perfume, $9.75 Carrington men's cologne, and medium-priced Forever Krystle women's perfume. The big-ticket items did poorly and were pulled off the market, while the lower-priced items did well. The mistake was selling high-priced items under the Dynasty label. One Dynasty executive said, "Your Dynasty viewer isn't going to be at the high end of the market, but we wanted to make things accessible to them with a little style." Another said, "If you make everything too high-priced, you alienate the great majority of the program's viewers. But if you cheapen it, you denigrate the audience."[29]

What to Learn, What Action to Take

The main problem with naming products and services after celebrities is this — what happens when a team loses, when a celebrity is involved in a scandal, or when a celebrity's popularity declines? In 1985, retailers sold about $150 million of products with the Dynasty labels, and the licensers received about 7 percent of the wholesale price. What would one point drop in Nielsen ratings do to retail sales? What will happen to the Newman's Own line of spaghetti sauce, popcorn, and salad dressings when Paul Newman dies? (He was in his mid-60s at the time I wrote this book.) In March 1980, viewers protested when New York's WABC-TV ran an American Express ad featuring Jesse Owens the day after the sports hero died. Here's what you can do about this.

Do what many companies do to minimize the potential impact of a lone spokesman's peccadillos — use a stable of celebrities, not just one, and use them sparingly, filling in with slice-of-life ads. Before you sign a contract with a celebrity, subject him or her to the same rigid standards to which the White House and Senate subject Supreme Court nominees. Cover your bets — don't put all your eggs in one sports team's basket. I'll reinforce some of these bits of advice shortly.

But should you use celebrities in the first place? They do attract attention, and they exert "stopping power" over advertising-saturated customers. However, they can be big trouble, as the examples you've just read indicate. Furthermore, when you drop an effective spokesman, your ad campaign loses momentum, and your customers feel abandoned. It's hard to make a seamless transition from one successful spokesman to another. On top of all that, these five U.S. research findings should disturb you:

- Only 19 percent of a large sample of consumers felt celebrities and athletes increase their interest in the product or service.
- Only 27 percent believed they use the products and services they promote.
- Half said they appeared in the ads only for the money they earned.
- Half avoided buying certain products and services because they believe the celebrity's expensive contract increased the price of the product or service.
- About 70 percent (mostly female) resented advice on household products from what they called "cutesy starlets."[30]

My advice is to use celebrities only under these conditions. First, the celebrity should have some kind of expertise in whatever he or she is promoting. Good U.S. examples include singer Stevie Wonder pushing TDK tape cassettes, actor and Beltone hearing aid wearer Eddie Albert touting that product, Dennis the Menace artist Hank Ketcham pushing Shaeffer pens, singer Ella Fitzgerald plugging Memorex audiotapes, and elderly Martha Raye, the comedienne who wears dentures and is nicknamed "the big mouth," pushing Polident denture adhesive.

Second, don't use controversial celebrities. I haven't seen Jane Fonda pushing too many products (other than her own exercise videos) after she took what many people called a controversial stand on the Vietnam War. In mid-1988, she apologized to U.S. veterans' groups for her actions in the 1960s and 1970s. Perhaps that action will make her less controversial. Perhaps not.

Make sure their Performer Q ratings are high, and monitor these ratings each year. Investigate noncontroversial celebrities as thoroughly as Supreme Court justices are investigated. You may find skeletons in their closets. If your market is the upscale professional customer, try well-known business executives instead. *Wall Street Journal* readers who see Chrysler Corporation chairman Lee Iacocca smoking Don Diego cigars in an ad may follow suit to emulate his success. Some U.S. executives will endorse products free or for very little money. They do it to enhance their own firms' visibility and to massage their egos. For example, Ted Turner of Turner Broadcasting System, Roger Enrico of Pepsi Cola, and Bill Marriott, Jr., of Marriott Hotels have all appeared, eyepatch and all, in ads for Hathaway shirts.[31] And P. J. Cundari, Regional Sales Manager for R. J. Reynolds Tobacco Co. appeared in a Doubletree Hotels ad. He's a regular customer.

SPELLING ERRORS

If you're going to spend a lot of money advertising, at least don't look like an idiot — spell the words correctly, and punctuate properly, too. Here are several examples of inexcusable grammatical carelessness, all from the United States.

The editor of *American Business* received a press kit from a California celebrity-contacts broker who said he could put his readers in contact with such stars as "Merl Haggard, Red Aurabauch, Julius Irving, Mohammed Ali, Sid Cessar, Ester Rolle, Ava Gabor, and Heather Lockleer." What's wrong with that? Ask Merle Haggard, Red Auerbach, Julius Erving, Muhammad Ali, Sid Caesar, Esther Rolle, Eva Gabor, and Heather Locklear. You'd think if the broker went to all the trouble of getting the photos shot, the artwork pasted up, the layout designed, and the ad copy written, he or she would have proofread the text for spelling errors.[32]

In 1985, Business Publications, Inc., a university textbook publisher specializing in business texts, sent out a letter to accounting professors publicizing the third edition of *Accounting Principals* by Hermanson, Edwards, and Salmonson. At least, when the book was published, *Accounting Principles* was spelled correctly.[33]

In the early 1980s, the Dean of a prestigious midwestern university was publicly humiliated when he sent a letter to the citizens' forum column of his local newspaper. The word, "ptomaine" was misspelled twice as "tomaine." The editor of the paper published a photocopy of the letter alongside an editorial entitled, "No Wonder Students Can't Spell . . . Even the College Dean Can't."[34]

Again in the early 1980s, Sears ran a correction in the Dallas *Morning News* for items that appeared in prior ads. There were five corrections. The last two sentences read, "We regret these erros. You can count on Sears." To do what? Make erros or errors?[35]

Probably the most common spelling error my university students made is "it's." They use it incorrectly. "It's" means "it is." "Its" is possessive. They usually use "it's" in place of "its." I've seen this in print ads over and over. I've got a collection, literally, of hundreds of ads with this particular error. I'll only print one here. In the middle 1980s in Jonesboro, Arkansas, O'Neal Motors ran a newspaper ad "to announce the association of Ken Bourland to it's award winning sales staff." (Oh, yes, the ad with Ken's picture in it was encased in a heavy black border, which reminded me of an obituary.)

In 1982, a large magazine ran a recipe in which "3/4 cup" was printed as "1/4 cup." Thousands of letters of complaint and cancelled subscriptions were received from upset readers.[36]

A public relations firm sent out a press release in which it offered to provide "legends in the making" press releases for new clients. The five-paragraph release had seven spelling or punctuation errors, spelled the term "free lance" three different ways, and assured the reader that "These aren't prima donna's," instead of "prima donnas." Who would hire a public relations firm that couldn't punctuate its own press releases properly — or spell correctly?[37]

The Musical Heritage Society, a classical music record and tape club, sent out a mailer with this printed on the envelope: "Was ist die Compact Disc? Was ist die Cassetten? Was ist das Langspielplatten?" The English translation is: What is the compact disk? What is the cassettes? What is the records?" Am I being picky, or is it important to correct the error of singular verbs with plural nouns? Is it important to spell "Kassetten" correctly? What do you think?[38]

This one is a lot more serious. In 1987, at an Atlanta computer trade show, Microlytics announced an agreement to supply its new spelling checker software package for the XyWrite III Plus Word Processor. Included in the announcement were two misspelled words — "tradmark" and "publishere."[39]

A government executive once wasted $3 million by not catching a hyphenation error when proofreading a business letter. When he dictated the letter, he said, "We want 1,000-foot-long radium bars. Send three in cases." The secretary typed instead "We want 1,000 foot-long radium bars. Send three in cases." Two months later, he received three huge crates containing 1,000 twelve-inch, cut-down, totally unusable radium bars.[40]

Woodrow Wilson got an undeserved reputation as a womanizer when he was president. After his first wife died in 1914, he began courting Edith Bolling Galt, whom he later married. During his courtship, the Washington *Post* ran an article with a typographical error: "The President spent much of the evening entering Mrs. Galt." Of course, it meant to say "entertaining Mrs. Galt."[41]

On a cold January day in 1986, I passed Wendy's Hamburger Restaurant in Jonesboro, Arkansas. Its marquee sign said ""WAR<u>N</u>ING HOT CHILI." I have a feeling it meant to say "WAR<u>M</u>ING HOT CHILI."

What to Learn, What Action to Take

Proofread your ads. Here are some hints on how to become a better proofreader:

- Reading your copy backwards makes it a lot easier to notice if a word is misspelled.

- Cut out a 4-mm tall slit in a 5" x 7" index card with a razor blade. Make sure the slit is as long as your typed lines are. Place the opening over one line at a time and critique it for grammar, spelling, and punctuation as it appears. Work from the bottom of the page to the top.

- Don't proofread each page in order. Shuffle them around. That keeps you from becoming distracted by your concentration on the overall content. You shouldn't care about the overall content when you're proofreading — you're looking for the minor, hard-to-catch errors. Before you shuffle the papers, though, make sure each page is numbered, so you can put them back together properly.

- Some of the most competent and least expensive proofreaders are people who run freelance typing services out of their homes.

- Always have at least two different people proofread. Don't rely on just one.

- Never proofread when you're tired. Always be fresh and alert.[42]

NOT MAKING SURE THE ADJACENT MATERIAL DOESN'T MESS UP THE EFFECTIVENESS OF YOUR AD

Advertisers have only limited control over what appears near their ads. Sometimes as a result, strange placements occur that receivers of the ads perceive as ironic or amusing — especially when cheerful ads collide with darker truths. Here are ten examples of terrible juxtapositioning. The first four occurred when an ad appeared next to damaging editorial material, and the last six occurred when an ad appeared next to another ad.

The December 19, 1988 issue of *Newsweek* magazine featured on its cover the story of the great earthquake in Soviet Armenia, calling it "The Agony." On the inside front cover and the next three pages was an ad for Smirnoff vodka, which most people perceive as a Russian vodka.

A full-page color ad for Colombian coffee appeared on the back cover of the March 8, 1987, *New York Times Magazine*. It cost $45,000. On the front cover was the headline "Cocaine Billionaires: The Men Who Hold Colombia Hostage." *El Tiempo,* a leading newspaper in Colombia, reported this mismatch in a long article. The advertiser, National Federation of Coffee Growers of Colombia, asked the *Times* to compensate it, and it got its compensation.

In the March 21, 1988, issue of *Newsweek* magazine, U.S. presidential candidate Michael Dukakis was pictured wearing a white cowboy hat, gray suit, and white shirt. The headline over the story read, "Quick-Change Artists: The Democrats Put on a Campaign Masquerade." On the facing page, to the right, was an Isuzu ad showing the sleazy salesman, Joe Isuzu, known as the "Big Liar," wearing an identical outfit — white cowboy hat, gray suit, and white shirt. The ad said, "Big Joe is a big liar."

On March 27, 1977, right after an NBC television newscaster told U.S. viewers about the collision of two jet planes in the Canary Islands killing 574 people, which was at that time the worst air disaster in history, an American Express ad appeared with spokesman Karl Malden telling everybody that the worst thing that could happen to you when you go on vacation is to lose your traveler's checks.[43]

In September 1987, Good Samaritan Hospital ran an ad in the Palm Beach (Florida) *Post* newspaper saying "Stop smoking in five days. No ifs, ands, or butts!" Right next to it was a K-Mart ad selling tobacco products at low prices.

In 1988, the Las Vegas Hilton and Flamingo Hilton hotels promoted its cable TV service in *Fun & Gaming* magazine, with the headline, "Only Tyson and Holmes will have a better view." The ad showed a picture of prizefighters Mike Tyson and Larry Holmes. There was no border around the ad. Directly below the borderless ad was a photo of chorus girls in bikinis from a revue playing at the Aladdin, another hotel.[44]

In 1986 in Los Angeles, California, a billboard saying "Come on down to San Diego" featured a blond woman underwater wearing a scuba mask and snorkel. The billboard next to it featured a huge gray shark with its toothy jaws pointed directly at the woman. It advertised an aquatic theme park.

In New York City, a billboard for Newport cigarettes claimed they were "Alive with pleasure!" Its location? Next to Calvary Cemetery. In a

New York City suburb, two billboards appeared next to each other in 1988 — a public-service ad warning that "People who do drugs go to hell *before* they die," and the red and black sign of the Red Devil Paint and Chemical Company.[45]

In early June 1988, the Manila (Philippines) *Bulletin* ran two ads next to each other. One advertised P. E. Martin Brandy, "The Love Potion." The second one was an ad that read, "The Holy Eucharist is The Body of Christ! Amen! Receive the Body of Christ in Holy Communion! Attend Holy Mass daily."

What to Learn, What Action to Take

What can you do to avoid these embarrassments? Not much. Even when you deal with reputable media, embarrassments happen. Make sure your ad agency knows you feel strongly about such things. If you have a good relationship with them, they'll do all they can to keep the media from embarrassing you, and make sure that your agency only deals with media that will compensate you for embarrassments.

HOW TO LEARN EVEN MORE BY DIGGING DEEPER

Aaker, David A. and Donald E. Bruzzone. "Causes of Irritation in Advertising." *Journal of Marketing*, (Spring 1985): 47–57.

Aaker, David A. and James M. Carman. "Are You Overadvertising?" *Journal of Advertising Research*, (August–September 1982): 57–70.

Abeele, P. Vandeh and J. Butaye. "Pretesting the Effectiveness of Industrial Advertising." *Industrial Marketing Management*, (February 1980): 75–83.

Axelrod, Joel N. "Advertising Wearout." *Journal of Advertising Research*, (October 1980): 13–20.

Benn, Alec. *The 27 Most Common Mistakes in Advertising*. New York: Amacom Books, 1978.

Koten, John. "After the Serious '70s, Advertisers are Going for Laughs Again." *Wall Street Journal*, 23 February 1984: 31.

Krugman, Herbert E. "What Makes Advertising Effective? *Harvard Business Review*, (March –April 1975): 96–103.

Lucas, Darrel Blaine and Steuart Henderson Britt. *Measuring Advertising Effectiveness*. New York: McGraw-Hill, 1963.

McNiver, Malcolm A. "Plan for More Productive Advertising." *Harvard Business Review*, (March–April 1980): 130–36.

Mitchel, F. Kent. "Advertising/Promotion Budgets: How Did We Get Here, and What Do We Do Now?" *Journal of Consumer Marketing*, (Fall 1985): 405–47.

Ogilvy, David and Joel Raphaelson. "Research on Advertising Techniques That Work — and Don't Work." *Harvard Business Review*, (July–August 1982): 14–18.

Ostle, Glenn V. and John K. Ryans, Jr. "Techniques for Measuring Advertising Effectiveness." *Journal of Advertising Research*, (June 1981): 19–24.

Pollay, Richard W. "The Distorted Mirror: Reflections on the Unintended Consequences of Advertising." *Journal of Marketing,* (April 1986): 18–36.

Schultz, Donald E., Dennis Martin and William P. Brown. *Strategic Advertising Campaigns.* Chicago: Crain Books, 1984.

"Special Report: Marketing to Hispanics." *Advertising Age,* 27 February 1986: 11–51.

Sternthal, Brian and C. Samuel Craig. "Humor in Advertising." *Journal of Marketing,* (October 1973): 12–18.

Swerdlow, Robert A. "Star-Studded Advertising: Is It Worth the Effort?" *Journal of the Academy of Marketing Science,* (Summer 1984): 89–102.

Swinyard, William R. "How Many Ad Exposures Is a Sales Call Worth?" *Journal of Advertising Research,* (February 1979): 17–22.

Tauber, Edward M. "How to Get Advertising Strategy from Research." *Journal of Advertising Research,* (October 1980): 67–74.

NOTES

1.   Michael McWilliams, "Burger King Ads Do Violence," *Advertising Age,* 9 September 1985, p. 55.

2.   *Arkansas Democrat,* Little Rock, 12 January 1986, p. 5-H.

3.   Irving L. Janis and S. Feshback, "Effects of Fear-Arousing Communication," *Journal of Abnormal and Social Psychology* 48 (1953), pp. 78–92; John R. Stutevile, "Psychic Defenses against High Fear Appeals: A Key Marketing Variable," *Journal of Marketing,* (April 1970), pp. 39–45; John J. Burnett and Richard L. Oliver, "Fear Appeal Effects in the Field: Segmentation Approach," *Journal of Marketing Research,* (May 1979), pp. 181–90; Michael Ray and William Wilkie, "Fear: The Potential of an Appeal Neglected by Marketing," *Journal of Marketing,* (January 1970), pp. 59–62; K. Higbee, "Fifteen Years of Fear Arousal: Research on Threat Appeals: 1953–1968," *Psychological Bulletin,* 72 (December 1969), pp. 426–44; Brian Sternthal and C. Samuel Craig, "Fear Appeals: Revisited and Revised," *Journal of Consumer Research,* (December 1974), pp. 22–34.

4.   *Arkansas Gazette,* Little Rock, 14 January 1986, p. 5-A; *Arkansas Gazette,* Little Rock, 16 January 1986, p. 1-A.

5.   Ronald Alsop, "Marketing: To Stir Up J&B Scotch Sales, Ads Hype Its British Heritage," *Wall Street Journal,* 17 October 1985, p. 27; Ronald Alsop, "Marketing: J&B Retreats from Its Toy Soldier Ads," *Wall Street Journal,* 15 January 1987, p. 21.

6.   Bernard Mendillo, "Pepsi's 'Real Thing' Spot," *Advertising Age,* 28 October 1985, p. 20.

7.   Ronald Alsop, "Marketing: Dr Pepper Is Bubbling Again After Its 'be a Pepper' Setback," *Wall Street Journal,* 26 September 1985.

8.   *Wall Street Journal,* 29 August 1985, p. 23.

9.   Alfredo Corchado, "Hispanic Supermarkets Are Blossoming," *Wall Street Journal,* 23 January 1989, p. B-1.

10.   All three examples from Humberto Valencia, "Point of View: Avoiding Hispanic Market Blunders," *Journal of Advertising Research,* (December 1983–January 1984), pp. 19–22.

11.   Ibid.

12. Examples 2 and 3 from Linda Gilliam, "Yardang Capitalizes on Hispanic Growth, Buying Power," *Adweek*, December 1982, p. 12.

13. Examples 4 and 5 from "How Ads Were Changed to Reach Minorities," *Advertising Age*, 7 April 1980, p. S-23.

14. Humberto Valencia, op. cit.

15. "Lost in Translation?" *Asiaweek*, 8 July 1988, p. 62.

16. Richard W. Brislin, Walter J. Lonner and Robert M. Thorndike, *Cross-Cultural Research Methods*, (New York: John Wiley and Sons, 1973), p. 10.

17. Oswald Werner and Donald T. Campbell, "Translating, Working Through Interpreters, and the Problem of Decentering," in *A Handbook of Method in Cultural Anthropology*, ed. Radul Narroll and Ronald Cohen. (Garden City, N.Y.: Natural History Press, 1970), pp. 398–420.

18. Recommendations 1, 2, and 5 from Humberto Valencia, op. cit.

19. Herbert C. Kelman and Carl I. Hovland, "Reinstatement of the Communication in Delayed Measurement of Opinion Change," *Journal of Abnormal and Social Psychology*, (July 1953), pp. 327–35; Carl I. Hovland, Irving L. Janis and Harold H. Kelley, *Communication and Persuasion: Psychological Studies of Opinion Change*, (New Haven, Conn.: Yale University Press, 1953), p. 225.

20. Alix M. Freedman, "Marriages Between Celebrity Spokesmen and Their Firms Can be Risky Ventures," *Wall Street Journal*, 22 January 1988, p. 29.

21. G. Christian Hill, "What Did Mr. Ehrlichman Know About the Ice Cream, and When . . ."*Wall Street Journal*, 18 May 1987, p. 19.

22. Alix M. Freedman, op. cit.

23. "In the News," *Arkansas Gazette*, Little Rock, 13 February 1987, p. 1-A; Albert R. Karr, "Let's Hope That People Magazine Doesn't Catch Cybill Eating Bacon," *Wall Street Journal*, 26 March 1987, p. 33.

24. Alix M. Freedman, op. cit.

25. William Mathewson, "Shop Talk: Does Anyone Focus on Monet's Finances, *Wall Street Journal*, 5 February 1988, p. 25.

26. "Donnay SA, Once a Star Performer, is Bankrupt," *International Herald Tribune*, Hong Kong, 20–21 August 1988, p. 9.

27. Phil Brown, "Johnson's Million-Dollar Image Now Worthless," *Times*, Chattanooga, Tenn., 28 September 1988, pp. D-1, D-4.

28. Ronald Alsop, "Marketing: Look Out, Paul Newman: Gloria's Back," *Wall Street Journal*, 13 August 1987, p. 21; and "Presstime," *Advertising Age*, 31 March 1980, p. 8.

29. Laura Landro, "Dynasty Shows Its Rivals How Not to License," *Wall Street Journal*, 22 January 1986, p. 27.

30. Ronald Alsop, "Jaded TV Viewers Tune Out Glut of Celebrity Commercials," *Wall Street Journal*, 7 February 1985, p. 35.

31. David Gregorio, "Executives Bask in Spotlight," *Commercial Appeal*, Memphis, Tenn., 16 September 1984, p. C-7.

32. Joseph M. Queenan, "Advertisements of Their Carelessness," *Wall Street Journal*, 1 December 1986, p. 18.

33. Undated letter to author from John R. Black, Accounting Editor, Business Publications, Inc., Plano, Tex.

34. Dennis E. Hensley, "The Cost of Crucial Errors," *Pace*, March 1986, p. 51.

35. "Selling It," *Consumer Reports*, July 1982, p. 368.

36.   Dennis E. Hensley, op. cit.

37.   Joseph M. Queenan, op. cit.

38.   William Mathewson, "Shop Talk: Sprechen Sie Deutsch? Yeah — Well, Sort Of," *Wall Street Journal,* 5 February 1988, p. 25.

39.   William M. Bulkeley, "Shop Talk: Reed Carefully," *Wall Street Journal,* 15 June 1987, p. 25.

40.   Dennis E. Hensley, op. cit.

41.   Walter Scott, "Personality Parade," *Parade,* 5 January 1986, p. 2.

42.   Dennis E. Hensley, op. cit., p. 52.

43.   Linda Ellerbee, *And So It Goes: Adventures in Television,* (New York: G. P. Putnam's Sons, 1986), pp. 244–45.

44.   *Las Vegas Fun & Gaming,* 15–21 January 1988, p. 4.

45.   Kathleen A. Hughes, "Slip-ups Can Put Ads — or News — in Right Place at the Wrong Time," *Wall Street Journal,* 17 March 1988, p. 27.

10
Personal Selling

NOT TRUSTING THE OTHER PERSON
ENOUGH IN NEGOTIATIONS

If you put too much trust in another person, you may end up the loser. But don't be so cynical that you never trust people, organizations, and systems ever again. Be aware of the need for caution. Of course, if you're too cautious, though, you'll never buy anything, sell anything, or hire anyone. For example, in 1899, Charles H. Duell, Director of the U.S. Patent Office, said, "Everything that *can* be invented *has* been invented." He was too cautious, and he was wrong. How many times have you asked yourself, "What if . . ."? What if you had signed that contract that your competitor later signed and made so much money on? What if you had listened to your stockbroker and bought that growth stock when it was selling at such a low price? What if you had bought that house in Greenwich, Connecticut, when you had the chance 25 years ago? Life is full of "what if's."

What to Learn, What Action to Take

In Figure 2, the other person (TOP) at first will try to negotiate with you in the northeast quadrant, and you'll try to negotiate with him or her in the southwest quadrant because neither one of you wants to give up your advantage. Eventually what usually happens is that after being in a stalemate for too long, you both take the risk of opening up to each other, and you both move to the southeast quadrant, where you finally conclude the deal. (Of course, nobody ever negotiates in the northwest quadrant.)

FIGURE 2 — The Negotiation Matrix

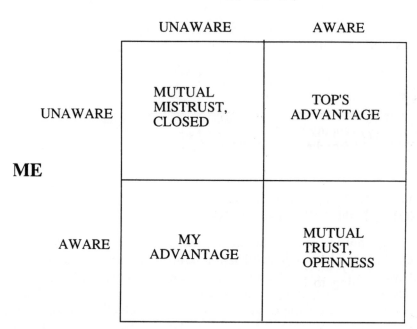

T. O. P.

	UNAWARE	AWARE
UNAWARE	MUTUAL MISTRUST, CLOSED	TOP'S ADVANTAGE
AWARE	MY ADVANTAGE	MUTUAL TRUST, OPENNESS

ME

At the beginning of my seminar, "How You Can Negotiate and Win," I give a quiz to the executives who attend to see which quadrant they are usually in when they begin to negotiate. Almost everybody prefers to be in the southwest quadrant. The southeast quadrant is in a very distant second place. Hardly anybody ever picks the two northern quadrants. By the end of the seminar, I give a somewhat different quiz, and almost everybody has moved into the southeast quadrant because by then they know it's the best place to be. That's because a win-win approach to negotiating a deal is the best one, and both sides can win only in one quadrant — the southeast one. Think about it — if they gave up too much and you won too much, they'll probably figure out some way of getting around the terms of the contract, possibly by using cheaper components in secret, which will be hard for you to catch. If both sides win, though, neither will feel cheated, and they'll live up to the agreement — both got what they wanted. And the seeds will have been planted for a long-term, mutually profitable relationship.

But it's hard to take the risk of opening up to TOP and laying your cards on the table because you don't trust him or her enough. You're afraid to give away your bottom line too soon. What you're doing is making the mistake of focusing on yourself. During the negotiation, you should focus on TOP. Be greedy for knowledge about TOP's wants and needs, for knowledge is power. The more you know about TOP, the situation, and yourself, the more powerful you are, and the more you'll win. The less you know about TOP, the situation, and yourself, the less powerful you are, and the more you'll lose. Sun Tzu Wu, the ancient Chinese general I talked about earlier in Chapter 3, said 2,500 years ago, "Know your enemy and know yourself, and you'll win every battle. If you know neither the enemy or yourself, you'll lose every battle."

Most of us think we know ourselves pretty well. We don't. I give several other short quizzes in my "How You Can Negotiate and Win" seminar that reveal different aspects of the participants' negotiating personalities to them. Most are quite surprised to find out things about themselves — their usual way of conceding, what really motivates them, and so forth.

Knowing yourself isn't enough. You've got to know TOP. The most important thing to know about TOP is his or her wants and needs. You've got to earn the right to learn TOP's needs before you can even begin to negotiate.[1] This won't be easy because their needs are among their most important possessions. They guard their needs and treat them as secrets because they are important to their future success. So you can't learn them quickly. And some, you'll never learn — just as you'll never learn all the needs of the person closest to you, your spouse.

For example, how many times have you awakened at 2 A.M., gotten up to go to the bathroom, and returned to bed, only to find your sleeping spouse smiling broadly. You'll never know what that smile was about, will you? Was it about a previous lover? Your spouse won't tell you. So if you can never learn all your spouse's secrets, how can you expect to learn all about your buyer's needs?

Like I said, you've got to earn the right to learn your buyer's needs. Until you've earned that right and have learned their needs, you're still only negotiating in the northwest or northeast quadrants, the two worst ones from your point of view. How can you earn that right? It's not enough to ask probing questions or to listen closely (with your eyes, watching their body language, as well as with your ears). Instead, accept the fact that it'll take a long time to gain their confidence — just as it'll take a long time for them to gain your confidence. You build up the buyer's confidence by getting out of the hard-sell mode and into the consulting mode. As indicated in Figure 3, when you're in the hard-sell mode, you're concentrating on yourself, and that's being production oriented. When you're in the consulting mode, you're concentrating on TOP, and that's being marketing oriented.

What do consultants do? They do their homework and learn ahead of time how the buyer's company markets its products or services. Impress them with this knowledge and by making sure they know you're putting their needs ahead of your own need to make a sale. That means sometimes you'll have to "bite the bullet" and tell your client that you don't think your products or services fit their needs at that time, and so you recommend somebody else's products or services. That goes against the grain, doesn't it? But don't be shortsighted. You'll lose the immediate sale, sure, but you'll probably make more sales in the long run with some of your other products or services because your client will begin to trust you more and more. Your short-run loss will pay for itself many times over in long-run dividends of future sales to a satisfied and trusting client. For example, J. P. Morgan & Co., the banking enterprise, encouraged its clients to become competitors in an ad it ran in the *Wall*

FIGURE 3 — The Difference Between the Hard-Sell Approach and the Marketing Approach

HARD-SELL	VARIABLE	MARKETING
on product	emphasis	on wants and needs of customers
make it first, then figure out how to sell it profitably	product	determine what customer wants and needs first, then figure out how to profitably make and deliver product to satisfy those wants and needs
on my company, internal	orientation	on the market, external
on my own company's (seller's) wants and needs	emphasis	on the market's (buyer's) wants and needs

Street Journal and *International Herald-Tribune* in June 1987. The ad said:

> Some might say encouraging clients to become competitors is the height of folly. We feel otherwise. There are times when helping clients meet a strategic need means helping them to do what we used to do for them. For example, with J. P. Morgan guidance, a number of multinationals have set up their own in-house banks to achieve better treasury management. . . . At J. P. Morgan, we welcome the fact that clients are dealing in the markets for themselves. The more professional our clients become, the more opportunities there are to interest them in new ideas.

Are you willing to take the risk of emulating J. P. Morgan's philosophy?

Let's talk some more about listening. You need to listen with your ears as well as with your eyes. A good technique to try in ear-listening is active listening, and a good technique to try in eye-listening is body language.

Active listening is nothing more than listening patiently to what TOP has to say, even though you may think it's wrong or irrelevant. Let TOP know you've accepted what he or she just said by nodding or using an occasional "I see." Try to understand TOP's feelings, as well as the content. It's harder to understand feelings, so pay special attention here.

The most important part of active listening is restating TOP's contents and feelings, briefly but accurately. By serving as a mirror, you're encouraging TOP to continue talking. In a neutral tone, say something like, "You feel that . . ." or "You think that . . ." Make sure you aren't trying to lead TOP to your own conclusions — that's not serving as a mirror. Don't get into a debate or argument with TOP. If this happens, you're really getting emotionally involved. You need to remain objective at all costs if you want to learn as much as you possibly can about TOP. Understand first, evaluate later on, after the conversation is over.

When TOP touches on a point you want to know more about, make sure you repeat his or her statement as a question. For instance, if TOP says, "Nobody can make a sale to Joe. He's just too tough," you should probe by saying, "You say nobody can sell anything to Joe?" What you're doing is encouraging TOP to expand on what he or she just said.

Active listening is a skill. It takes time to learn, so you need to practice it over and over. Knowing body language is a skill, too. It's one of the most important skills I've ever developed. It's helped me immensely, not only when I'm dealing with clients and university students, but also in my personal life. It's a way of knowing what's on

TOP's mind without TOP knowing that you know this. You can tell through body language if you're winning TOP over or alienating TOP. You can even tell if TOP is lying to you or not — although that's a little harder.

I think it's simple to learn. I teach the participants in my seminars the basics of body language in just 45 minutes. Here's a sample of ten gestures in Figure 4: That's not enough for you to know about, for there are hundreds of gestures for which a person skilled in body language watches.

When you watch TOP, never judge what's on his or her mind based on just one gesture. That can really mislead you. Instead, watch

FIGURE 4 — The Basics of Body Language

SHOW NEGATIVE FEELINGS	GESTURES	SHOW POSITIVE FEELINGS
Crossed	Arms	Open
Crossed	Legs	Open
Lean back	Overall position of body	Sit forward
Turned away from you	Position of head	Turned toward you
Doodling	Writing during sales pitch	Taking notes
Always very straight	Back	Curved, more flexible
Far away	Distance from you	Fairly close
Left on top of right	Positions of thumbs when hands are together	Right on top of left
Raised high	Shoulders	Normal position
Rubbing the nose	Hand-to-face gestures	Patting the head

Source: Donald W. Hendon, *Battling for Profits* (Jonesboro, Ark.: Business Consultants International, 1987), p. 270.

TOP for a few minutes, until you've seen several gestures. If they are all mostly negative, you can be pretty sure TOP's attitude is negative. If they're all mostly positive, you can be pretty sure TOP's attitude is positive.

If you're getting lots of negative gestures, don't respond with negative gestures of your own. Instead, give TOP as many positive body language gestures as you can. Even if TOP doesn't know body language — and chances are, he or she won't — your positive gestures will usually lead to positive body language gestures on TOP's part. And since our body language echoes what's going on in our heads, TOP's newly positive body language will probably lead to positive thoughts and positive acceptance of what you're saying.

And never let TOP know you can "read" his or her body language. If you do, TOP will immediately tighten up and won't trust you. Always keep your knowledge a secret, and use it to your advantage.

When I first begin talking about body language in my seminars, I can tell that the majority of the audience has a closed mind and thinks it's a bunch of garbage. Perhaps you do, too. By the end of the session, though, especially after several exercises on how to influence TOP with your own body language and how to tell if TOP is lying to you, the audience's body language indicates belief in the power of this skill. Let me try to convince you of its power just with these words.

Body language is not voodoo or witchcraft. It's taught in universities under its more formal title, kinesics. Social scientists have written papers in academic journals about it. Research usually involves filming or videotaping people's actions and then asking them what was going on in their minds when they made a particular gesture. There is always a high correlation between a given gesture, such as putting you hands together in a "steepling" gesture, and the mental meaning behind the gesture — in the case of "steepling," it's a sign of superiority.

One social scientist, Betty Grayson, videotaped many people on the streets of New York City. She took the tapes to Sing Sing Prison and showed the tapes to individual prisoners — one-on-one, not in groups — who had been convicted of robbery. She asked each convict which people they would rob and which people they would stay away from. Almost every convict agreed on whom they would rob and whom they would stay away from. She then figured out the differences between gestures of the robbable victims and of those whom the prisoners avoided and published these findings.[2]

I hope what I just said convinces you that body language is a useful skill and not garbage. Use it and see!

HOW TO LEARN EVEN MORE BY DIGGING DEEPER

Allesandra, Tony, Phil Wexler and Jerry D. Dean. *Non-Manipulative Selling*. San Diego, Calif.: Courseware, 1979.

Fisher, Roger and William Ury. *Getting to Yes*. New York: Penguin Books, 1983.

Hendon, Donald W. and Rebecca A. Hendon. *How to Negotiate Worldwide*. London: Gower Publishers and New York: John Wiley & Sons, 1989.

Jolson, Marvin H. "Selling Assertively." *Business Horizons*, (September–October 1984): 71–77.

Karrass, Chester L. *Give and Take*. New York: Thomas Y. Crowell Co., 1974.

Lockeman, Bradley D. and John H. Hallaq. "Who Are Your Successful Salespeople?" *Journal of the Academy of Marketing Science*, 10, no. 4 (Fall 1982): pp. 457–72.

Main, Jeremy. "How to Sell by Listening." *Fortune*, 4 February 1985: 52–54.

Mayer, David and Herbert M. Greenberg, "What Makes a Good Salesman?" *Harvard Business Review*, (July–August 1964): 119–25.

McMurry, Robert N. "The Mystique of Super-Salesmanship," *Harvard Business Review*, (March–April 1961): 113–22.

Oskam, Bob and Henry Calero. *Negotiate Any Deal You Want*. New York: Dodd, Mead and Co., 1983.

Reichard, Clifford J. "Industrial Selling: Beyond Price and Persistence." *Harvard Business Review*, (March–April 1985): 127–33.

Winkler, John. *Bargaining for Results*. New York: Facts-on-File, 1984.

NOTES

1.   Donald W. Hendon, *Battling for Profits*, 2d ed. (Jonesboro, AR: Business Consultants International and Singapore: Executive Data Centre, 1987), p. 269.

2.   *Express-News*, San Antonio, Tex., 11 January 1981, p. 2-J.

Subject Index

Activities–interests–opinions, 162–63, 165–66

Advertising, 65, 113–18, 144, 161–80

Advertising blunders aimed at the Hispanic market, 161–70

AIOs, 162–63, 165–66

American values, 28, 171

Anderson, Charles, 24

Argentina, 4, 26, 28, 33

Asia, 43, 106

Bait-and-switch, 58–59

Belgium, 4, 173

Body language, 5, 187, 189–91

Boesky, Ivan, 143

Bottner, Irving, 18–19

Brand name products: Airbus A-320, 69–70; American Express credit cards, 167, 174, 179; American Flyer trains, 42; Apple personal computer, 69; Apple software, 129; Audi automobiles, 74; Ayds diet candy, 130; Baker Tom's Baked Cat Food, 3; Barbie Sticker Album, 12; Batman Crazy Foam, 2; Beauty Bronze U.V.A. Sunbed and Sunroof, 127; Beer Hausen beer, 46; Benedictin, 72; Big John canned goods, 131; Bill Blass chocolates, 174; Billy Beer, 131; Bounce anti-static laundry aid, 125; Bright Moment coffee, 133; Bubble Yum bubble gum, 89; Budweiser beer, 168; Buffalo Chip chocolate cookies, 3; Burger King, 117–19; Campbell's Tomato Soup, 78; Champion car batteries, 162; Chase and Sanborn coffee, 133, 164; Chevrolet Corvair, 83; Coca-Cola soft drink, 4, 31–33, 43, 45–46, 89; Coca-Cola clothing, 30–31, 33; Commence herbicide, 14–15; Contac cold remedy, 77–79; Coors beer, 168; Copper 7 inter-uterine device, 72; Corona beer, 90; Cosmic Candy, 89; Crisp 'N Tender batter, 124–25; Dalkon Shield inter-uterine device, 71; Darkie toothpaste, 21–22; Designer Diapers, 3; Dietac appetite control pills, 77–79; Dowtherm 209 antifreeze-coolant, 120, 122; Dr Pepper soft drink, 134, 166; Dreyer's Grand Ice Cream, 171–72; Duncan Hines muffin mix, 67; Dynasty evening dresses, 174; Dynasty furs, 174; Dynasty pantyhose, 174; Dynasty perfume, 174; Easyseat bicycle accessory, 128; Edsel, 6, 7, 109–10, 126; Electrostatically Enhanced Game, 109; Enco gasoline, 135; Erector set toys, 42; Esso gasoline, 135; Estee Lauder perfume, 167; Excedrin headache remedy, 77, 79; F-20 Tiger Shark airplane, 69; Famolare shoes, 25; Ford Escort, 74; Ford Model T, 55; Ford Pinto, 74; Fruit of the Loom laundry detergent, 111; Fuji film, 134; GEM software, 60; Gerber's baby food, 77, 79–80; Gillette Super Blue Blades, 56; Gimme Cucumber hair conditioner, 3; Girl Scout cookies, 78–79; Gleason's coffee, 133; Gloria Vanderbilt chocolates, 174; Gloria Vanderbilt frozen tofu, 174; Guinness Stout, 6; Gulf No-Nox gasoline, 6; Hagar the Horrible Cola soft drink, 3; Hygrade Ball Park frankfurters, 88; I Hate Beets canned food, 3; I Hate Peas canned food, 3; I Hate Spinach canned food, 3; IBM PC jr computer, 127; Interferon software, 129; Ivory Snow detergent, 172; J & B whisky, 163–64; Jalisco cheese, 77–78; Jazz software, 127; Jeep Wagoneer, 54; Jockey underwear, 89; Kickapoo Joy Juice soft drink, 3; La Valtromplina nut and bean roaster, 128; Lexicon software, 126; Liquid Plum'r drain cleaner, 132; Little Black Hanna books and toys, 20; Little Black Sambo books and toys, 20; Love cosmetics, 156–57; Meow Mix cat food, 12–13; Mercury Lynx, 74; Mercury station wagon, 167; Michelin tires, 25; Moonshine aftershave, 3; Moonshine Sippin' Citrus soft drink, 3; Mr. PiBB soft drink, 21; Multiplan software, 127; Nescafe Gold coffee, 133; Nestle food products, 134; Newport cigarettes, 179; Nine Lives cat food, 168; Nova, 131; Nutrimato beverage, 3; Oasis deodorant, 3; Oggi hair care, 27; Okeechobee Orange Pokem soft drink, 3; Opium perfume, 135; P. E. Martin brandy, 180; Pac-Man video game, 131; Pacer, 105; Panda Punch soft drink, 3; Paul Masson wines, 171; Pepsi Cola soft drink, 43, 89, 165, 172; Perdue chicken, 168; Pink Panther cereal, 131; Playboy magazine, 61–62; Polavision instant motion pictures system, 101–02, 126; Pop Rocks candy, 89; Premier cigarettes, 121–22, 126; Pussyfoot cat feeder, 128; Putnam's Inn coffee, 133; Rambler, 114; Real cigarettes, 121–22, 126; Realistic beauty care, 19; Reggie candy bar, 174; Rely tampons, 71; Riunite wine, 77–78; Roux beauty care, 19; Royal Crown Cola soft drink, 114; Royal no-bake cheesecake mix, 114; Saturn, 88; Savin photocopiers, 114; Schick razor blades, 173; Schlitz beer, 161–62; Seagram's Golden wine cooler, 172; SelectaVision video disc, 101–02, 126; Sine-Off sinus remedy, 77, 79; Skin Cancer Garde sunblock lotion, 162; Skunkguard repellent, 117, 119; Slime toys, 69; Smirnoff vodka, 179; Snuggles the Seal toys, 12; Solar Rover dog house, 109; Standard Oil petroleum products, 134; Stroh's beer, 17–18, 88; Sudden Soda soft drink, 3; Sunkist raisins, 167; Sutter's Gold coffee, 133; Symphony software, 126–27; Tab cola, 90–91; Tanduay Rhum, 43; Tatum T I.U.D., 72; Teldrin antihistamine, 77–79; Thalidomide medicine, 72; Tingle Pants radio-clothing combination, 102; Trips magazine, 111; TRS-80 computer, 127; Tuna Twist, 3; TV-Cable Week magazine, 123; "Two-Potato Clock," 117, 119; Tylenol, 77–78, 80–82; Ultra Pampers disposable diapers, 71–72; Ultralife batteries, 108; Ultrashock game, 109; Univac computers, 114; Volkswagen, 114; Wang computers, 114; Wankel rotary engine, 105; Westinghouse, 114; Whopper Burger, 117–19, 162; Wild Life beans in sauce with wild boar meat, 3; Wine and Dine frozen dinner, 3; Wristmatic wrist camera, 128; Xerox copiers, 55; XyWrite III Plus word processor, 177; Yabba Dabba Dew soft drink, 3; Yellobags garbage bags, 68

Brazil, 3, 4, 44, 74, 149
Brennan, Robert, 142
Brunei, 4, 21–22

Canada, 4, 11–12, 16, 25, 27, 44, 67, 70, 90, 131, 149, 173
Canary Islands, 4, 179
Cannibalization, 32, 56, 125, 158
Celebrities, 170–76
Channel relationships, 155–59
Channels of distribution, 155–59
Chile, 4, 78
China, People's Republic, 4, 37, 66, 107, 129, 134–35, 187
Community groups, 11–16

Companies (manufacturers, middlemen): A.
C. Gilbert Toy Company, 42; A.H.
Robins, 71; A.i.d.s. Ambulance
Service, 130; AID Insurance Company
Mutual, 130; Airbus Industrie,
69–70; Aladdin Hotel, 179;
Allegheny Airlines, 132; Allegis
Corporation, 132; Allied Roofing &
Siding Company, 69; American
Airlines, 76; American Bullion and
Coin, 29–30, 33; American Express,
14; American Express Canada, 173;
American Institute of Decision
Sciences, 130; American Motors,
53–54, 105, 114; Arkwright Boston
Insurance Company, 65; Arrow Air,
70; Asia Breweries, 46; Atlantic
Richfield Company, 141; Audi of
America Inc., 74; Australian Mint,
118–19, 129; Banana Republic, 111;
Bank of America, 142; Bank of New
England, 142; Beef Industry
Council/National Live Stock and Meat
Board, 172; Better Book Inc., 30, 33;
Better Business Bureaus, Council of,
29–30, 33; Big 20 Restaurants, 88;
Booz Allen and Hamilton, 128;
Bristol-Myers Company, 79; Burger
Chef, 111; Burger King, 162;
Burgerville USA, 31; Business
Publications Inc., 176; Cadillac
Motor Car Division, 74; Campbell
Soup Company, 78; Canadian
Imperial Bank of Commerce, 16;
Canpak, 68; Cavalry Cemetery, 179;
Chase Manhattan Bank, 142; Chattem
Inc., 156; Chemical Bank, 142;
Chevrolet Motors, 131; Chrysler
Corporation, 171; Church's Fried
Chicken, 89; Citibank, 23; Coca-Cola
Bottlers, 59–60; Coca-Cola USA, 4,
21, 30–33, 45–46, 62–63, 90;
Coleco Industries, 57–58; Colgate-
Palmolive Co., 21–22; Columbia
Pictures, 62–63; Comrealty Ltd.,
13–14; Continental Airlines, 27,
74–75; CPC Corporation, 130; Decca
Records, 5; Delta Airlines, 75;
Democratic Party, 179; Dep
Corporation, 130; Diadora, 173;
Digital Research Inc., 60; Dow
Chemical Company, 82–83, 120,
123; Dragon Airlines, 107; Drexel
Burnham Lambert, 142; E. F. Hutton
Company, 142; E. R. Squibb
Company, 172; Eastern Airlines,
74–75; Eastman Kodak Company,
104, 108; Eclipse Laboratories, 162;
Elanco, 15; Eli Lilly & Co., 15; Estee
Lauder, 167; Exxon Corporation, 111,
135, 141; Exxon Office Systems, 45;
Fallon McElligott, 24–25, 27; Federal
Express, 128–29; Fingerhut
Corporation, 67; First Jersey
Securities, 142; First National Stores,
142; Flamingo Hilton Hotel, 179;
FMC Corporation, 14–15; Ford Motor
Company, 55, 74–75, 110, 167; Fruit
of the Loom Inc., 111; G. D. Searle &
Co., 72; GAF Corporation, 130;
Gallo Wine Company, 91; General
Cinema Corporation, 59; General
Dynamics Corporation, 141; General
Electric Company, 107–08, 124, 141;
General Foods Corporation, 89, 111;
General Mills, 124–25; General
Motors Corporation, 83–84, 88;
Gillette Company, 56; Girl Scouts,
78–79; Godfather's Pizza, 20; Good
Samaritan Hospital, 179; Gulf Oil
Co., 6; Hammacher Schlemmer and
Co., 128; Harcourt Brace Jovanovich,
13; Harry M. Stevens Inc., 29, 33;
Hawley & Hazel Chemical Co.,
21–22; Hewlett-Packard, 5; Hitachi
Corporation, 45; Holly Farms
Corporation, 119–20; Hunt-Wesson
Corporation, 131; IBM Corporation,
104, 127; Insurance companies trade
association, 15–16; Interconnect
Planning Corp., 69; Irving Trust
Company, 142; Isuzu Motor
Company, 179; J. P. Morgan and
Company, 188–89; Jalisco Mexican
Products, 77–78; Jollibee Restaurants,
88; Kentucky Fried Chicken, 88;
Kmart Stores, 89, 179; Kongsberg
Vaapenfabrikk, 33; Kyodo Oil
Company, 173; Las Vegas Hilton
Hotel, 179; Liggett Group Inc., 72;
Lincoln Mercury Division, 167;
Lotus, 126–27; Lowe Marschalk, 17;
Lucio Tan Group, 46; Lucky Stores
Inc., 111; Manufacturers Hanover

Trust Company, 142; Manville Corporation, 71; Mattel Inc., 12, 69; Mazda Motor Company, 173; McCall Publishing Co., 59; McDonald's Restaurants, 88, 92; McDonnell Douglas Corporation, 141–42; Merrell Dow Pharmaceuticals, 72; Michael Max's Leather Stores, 162; Microlytics, 177; Microsoft, 127; Montgomery Ward Company, 57; Morgan Stanley Company, 142; Morton Thiokol, 65; Murjani International, 30; Musical Heritage Society, 177; Nash Motor Cars, 53; National Aeronautics and Space Administration, 70–71; National Federation of Coffee Growers of Columbia, 179; NBC-TV, 179; New York Times Magazine, 179; Newsweek Magazine, 179; Northeastern Software Inc., 105; Northrop Corporation, 69, 142; Northwest Airlines, 75; O'Neal Motors, 177; Pacific Coast Publishing, 68; Pacific Telesis, 30; Panasonic Corporation, 142; Parker Brothers, 104; Pepsi Cola Bottlers, 59–60; Peterson Outdoor Advertising Co., 27; Playboy Enterprises, 61–62; Polaroid Corporation, 101–02; Preco Turbine Services, 45, 48; Procter and Gamble, 67, 71–72, 86–88, 92, 125; PSA Airlines, 161; R. J. Reynolds Tobacco Company, 121; Radio Shack stores, 127; Ralston Purina Company, 12–13; RCA Corporation, 101–02; Red Devil Paint and Chemical Company, 180; Revlon's Professional Products Division, 18–19; Riunite Wine, 77–78; Robinson's Department Store, 89; Rockwell International, 141; San Jose Mexican Restaurant, 112; SCM Corporation, 130; Sears Roebuck Company, 58–59, 177; Seven-Eleven Stores, 60; Shiley Inc., 73; Siemens Corporation, 134; Smith Kline and French, 156–57; Smith Kline Beckman Corporation, 78–79; Snell Division of Booz Allen Hamilton, 128; Standard Brands, 133; Standard Oil Corporation of New Jersey, 135; Starr National Manufacturing Corporation, 84; Stevedoring Services of America, 73; Stop and Shop Stores, 142; Tandy Corporation, 127; Texas Air Corporation, 27, 74–75; Time Inc., 91, 123; Toshiba Machine Co., 33; TRW Corporation, 130; U.S. Mint, 118–19; UAL Inc., 132; Union Carbide, 73, 77; Unisys Corporation, 142; United Airlines, 106–07; United Technologies Corporation, 142; Universal Studios, 60; USM Corporation, 130; Valio, 173; Vallco Fashion Park, 25; Vintners International, 171; Volkswagen AG, 74; WABC-TV, 174–75; Waldbaum Stores, 142; Walt Disney Studios, 125–26; Warner Brothers Studios, 104; Washington Post, 178; Wells Rich and Greene, 156; Wendy's Hamburger Restaurant, 178; Wendy's Restaurants, 88; Western Airlines, 75; Westinghouse Electric Corporation, 141; WHBQ Radio, 28–29, 33; Xerox Corporation, 55; Yamato Mannequin Co., 20; Yves St. Laurent Company, 134–35

Company's resources and objectives, 62–63
Competitors, 37–49, 53–55, 93, 124–25, 164–65
Concessions, price, 149–51, 187
Confidence, 185–91
Consulting mode, 188
Consumer protection and consumerism, 29, 39, 83–84, 105, 141–43
Contamination, 43, 77–80, 90–91
Contests, 21, 120
Crandall, Bob, 76
Creativity, 104, 114
Customers, 11–34

Demographics, 92–93, 122
Denial of failure, 4
Disasters, 65–82, 179
Distributors, 155–59

Egypt, 4, 33
Environment, 155; changes in, 125–26; cultural-social, 61–62; economic, 56–58; legal, 58–60; technological, 55–56

Erlichman, John, 171–73
Espionage, 44–46
Ethics, 29, 46–49, 108
Europe, 76

Fear appeal, 116–62
Finland, 4, 173
Follow the leader, 43–44
Fonda, Jane, 175
Ford, Henry, 55, 110
France, 4, 69–70, 77–78, 134–35
Franchises and franchising, 113, 156
Fraud, 141–43

Gap analysis, 113–17
Garner, James, 172–73
Goals, defined, 102

Hong Kong, 4, 6, 21–22, 44, 107, 142, 150

Image, 54, 61, 159
India, 4, 6, 44, 73, 150
Indonesia, 4, 6, 44, 89, 150
Industries: advertising agencies, 17–18, 24–25, 156, 166, 173, 180; advertising media, 178–80; airlines, 5, 16, 27, 69–70, 74–76, 106–07, 112, 132, 161; ambulance services, 130; amusement parks, 13, 126, 179; archaeology, 164; athletic programs, 77; auto repairs, 112; automation, 107–08, 124; automobile dealers, 112; automobile rental agencies, 132; bakeries, 66, 169; banks and financial services 14, 16, 23, 47, 84–85, 113, 130, 142, 188–89; baseball, 5–6, 19, 29, 33, 165; biotechnology, 38; capital intensive industries, 43; casinos, 179; chambers of commerce, 48; commodities market, 84–85; computer software, 45, 60, 105, 115–17, 124, 126–27, 129, 135–36, 177; computer stores, 127; conglomerates, 130, 134; construction, 6, 13–14; consulting, 187–89; courier service, 128, 173; day-care centers, 163; defense, 65, 69–71, 88, 141–42; department stores, 57–59, 156–57, 177; discount stores, 89, 179; educational institutions, 164, 191; electric power/public utilities, 48, 54; executive search firms, 47; facsimile services, 128–29; factory automation, 107–08, 124; gas power/public utilities, 54; gasoline stations (service stations), 112; government, 48; hospitals, 73, 127, 179; hotels and motels, 23, 132-34, 176, 179; importers, 66–67, 73; insurance companies, 15–16, 65, 71, 76–77, 129–30; insurance agencies and brokers, 20, 112; investment brokers, 142; journalism, 89, 91; legal services, 45; mail delivery services, 128–29; mail order companies, 59, 128, 177; management consultants, 128, 135; motion picture, 5, 6, 56, 59–60, 62–63, 104, 125–26, 134, 163–64, 174; music, 5, 167, 177; nuclear plants, 4–5; politics and political campaigns, 5, 20–22, 84, 88–90, 163, 179; professional associations, 130; public relations, 4, 68, 70–71, 82–83, 94, 176–77; publishing, 20, 59, 61, 62, 105–06, 111, 123, 142, 172–73, 176–77, 179; restaurants, 20–21, 31, 88, 92, 108, 111–12, 113, 117–19, 162, 178; retailers, 65–66; scientific consultants, 6; security consultants, 47; sexual services, 118; small businesses, 112; snow-removal services, 69; space program, 65, 70–71, 88; sports, 173–74; supermarkets, 111, 119–20, 129, 142, 146; telephone companies and systems, 30, 33, 38, 69, 168; tourism, 169; trade associations, 92, 173; travel agencies, 20
Information, 46–48
International marketing, 65–67, 76, 131, 135
Ireland, 4, 6
Italy, 4, 6, 12, 20, 44, 163, 173

Jackson, Reggie, 174
Japan, 4, 19–20, 33, 37–42, 44–45, 68–69, 72–73, 76, 106–07, 126, 128, 134–35, 173
Johnson, Ben, 173–74

Kenya, 4, 150

Latin America, 131
Liabilities, products and services, 71–76
Lifestyle, 162–63, 165–66, 168

Madagascar, 4, 45–46
Malaysia, 4, 21–22, 37, 44, 89, 150
Market definition, 102
Market research, 80, 110, 113–14,
    120–23, 133, 159, 170
Market segmentation/market niching,
    53–54, 108, 113–14, 146, 162–63,
    167
Marketing mix, 11, 62, 119, 143–46,
    148
Marketing-oriented, 62–63, 188
Me-too strategy, 43–44
Mexico, 4, 33, 44, 65–66, 90, 131
Middlemen, 119, 143, 155–59
Minority groups, 17–22
Monitoring launch, 102, 109, 125–26
Monitoring the environment, 63, 125

Namath, Joe, 171
Names: choice of, 132–33; use of, 129–35
Negotiating, 54–55, 148–51, 185–91
Netherlands, 4
New Zealand, 4, 149
Nixon, Richard M., 84, 171
Norway, 4, 33

Overenthusiasm, 105–08
Overselling, 105–08

Packaging, 46
Patriotism, 32, 93
Perdue, Frank, 168
Persian Gulf States, 4, 44
Personal selling, 185–91
Philippines, 4, 43–44, 46, 56, 88–89,
    94, 128, 150, 180
Positioning, 61, 113–17, 121, 125, 164,
    168
Power, 156–59, 187–91
Pressure groups, 11–16
Price concessions, 149–50
Price fixing, 59–60, 146, 149
Price wars, 43, 54–55, 94, 144–49, 158
Pricing, 141–51
Products: aircraft, 38; antifreeze, 78, 120,
    122; asbestos, 71;
    audiocassettes/tapes, 175; auto
    rentals, 114; automatic teller

machines, 113; automobiles, 6–7,
38–39, 55, 61, 74, 83–84, 88, 105,
109–10, 112, 114, 126, 129, 131,
167, 171, 173, 177, 179; baby food,
77, 79–80; baby products, 71–72,
87; bath towels, 115–17; batter,
124–25; batteries (automobile), 133,
162; batteries (household), 108;
bicycle accessories, 128; birth
control devices, 71–72; blood,
72–73; board games, 104; boats,
123; cable television, 61–62;
camcorders, 101, 126; cemeteries,
179; ceramics, 38; chemicals, 43, 73,
77, 82–84, 180; cigarettes, 72,
89–90, 115, 121–22, 126, 164, 176,
179; cigars, 176; clocks, 117, 119;
cloth towels, 115–17; clothing, 20,
30–31, 33, 65–67, 89, 102, 111,
162, 171, 173–74, 176; clothing
boutiques, 57, 111, 162; coins, 29,
33, 118, 128; computer software, 45,
60, 105, 115–17, 124, 126–27, 129,
135–36, 177; computers, 5, 38, 43,
45, 47, 60, 114, 127, 129, 135, 177;
consumer electronics, 33, 38, 56, 65,
101–02, 130, 142; consumer
packaged goods, 147; cooking oil,
72, 87; coolants, 120, 122; credit
cards, 167, 173–75; de-icers, 84;
denture adhesives, 175; dentures, 175;
detergents, 87, 172; diet products,
130; directories, 29–30, 33; drain
cleaner, 132; drinks: alcoholic, 6,
17–18, 26–27, 43, 46, 77–78, 88,
90–91, 131, 161–64, 168–69,
171–73, 179–80; drinks:
nonalcoholic, 3–4, 21, 27, 30–33,
43, 45–46, 59–60, 62–63, 87,
89–91, 114, 132–34, 164–66, 172,
175, 179; food, 3, 19, 26–27, 29,
33, 65–67, 77–79, 87–90, 111, 114,
117–20, 129–31, 134, 167–69,
171–74; garbage bags, 68; hardware,
76; health and beauty aids, 3, 18–19,
21–22, 27, 41, 72, 76–82, 87–88,
91, 112, 114, 117, 119, 127–28,
132, 134–35, 156–57, 162–63, 167,
172, 174–75; hearing aids, 175; heart
valves, 73; herbicides, 14–15;
household appliances, 68–69, 114;
industrial bathroom cleaner, 115–17;

industrial robots, 107–08, 124; insecticides, 169; laundry detergent, 111, 161–62; leather, 162, 171; light bulbs, 54; lubricants, 123; luggage, 67; machinery and tools, 76–77; machine tool controls, 107–08, 124; mannequins, 20; metal containers, 43; money, 118, 128; novelties, 68; office products, 130; office systems, 111; oil and petroleum, 6, 92, 111, 131–32, 134–35, 141, 173; outboard motor, 123, 173; paints, 180; paper, 43, 61, 87, 115–17; pet food and pet care, 12–13, 109, 128, 163; photography and film, 6, 104, 128, 130, 134; pipelines, 131–32; radiation therapy machines, 127; radio, 28–29; radium bars, 177; rags, 115–17; roasting devices, 128; sanitary napkins, 71–72; self-protection devices, 117, 119; semiconductors, 38; sewing kits, 67; sewing machines, 58–59; shoes, 25; solar power, 109; solvents, 78; sponges, 115–17; sports equipment, 173; steel, 43, 130; suntanning equipment, 127; surveillance devices, 46–47, 84; television, 19, 165, 172, 174, 176, 179; textiles, 76; tires, 25; toys, 12, 20, 42, 57–58, 69, 73, 104; travelers checks, 179; turbines, 45; vacuum cleaners, 94; video cameras, 101, 126; video cassette recorders, 61, 101, 165; video games, 60, 109, 131; video cassettes, 175; W.A.T.S. lines/800 numbers, 68; writing instruments, 175

Product: launches, 101–02, 104–14, 117–21, 123–29; liability, 71–80; life cycle, 145; recalls, 74, 77–80

Product line extension, 32, 132

Production-oriented, 63, 188

Promotion, general, 120

Psychographics, 162–63, 165–66

Public relations/publicity, 141, 149, 165

Repositioning, 61

Return on investment (R.O.I.), 109–10

Risk-taking, 56, 112–13

Rumors, 43, 81–94, 125

Sabotage, 82–90, 125

Safety, 71–80, 161

Sales forecasting, 102, 104, 107–10, 123–24, 126

Sales representatives, 124–25, 143–44, 156–57

Service, 144, 158

Setting prices, 141–43

Sex appeal, 163

Sexism, 23–27, 163

Shepherd, Cybil, 172–73

Shortsightedness, 124–25

Singapore, 4, 21–22, 37, 44, 89, 129, 150

South Africa, 4, 19, 149

South Korea, 4, 39, 44, 69, 174

Suppliers, 155–59

Sweden, 4, 173

Switzerland, 4, 132–33

Taiwan, 4, 21–22, 44, 72–73, 89, 134, 149

Tampering, 77–80

Target markets, 163

Technological changes, 101

Test-marketing, 102 110, 119–20, 122–25, 129, 159

Thailand, 4, 21–22, 44, 89, 107, 149

Trust, 185–91

Uncontrollable environment, 53–63

Uniqueness, 167

United Kingdom, 4–6, 127, 129, 163–64, 171

Values, 28–33

Vanderbilt, Gloria, 174

Vietnam, 4, 175

West Germany, 4, 72, 90, 134

Willis, Bruce, 172–73

Wrong advertising appeals, 161–70

Wrong assumptions, 38–42

Author Index

Aaker, David A., 180
Aames, B. Charles, 160
Abeele, P. Vandeh, 180
Adams, James L., 136
Adler, Lee, 159
Agnew, Joe, 35
Alexander, Ralph M., 160
Alford, C. L., 136
Allesandra, Tony, 192
Allport, Gordon W., 94
Alreck, Pamela L., 49
Alsop, Ronald, 138, 181, 182
Alter, Jonathan, 138
Anderson, L. K., 152
Anderson, Susan Heller, 137
Anderson, M. Jack, Jr., 50
Ansberry, Clare, 137, 138
Armbrister, Trevor, 138
Assael, Henry, 36
Avis, Warren, 137
Axelrod, Joel N., 180

Bauer, Raymond A., 94
Bellenger, Danny N., 49
Benn, Alec, 180
Bennett, Amanda, 137
Berthelsen, John, 137
Beveridge, J. M., 136
Birnbaum, Jeffrey N., 50
Bishop, Jerry E., 97
Black, John R., 182
Black, Norman, 152
Bloom, Paul N., 94
Bobrow, Edwin E., 136
Bonasegna, Christina, 35

Borchard, William M., 64
Borrus, Amy, 50
Bose, Romen, 139
Boyd, Harper W., Jr., 160
Bradford, Hazel, 50
Brendel, Louis H., 160
Brion, John M., 160
Brislin, Richard W., 170, 182
Britt, Steuart Henderson, 180
Brody, Michael, 95, 96
Brown, F. E., 152
Brown, Phil, 182
Brown, Robert L., 50
Brown, William P., 181
Bruzzone, Donald E., 180
Bryer, Jack E., 160
Buckler, Arthur, 138
Buckner, H. Taylor, 94
Bulkeley, William M., 139, 183
Burnett, John J., 181
Buss, Dale D., 97
Bussey, John, 97, 98
Butaye, J., 180
Buzzell, Robert D., 153

Calantone, Robert, 136
Calero, Henry, 192
Campbell, Donald T., 182
Carlisle, Howard W., 137
Carman, James M., 180
Carrington, Tim, 152
Cauley, Leslie, 36
Cavanaugh, Gerald F., 34
Charmasson, Henri, 136
Chay, Richard F., 136

Chisholm, R. K., 124
Chisum, James, 97
Church, George J., 50
Churchill, V. B., Jr., 138
Cimball, Richard S., 153
Clark, Terry, 98
Cohen, Laurie P., 138
Cohen, Ronald, 182
Cohen, Stanley E., 138
Cohen, Willliam A., 49
Cohn, Bob, 51
Colvin, Geofrey, 98
Connant, Jennet, 50
Cooke, James, 160
Cooney, John E., 98
Cooper, Arnold C., 50, 63
Cooper, Robert G., 136
Corchado, Alfredo, 181
Courter, Eileen, 98
Craig, C. Samuel, 181
Cravens, David W., 63
Crawford, C. Merle, 136
Cross, James S., 160
Crossen, Cynthia, 95, 138, 139
Curry, David J., 151

Dahl, Jonathan, 96
Davis, Bob, 96, 138
Day, George S., 49
Dean, Jerry D., 192
Diamond, William T., 160
Dietrich, Robert, 152
Dishneau, David, 64
Dodge, H. Robert, 160
Dorfman, John R., 137
Doyle, John M., 152
Drucker, Peter F., 136
Dubrin, Andrew J., 102, 137
Dwyer, Paula, 97

Eastlack, J. O., Jr., 160
Egan, Timothy, 97
Eichenwald, Kurt, 96, 152
Ellerbee, Linda, 183
Elliott, Dorinda, 50
Emshwiller, John R., 36
Enrico, Roger, 31
Esposito, J. L., 94

Fanelli, Louis A., 137
Farago, Ladislas, 97
Fenn, Dan H., Jr., 94

Feshback, Seymour, 181
Fialka, John J., 50
Fine, Gary A., 94, 98
Fisher, Roger, 192
Fisher, Glen, 34
Fitz Simmon, Jane, 64
Flinn, John, 138
Flynn, Leslie, 94
Foltz, Kim, 139
Foster, Robert, 160
Freedman, Alix M., 98, 182
Freeman, Alan, 34, 138
Fueroghne, Dean K., 63
Fuld, Leonard M., 50

Gabor, Andre, 152
Gale, Bradley T., 153
Gang, Christine Arpe, 96
Gaskie, John F., 159
Geczi, Michael, 50
Gellene, Denise, 152
Ghemawat, Pankaj, 63
Gibney, Frank, Jr., 50
Gibson, Richard, 35
Gilliam, Linda, 182
Gilly, Mary C., 136
Gilman, Hank, 97, 137
Glaberson, William B., 95
Goldberg, M. Hirsh, 7, 95, 137
Goldstucker, Jac, 49
Gonik, Jacob, 136
Gonzalez, David L., 97
Graham, Margaret B. W., 64
Granger, Clive W. J., 152
Greenberg, Barnett A., 49
Greenberg, Herbert M., 192
Greene, Bob, 138
Gregorio, David, 182
Greyser, Stephen A., 94
Grimmer, Russell, 96
Guerts, Michael, 136
Guyon, Janet, 138

Haas, R. M., 152
Haberman, Clyde, 36
Hagedorn, Ann, 152
Hager, Mary, 97
Haines, George, 152
Hallaq, John H., 192
Hammermesh, Richard G., 50
Hansen, Richard W., 136
Harding, Harold F., 137

Haring, Robert C., 95
Harris, Roy J., Jr., 35, 95
Harris, J. Elizabeth, 50
Hartley, Robert F., 50
Harvey, Michael G., 136
Heany, Donald F., 153
Hendon, Donald W., 31, 36, 49, 54, 95,
    97, 101, 139, 149–50, 153, 160,
    186–87, 190, 192
Hendon, Rebecca A., 36, 54, 149–50,
    153, 186–87, 192
Henion, Karl E., 63
Henry, Waleter A., 34
Hensley, Dennis E., 182, 183
Hershey, Robert, 49
Hiatt, Fred, 96
Higbee, K., 181
Hill, G. Christian, 182
Hill, Richard M., 160
Hisrich, Robert D., 136
Hlavacek, James D., 159, 160
Holloway, Robert J., 152
Holusha, John, 94
Holz, Michael Wald, 97
Hovland, Carl I., 182
Hughes, Kathleen A., 95, 183
Huse, Edgar F., 137
Hutchins, Dexter, 152

Jacoby, Jacob, 153
James, Barry, 95
Janis, Irving L., 181, 182
Jeffrey, Nancy, 97
Johnson, Robert, 34–35
Jolson, Marvin H., 192
Jones, John P., 136

Kaikati, Jack G., 151
Karr, Albert R., 182
Karrass, Chester L., 192
Kasindorf, Martin, 97
Katz, Elihu, 152
Keil, John M., 136
Kelley, Harold H., 182
Kelman, Herbert C., 182
Kent, Mitchel F., 180
Kerin, Roger A., 136
Kilman, Lawrence, 152
Kneale, Dennis, 138, 139
Knopf, Terry, 94
Koenig, Frederick, 98
Kornbluth, Jesse, 31

Koten, John, 180
Kotler, Philip, 50, 136
Kovach, Jeffrey L., 50
Krugman, Herbert E., 180
Kurland, Mark A., 50

Lamont, Lawrence M., 34
Landro, Laura, 182
Lazarsfeld, Paul F., 152
Lazer, William, 63
Lear, John, 95
Lerbinger, Otto, 94
Levingston, Steven E., 95
Levitt, Theodore, 63
Lipman, Joanne, 7
Lockeman, Bradley D., 192
Lonner, Walter J., 170, 182
LoScuito, Leonard A., 152
Lucas, Darrel Blaine, 180
Lynagh, Peter M., 159

Magnet, Myron, 34
Main, Jeremy, 192
Malone, Maggie, 35
Maloney, John C., 108–09, 138
Manela, Stewart S., 48, 51
Mantrala, Murali K., 136
Marcom, John, Jr., 139
Martin, Dennis, 181
Marx, Gary S., 48, 51
Mason, J. Barry, 136
Massy, William F., 160
Mathewson, William, 182, 183
Matthew, William, 137
Mauser, Ferdinand F., 160
Mayer, David, 192
McAlevey, Peter, 64
McCarthy, Michael J., 64
McCuistion, Tommy J., 159
McGill, Douglas C., 35
McGinley, Laurie, 95
McMurray, Scott, 152
McMurry, Robert N., 192
McNiver, Malcolm A., 180
McWilliams, Michael, 181
Meier, Barry, 96
Melloan, George, 49
Mendillo, Bernard, 181
Metz, Tim, 138
Michman, Ronald D., 64
Millar, Victor E., 49
Miller, Cyndee, 35

Miller, Michael M., 7
Mitchell, Arnold, 34
Moffett, Matt, 95
Monroe, Kent B., 151, 152
Montgomery, Jim, 98
Moore, William L., 49
More, Roger A., 136
Morgan, Hal, 94
Mufson, Steve, 50
Myers, Gerald C., 94

Nagle, Thomas, 151
Naisbitt, John, 64
Narroll, Radul, 182
Narus, James A., 159
Newman, Joseph, 152
Nicholson, Thom, 50
Nierenberg, Gerard I., 137
Nimer, Daniel A., 151
Nonaka, Ikujuro, 137

O'Donnell, Thomas C., 50
O'Neill, Tom, 139
Odiorne, George S., 137
Ogilvy, David, 180
Oliver, Richard L., 181
Oliver, Thomas, 31
Olson, Jerry C., 153
Ono, Yumiko, 35
Osborn, Alex F., 137
Oskam, Bob, 192
Ostle, Glenn V., 180
Oxenfeldt, Alfred R., 49, 151

Panat, Charles, 64
Paris, Ellen, 138
Parnes, Sidney J., 137
Pasztor, Andy, 64, 96, 152
Pave, Irene, 50
Payne, Stanley L., 49
Pearson, Michael M., 160
Pegram, Robert M., 160
Perry, Nancy J., 64
Peters, Michael P., 136
Peterzell, Jay, 50
Petre, Peter, 137
Poist, Richard S., 159
Pollay, Richard W., 181
Porter, Michael E., 49
Postman, Leo, 94
Potts, Mark, 50
Powell, Bill, 97

Power, William, 36, 97
Prestowitz, Clyde V., Jr., 50
Purushothaman, Shoba, 95
Pusateri, C. Joseph, 34

Queenan, Joseph M., 182, 183
Quinn, James Brian, 137

Rajaratnam, Daniel, 160
Rao, Vithala, 151
Raphaelson, Joel, 180
Ray, Michael, 181
Recklefs, Roger, 139
Reetz, John, 98
Reibstein, David J., 36
Reibstein, Larry, 64
Reichard, Clifford J., 192
Reinmuth, James, 136
Reynolds, William H., 138
Richins, Marsha L., 34
Ricks, David A., 7, 96, 139
Ries, Al, 137
Risen, James, 35
Rivers, Colin, 50
Rogers, Michael, 138
Rosenbloom, Bert, 160
Rosnow, Ralph L., 94
Ross, Elliot B., 151
Rotbart, Dean, 94
Roth, Terence, 96
Rothe, James T., 136
Rothman, Andrea, 35
Rotschild, William, 49
Rudolph, Barbara, 36
Russell, Cheryl, 64
Ryans, John K., Jr., 180

Salwen, Kevin G., 138
Samghabadi, Raji, 50
Sammon, William L., 50
Sanger, David E., 35
Scanlon, Sally, 138
Schendel, Dan, 63
Schmitt, Richard B., 138
Schoeffler, Sidney, 153
Schuler, Randall S., 137
Schultz, Donald E., 181
Schwadel, Francine, 95
Schwartz, John, 51
Scott, Jerome E., 34
Scott, Walter, 183
Settle, Robert B., 49

Shafer, Dennis W., 136
Shapiro, Benson P., 153
Shay, Paul, 34
Shenon, Philip, 152
Shibutani, Tomatosu, 95
Siconolfi, Michael, 138
Siegel, Lee, 96
Simpson, Janice C., 7
Sims, J. Taylor, 160
Smart, Carolyne, 94
Smith, Timothy K., 139
Solomon, Jolie, 95
Spitalnic, Robert, 50
Starfire, Brian, 139
Sterngold, James, 152
Sternthal, Brian, 181
Stevens, Charles, 98
Stewart, Doug, 51
Stone, Gregory P., 152
Strauss, Lawrence, 64
Stuller, Jay, 50
Stutevile, John R., 181
Sultan, Ralph G. M., 153
Swan, John E., 95
Swartz, Steve, 35
Swerdlow, Robert A., 181
Swinyard, William R., 181

Takeuchi, Hirotaka, 137
Tauber, Edward M., 181
Taylor, J. R., 152
Tellis, Gerald J., 151
Thomas, Paulette, 96
Thomas, Philip S., 64
Thorndike, Robert M., 170, 182
Toffler, Alvin, 64
Trost, Cathy, 34
Trout, Jack, 137
Tsiantar, Dody, 51
Tucker, Kerry, 94

Ury, William, 192

Valencia, Humberto, 181
Valentine, Judith, 137
Varadarajan, P. "Rajan," 160
Velton, E. J., 136
Venkatesh, Alladi, 34
Vertinsky, Ilan, 94
Vinson, Donald E., 34

Waldholz, Michael, 97
Wall, Jerry L., 49
Wang, Penelope, 35
Weaver, Earl, 7
Webdale, Adrienne M., 153
Webster, Frederick E., 160
Weiner, Elizabeth, 50
Weinrauch, J. Donald, 138
Welch, Joe L., 64
Wells, William D., 152
Wenger, Scott, 36
Werner, Oswald, 182
Wexler, Phil, 192
Whitaker, G. R., 124
White, George R., 64
White, Irving S., 152
Wiersema, Frederik D., 153
Wilkie, William, 181
Winkler, John, 153, 192
Winter, Ralph E., 153
Witcher, S. Karene, 35
Witkin, Richard, 96
Wolkomir, Richard, 50
Wollenberg, Skip, 97
Woo, Carolyn Y., 50
Woodside, Arch G., 160
Woolley, Suzanne, 137
Wright, Lynda, 51
Wynter, Leon E., 152

Yang, John E., 96
Yankelovich, Daniel, 64

Zaslow, Jeffrey, 64, 97
Zweig, Philip L., 152

ABOUT THE AUTHOR

DR. DONALD W. HENDON is President of Business Consultants International. He is also Professor of Marketing and Director of the International Business Program at Northern State University, Aberdeen, South Dakota.